WITHERNSEA
HUMBER
CLEETHORPES
MABLETHORPE*
SKEGNESS*
HUNSTANTON
WELLS*
SHERINGHAM
CROMER*
HAPPISBURGH*
GREAT YARMOUTH AND GORLESTON
LOWESTOFT
SOUTHWOLD
ALDEBURGH
HARWICH
WALTON AND FRINTON
WEST MERSEA
CLACTON-ON-SEA
BURNHAM-ON-CROUCH
SHEERNESS
SOUTHEND-ON-SEA
MARGATE
RAMSGATE
WALMER
DOVER
WHITSTABLE
LITTLESTONE-ON-SEA
DUNGENESS
RYE HARBOUR
HASTINGS
EASTBOURNE
NEWHAVEN
BRIGHTON
SHOREHAM HARBOUR
LITTLEHAMPTON
SELSEY
HAYLING ISLAND
PORTSMOUTH
CALSHOT
LYMINGTON
BEMBRIDGE
YARMOUTH
MUDEFORD
SWANAGE*
POOLE
WEYMOUTH
LYME REGIS
EXMOUTH
TORBAY
SALCOMBE
PLYMOUTH
LOOE
FOWEY
FALMOUTH
THE LIZARD
MARAZION*
PENLEE
SENNEN COVE*
ST IVES
ST AGNES*
NEWQUAY
PADSTOW
ROCK
PORT ISAAC*
BUDE*
TEIGNMOUTH
APPLEDORE
ILFRACOMBE*
MINEHEAD
WESTON-SUPER-MARE
PENARTH
BARRY DOCK
ATLANTIC COLLEGE (ST DONATS)
PORTHCAWL
PORT TALBOT
THE MUMBLES
HORTON AND PORT EYNON
ANGLE*
TENBY
BURRY PORT
NEW QUAY
CARDIGAN
FISHGUARD
ST DAVIDS
LITTLE AND BROAD HAVEN
ABERYSTWYTH
BORTH
ABERDOVEY
BARMOUTH
CRICCIETH
PORTHDINLLAEN
ABERSOCH
PWLLHELI
MOELFRE
HOLYHEAD
TREARDDUR BAY
BEAUMARIS
CONWY
LLANDUDNO*
RHYL
FLINT
HOYLAKE
WEST KIRBY
NEW BRIGHTON
LYTHAM ST ANNES

ST MARY'S

Channel Islands
ALDERNEY   ST PETER PORT
ST CATHERINE   ST HELIER

SKERRIES
HOWTH*
DUN LAOGHAIRE
WICKLOW
ARKLOW
COURTOWN*
ROSSLARE HARBOUR
KILMORE QUAY
DUNMORE EAST
TRAMORE*
YOUGHAL
BALLYCOTTON
COURTMACSHERRY HARBOUR
BALTIMORE
GALWAY CITY* (To be established 1995 for one year's evaluation)
KILRUSH (To be established late 1994)
Fenit (Established 1994 for one year's evaluation)
CLIFDEN
GALWAY BAY
VALENTIA

STRONG
TO SAVE

Other books by Ray Kipling:

Rescue by Sail and Oar

A Source Book of Lifeboats

Patrick Stephens Limited, an imprint of Haynes Publishing, has published authoritative, quality books for enthusiasts for more than 20 years. During that time the company has established a reputation as one of the world's leading publishers of books on aviation, maritime, military, model-making, motor cycling, motoring, motor racing, railway and railway modelling subjects. Readers or authors with suggestions for books they would like to see published are invited to write to: The Editorial Director, Patrick Stephens Limited, Sparkford, Nr Yeovil, Somerset, BA22 7JJ.

STRONG TO SAVE

Dramatic first-hand accounts of RNLI lifeboat rescues around the British Isles

Ray and Susannah Kipling

Patrick Stephens Limited

First published in 1995

British Library Cataloguing in Publication Data:
A catalogue record for this book is available from the British Library.

ISBN 1 85260 495 6

Library of Congress catalog card no. 95 78118

Patrick Stephens Limited is an imprint of Haynes Publishing, Sparkford, Nr Yeovil, Somerset, BA22 7JJ.

Typeset by Haynes Publishing, Sparkford, Nr Yeovil, Somerset BA22 7JJ.
Printed and bound in Great Britain by
BPC Hazell Books Ltd
A member of
The British Printing Company Ltd

Contents

Acknowledgements   6

Introduction   7

Chapter 1: The North West – birth of an institution   9

Chapter 2: The North East – designed for danger   30

Chapter 3: The Second World War – under fire   56

Chapter 4: The East – exposed to peril   67

Chapter 5: The South East – hurricane!   82

Chapter 6: Animal rescues – tails from the deep   107

Chapter 7: The South West – air and sea rescue   111

Chapter 8: Wales – boats and bards   142

Chapter 9: Children of courage   166

Chapter 10: Scotland – disaster and triumph   173

Chapter 11: Ireland – Hibernian future   211

Chapter 12: Survivors' stories – saved from the sea   245

Appendices

'The lifeboatman's VC': Gold Medal awards in the 20th century 252

Lifeboat disasters in the 20th century   254

Index   255

Colour section between pages 128 and 129

Acknowledgements

THE AUTHORS WOULD like to express their gratitude to scores of people who helped to provide information for this book. In particular we thank Brian Miles, Leslie Vipond and Michael Vlasto for their recollections as lifeboat inspectors; Roger Smith, Myra Searle and Helen Hallam at RNLI Headquarters for their patient help with checking facts; and, most of all, we are grateful to the lifeboatmen and women who were good enough to spend time talking to us about their experiences.

Picture credits
We would like to express our gratitude to the following for the use of their photographs:

Brian Stevenson, *Lancashire Evening Post*, Cumbria Newspapers Ltd, GEC Alsthom, Rick Tomlinson, Peter Hadfield, *Scarborough Evening News*, North News & Pictures, Clem James, *Daily Mirror*, Doran Bros, Yorkshire Regional Newspapers, Simon Kench Photography, *Evening News*, L. F. Gilding, *Leicester Mercury*, Mike Richford, *Grimsby Evening Telegraph*, *East Anglian Daily Times*, Richard Davies, Jim Bellinghall, Portsmouth Publishing & Printing, Michael Pett, Trafalgar Photographic Agency, Bournemouth News & Picture Service, Mercury Press, Paul Singer Photographic, Peter Hodges, Times Newspapers, F. E. Gibson, Focus Press, Norman Childs Photography, *Western Morning News*, Steve Guscott, R. Bishop, John Watts, Cornish Photonews, Torbay News Agency, Brian Green, Basil Tierney, A. J. Levine, Martin Cavaney Photography, *South Wales Evening Post*, David Jenkins, Phil Michell, Gareth Davies Photography, *Western Mail & Echo*, Photopress, *Great Yarmouth Mercury*, Peter Phillips, Maggie Murray, *Scottish Sunday Express*, Edward Foster, Dave Cutler, John Mowatt, Terry Freeman, Bristow Helicopters, Bill Runciman, *Sunday Telegraph*, F. H. McCarlie, D. M. Smith, D. C. Thomson, Aberdeen Journals, Rothmans Sailing; Malory Maltby, *Evening Herald*, Jerry Kennelly, Ambrose Greenway, Colin Watson, *Belfast Newsletter*, Ian Watson, Max Hess, Roger Oram, Zac Austin, *Cork Examiner*, RNAS Culdrose, Ian Leask, John Mercer, *Daily Telegraph*, Roger Lean-Vercoe, Express Newspapers, Campbell MacCallum, Ken Farrow, Captain I. Fyffe, Dave Trotter, Paul Whittle, Mike Horton.

Over the years, photographs often become impossible to trace to their origin. If we have inadvertently failed to acknowledge any photographer, we extend our apologies.

Introduction

'BY NOW, THE wind had risen to storm force 10. Coxswain Bowry brought the lifeboat towards the casualty through peaking, confused seas. A number of approaches had to be made before all survivors were safely taken off, and soon after the lifeboat had pulled away the *Mi Amigo* sank.'

The dry, terse language of an official RNLI report has a drama of its own, but can never tell the story as seen by a lifeboat crew. Charlie Bowry, late coxswain of the Sheerness lifeboat, gave an account that made much more entertaining reading:

'Well, we took one man off, did all the business and went in for the next. We grab him off. Then another comes running across the deck with this canary in a cage and throws himself on board. This canary, I could see it in the light of the searchlight, he's pressed up against the side of the cage and there's gales of wind blowing through his feathers. Once we'd got clear of the sandbanks I opened the cabin door and they were all down there smoking away and the cabin was black with smoke. And this old canary is on the table, wheezing and coughing and his eyes are popping. I said "That's going to have a cardiac arrest if you don't get it out of here".'

There's a rare humour, a musketeer spirit that binds lifeboat crews together in the face of adversity. When the Teesmouth lifeboat was overwhelmed by a 40-foot wave and rolled to 90 degrees, nearly capsizing, a videocamera that had been loaned to film rescues kept running. As the boat shook herself free of the immense weight of water and came upright, the first remark picked up by the camera was: 'I hope that bloody video's insured'.

Or take Malcolm Keen, one of Charlie Bowry's crew. A cabin cruiser was stuck hard on a sandbank being battered by the surf. The lifeboat could get no closer than 200 feet before grounding herself. Charlie takes up the tale:

'The seas washed right through us. All you could see was the top of the wheelhouse and the mast. All the rest was under the 'oggin. A helicopter, he's arrived now and he's doing his sort of fluttering bit up there; he told the coastguard he thought I had sunk because he couldn't see a lot of me, know what I mean? Now I'm drawing 4 ft 9 in and I'm in 4 ft 9 in of water and the breakers are rolling through. So we are wading round the deck and I'm beginning to run out of ideas. Then I come across this big lad of mine, Malcolm. I says to him, "How tall are you, Malcolm?" He says, "I'm 6 ft 3 in, aren't I?" "Well," I said, "there's only 4 ft 9 in of water here, cock. Off you go!"'

Malcolm inflated his lifejacket and with a line round his waist waded the 200 feet to reach the cruiser.

'He climbs aboard and says "Morning, Harry" because we know the bloke quite well. "Have you off here in a minute, mate." And that's another little situation dealt with.'

Every year lifeboat crews deal with over 5,000 'little situations'. This book tells their story, from their perspective and using their personal accounts. It is a human story rather than the dusty history of an organisation. For the RNLI, one of the nation's best-loved and oldest charities, is an organisation of thousands of people, nearly all volunteers. The crews are always ready to go out, in blizzards, hurricane-force winds, towering waves – or on calm, sunny summer days. They find it hard to tell you why they do it. You might get a gruff 'Well somebody's got to' or 'If I was out there I'd like to think someone would come for me'.

Perhaps Joe Martin, former coxswain of the Hastings lifeboat, got nearer the mark. 'Just the look on their faces when they know they're not going to die. That's enough.'

CHAPTER ONE

The North West – birth of an institution

'With courage, everything is possible.'

Motto of Sir William Hillary

THE SEAFARERS' HYMN 'Eternal Father Strong to Save' offers a prayer for seamen: 'From rock and tempest, fire and foe, protect them wheresoe'r they go'. Many times rock and tempest have combined to send ships and their crews to the bottom of the ocean. In the days of sail, ships were virtually helpless as they were driven ashore by ferocious storms, while powerless bystanders would watch despairingly as seamen dropped from the rigging to their deaths. The same fate seemed to await the men on the steamer *St George* when a storm pushed her onto the rocks in Douglas Bay in 1830. The only lifeboat available was a new one, not yet tested or ready for service, but, undaunted, 16 Manxmen put out into the storm with a 63-year-old Yorkshireman as coxswain.

As they strained at the oars, the lifeboat was badly battered.

Six of her ten oars were broken or lost, air cases and wooden planks were smashed. Then a huge wave crashed over the open boat, washing three men overboard. The coxswain, who could not swim, managed to grab a rope hanging from the *St George* and was eventually pulled on board, severely injured. His chest was badly crushed and six of his ribs were broken. His disabled lifeboat was trapped between the wreck and the rocks, unable to get out. For the next two hours the men desperately hacked through fallen rigging to make a clear passageway while the tide rose and swept over both vessels.

The *St George* was now awash and her crew of 22 joined the 18 lifeboatmen. The lifeboat was bailed out, the remaining oars were manned and the desperate struggle for the shore began. As soon as she was cast off, the lifeboat hit a rock, filled with water, filled again and was swept over the reef. Then a sea lifted her and drove her

Sir William Hillary, founder of the RNLI.

broadside on to the waves, usually a fatal position.

Somehow the boat survived and the same sea pushed her into calmer waters where the men were able to row her to the shore.

The coxswain on this rescue was Sir William Hillary, founder of the Royal National Lifeboat Institution, who was described on his tombstone as a soldier, author and philanthropist. He could equally well have been labelled as a baronet, bankrupt and bigamist, for his was a stormy life, driven by a heady mixture of impetuousness and sharp intelligence.

He was a great campaigner who raised a huge home guard in Essex against the feared French invasion; he also devised schemes for a tower of refuge in Douglas Bay (which was built in 1832) and for steam lifeboats (which were not built until the 1890s, years after his death). He even wrote a pamphlet entitled 'Suggestions for the Improvement and Embellishment of the Metropolis', with his views on how the streets of London should be widened and an enormous monument erected to Britain's naval supremacy, set on a granite base in the River Thames and big enough to provide accommodation for retired seafarers. His Tower of Refuge moved William Wordsworth to praise him in verse, perhaps not the poet's most distinguished:

'A Tower of Refuge built for else forlorn,
Spare it, ye waves, and lift the mariner,
Struggling to life, into its saving arms.
Spare too the human helpers! Do they stir
Mid your fierce shock like men afraid to die?
No; their dread service nerves the heart it warms,
And they are led by noble Hillary.'

The tower still stands in Douglas Bay, but Hillary's greatest achievement was the founding of the RNLI. Lifeboats had existed long before he came on the scene; marine insurers Lloyds of London had provided over 30 and individual harbour authorities and philanthropists had bought others. But rescue cover was patchy, the boats very variable in quality and there was no provision for the families of any men who drowned during rescues.

Sir William issued a stirring 'Appeal to the British Nation on the Humanity and Policy of Forming a National Institution for the Preservation of Lives and Property from Shipwreck'. He saw that there would always be danger at sea, 'so long as men shall continue to navigate the ocean, and the tempest shall hold their course over its surface, in every age and on every coast, disasters by sea, shipwreck and peril to human life must inevitably take place'.

Equipped with well-found lifeboats and the assurance of pensions for their families, he was sure that men would willingly respond. 'To expect a large body of men to enrol themselves, and be in constant readiness to risk their own lives for the preservation of those whom they have never known or seen, perhaps of another nation, merely because they are fellow creatures in extreme peril, is to pay the highest possible compliment to my countrymen; and that on every coast there are such men, has been fully evinced, even under the present want of system, when the best means for their purpose are not supplied; when they are without any certainty of reward; and act under the peculiarly appalling consideration that, if they perish, they may leave wives, children and every one destitute who depend on them for support.'

As for funds, Hillary was equally confident of support. 'Who is there, to whom such an Institution once became known, that would refuse his aid? It is a cause which extends from the palace to the cottage, in which politics and party cannot have any share, and which addresses itself with equal force to all the best feelings of every class in the state.'

He had originally tried to get the Admiralty to take responsibility for a national lifeboat service but they refused. Had they accepted, the wonderful voluntary traditions of the RNLI, so clearly spelled out by Hillary almost two centuries ago, would never have developed. Having been rebuffed by government, he went on to gather the support of influential men, the nobility and MPs, and on 4 March 1824 the National Institution for the Preservation of Life from Shipwreck was founded, gaining royal patronage and adding Royal to the title within weeks.

The new Institution soon took over many existing lifeboats, but to this day nobody has been able to give a definitive answer to the question of where the world's first lifeboat was stationed. The strongest claim is Formby Point, Merseyside, where there was certainly a boat dedicated to lifesaving as early as 1776. The evidence is a footnote to a chart of the Harbour of Liverpool: 'On the strand about a mile below Formby Lower Land Mark there is a boathouse and a boat kept ready to save lives from vessels forced on the shore on that coast and a guinea or more reward is paid by the Corporation for every human life that is saved by means of this boat'. The Liverpool Dock Trustees set up six lifeboat stations in all and the Mersey Docks and Harbour Board maintained them until 1894 when the RNLI took over. Liverpool's great contribution to lifesaving has been recognised by naming different classes of lifeboats Liverpool and Mersey.

THE FIRST FUND-RAISERS

The North West of England was also the birthplace of organised fundraising. In 1886 the worst disaster in the RNLI's history led to the introduction of street collections, and eventually to the establishment of the successful fundraising structure on which the organisation still relies.

On a tempestuous December night in that year, three Lancashire lifeboats went to the aid of the ship *Mexico*, bound from Liverpool to Guayaquil in South America. The ferocity of the storm had driven the ship on to a sandbank between Southport and Formby, and the lifeboat crews from Southport, Lytham and St Annes had put out to the rescue. The **Lytham** lifeboat was filled with water four or five times, and three of its oars were broken when the boat nearly capsized. Yet the crew managed to manoeuvre the boat alongside the *Mexico*, where the men aboard had lashed themselves to whatever rigging remained and prepared themselves for the worst. The coxswain of the Lytham lifeboat, J. Clarkson, in an interview given to the *Southport Guardian*, takes up the tale:

The loss of the Southport lifeboat Eliza Fernley.

'We had great difficulty getting at the men on the boat, for the sea was constantly breaking over her in great mountain waves. . . She had only her mizzen mast left standing. The men jumped safely into our lifeboat, except one who missed the boat, but was fortunately caught by one of our crew, and had a most miraculous escape.'

But the crews of the **Southport** and **St Annes** boats were not so lucky. The former had just reached the *Mexico* when a huge wave struck the lifeboat and capsized it.

'We had just got alongside [the ship] and were just getting ready to cast anchor when a wave came and capsized us in a jiffy,' recalled John Jackson, one of the two men who survived from the crew of 16. 'Why, mate, believe me but the weight of the water alone was enough to have killed us. . . Well, when I got round a bit, I found myself clinging to the side of the boat.'

Hanging grimly on to the boat with Jackson were four other crew members.

'Poor Dick got hold of my arm . . . and said to me, "Jack, will 'ta help me?" I raised his head a bit, but a heavy sea came and took Dick clean away from me. I could now feel the cramp (what I was most frightened of) coming into my legs, but I managed to keep it off a bit by keeping kicking.'

Eventually the boat drifted into shallower water and John Jackson managed to struggle ashore. He finally reached home 'in such a state that I thought I had come home only to die'. But he was alive, while all 13 men on the St Annes lifeboat were drowned. The boat was found, bottom up, on the beach the following morning. There was no trace of the crew and no one really knows what happened to them.

Horrified by this appalling tragedy, a Manchester businessman, Sir Charles Macara, launched a national appeal to help the orphans and widows of the 27 lost lifeboatmen. He was a successful cotton manufacturer with shrewd financial acumen who spent his weekends and holidays at the family home in St Annes. From his windows Sir Charles could see the remains of some of the many ships wrecked by the treacherous currents along this exposed coastline, and he was deeply impressed by the bravery of the local lifeboatmen. He became an enthusiastic RNLI supporter and was chairman of the St Annes branch at the time of the disaster. When exhausted lifeboatmen arrived back from a rescue mission in the middle of the night, they would find a hot meal waiting for them at the Macaras' home.

Through Sir Charles's efforts thousands of pounds were raised for the families of the men who had died. But he realised that the RNLI should not have to rely on occasional collections, and that, as he wrote in his autobiography many years later, 'to offer a widow and family a grant of £100, as had hitherto been the custom of the Institution, when the breadwinner had given his life voluntarily, was utterly inadequate.

'At least every lifeboatman ought to have the satisfaction of knowing that, if he never returned, those dependent on him should not suffer pecuniary loss through his self-sacrifice.'

As he started to delve into the RNLI's finances, Sir Charles found that they were in a sorry state; the Institution's outgoings were double its income. To his amazement, he also discovered that two-thirds of the RNLI's income came from just 100 of the country's wealthiest people. Sir Charles believed strongly that lifeboatmen deserved the support of everyone, so he decided 'to bring charity into the streets and streets into charity', and set up the world's first ever street collection for charity.

With the Mayor, Sir Charles organised a street parade through the streets of Manchester on Saturday 1 October 1891. There were three bands, many decorated floats and two lifeboats drawn by horses; 30,000 people lined the streets and watched from windows or the tops of trams. Charles's wife, Marion, and her friends went round with tins and buckets to collect the money. To reach the spectators at the windows, they fixed purses to long poles. More than £5,000 was collected, and the parade was so successful that 'Lifeboat Saturdays' spread to other towns all over the country, ensuring a healthy income for the RNLI for the first time ever.

Lifeboats had traditionally been supported by seafaring communities; these street collections swelled lifeboat funds by firing the imaginations of town and city dwellers inland.

During one of Sheffield's 'Lifeboat Saturdays' there was a procession three miles long, while Birmingham's aquatic gala drew crowds of 40,000. Encouraged by the success of the street collections, Marion

Early flag day collectors.

Macara began to set up ladies' fundraising committees all over the country. Meanwhile, Sir Charles established six district committees to co-ordinate fundraising throughout the UK.

Today the RNLI's highly successful fundraising structure is still partly based on the system introduced by Sir Charles Macara. Flag days are a vital part of the Institution's income, but the greatest source of money is from legacies, and these are usually inspired by an admiration of the work of lifeboat crews. Harry Jones, former coxswain of the **Hoylake** lifeboat, can take a particular pride in having inspired a West Midlands man to leave a huge sum to the RNLI in his will.

Frank Clifford was a friend of one of the RNLI's fundraising volunteers in Stourbridge, who invited him to hear a talk by Harry Jones. In straightforward language Harry told of the rescue in 1979 that earned him a Bronze Medal. The weather was so rough that even the launch was hazardous, the launching tractor so badly swamped that only the exhaust pipes could be seen above the waves. The lifeboat found a catamaran anchored but pitching violently with the seas smashing over her. There were no signs of life, so second coxswain John McDermott prepared to board. Then a man appeared on deck and asked for the two women crew to be taken off and the catamaran to be towed.

Getting the lifeboat alongside in the rough seas was dangerous and difficult, but Harry Jones succeeded and John McDermott judged his moment and jumped. The lifeboat went in again and lifeboatman David Dodd jumped across. Now the lifeboatmen could make their own assessment of the situation.

They found the crew too exhausted to be transferred safely in the very rough seas. The catamaran was in danger of being wrecked if the strained anchor cable snapped, so Harry Jones decided he must tow her off. It was a difficult job and a plastic dustbin had to be towed behind the catamaran to act as a drogue. Seamanship of the highest order was needed to coax the tow around and into the shelter of Mostyn Harbour, and to land three very grateful people.

Hearing the tale in Stourbridge, Frank Clifford was so impressed that he decided to change his will. When he died he left the RNLI £300,000 to help provide the New Quay lifeboat, *Frank and Lena Clifford of Stourbridge*. Harry and Margaret Jones were among the crowd at the naming ceremony, and had to be prised out, somewhat reluctantly, to meet the various VIPs present.

INSHORE ANTICS

West Kirby, Hoylake's near neighbour, has an inshore lifeboat in a spanking new boathouse on the promenade overlooking the River Dee; the old boathouse was seriously damaged and flooded in storms in 1990 and had to be demolished. At one stage during the floods the whole boathouse was awash and the crew and honorary secretary were nearly trapped inside.

The other lifeboat on the Wirral is at **New Brighton**, which clocked up the RNLI's 100,000th life saved in 1975 when a 13-year-old boy drifting out to sea in a rubber dinghy was pulled in. Instead of getting a telling off, a surprised Stuart Dixon was later presented with a framed certificate.

New Brighton is a station that has made the transition from an all-weather to an inshore lifeboat with great success, and the new Atlantic 21 was in dramatic action within a year of the big boat leaving.

Helmsman Bev Brown had to drive the lifeboat on to the deck of a fishing boat so that lifeboatman Robin Middleton could leap on to the deck and drag an injured fisherman through tangled nets and deck tackle to safety. Both lifeboatmen won Silver Medals. Bev Brown went on to win a Vellum for a difficult search in darkness, then a Bronze Medal for saving a yacht and two people in gales and rough seas.

Then in 1987 Helmsman Anthony Clare rescued three people and their yacht in very bad conditions and was given the award for the bravest inshore lifeboat rescue of the year.

Awards bring publicity which not everyone enjoys. Keith Willacy, the honorary secretary of the **Morecambe** lifeboat station, is one of those who will not like seeing his name in this book. Not that he has anything

Bev Brown and Robin Middleton of the New Brighton lifeboat.

Keith Willacy of Morecambe.

to hide; far from it, he is a distinguished figure at the Morecambe station, a founder lifeboatman and a medal winner, who now has a son in the crew. With his gruff exterior and no-nonsense outlook, Keith hates personal publicity, but it is difficult to stay out of the limelight when you win a Bronze Medal for rescuing two men stranded on a sandbank in a gale-force wind, an official letter of appreciation for rescuing two people in an inflatable dinghy from under a sea wall, and a Silver Medal for outstanding courage and seamanship in saving a man stranded on a concrete marker pillar after he lost his sailboard in a gale.

Even as honorary secretary, Keith has carried out rescues. He is a local Sea Fisheries Officer and, on a stormy February night in 1990, when a call came that a yacht anchored off Glasson Dock, on the River Lune near Lancaster, was flashing SOS messages with a torch, he decided to take the Sea Fisheries inflatable to the scene by road to save time. Two lifeboatmen went with him and, even though the force 9 gale blowing from the north-west was gusting to force 11, with hail and rain squalls, they decided to launch their boat.

Weaving in and out of moorings, branches of trees and other floating debris, with hardly any visibility in the spray, they managed to reach the yacht and, before they could even get aboard, a man jumped into their boat. He was the only occupant and after waiting for a stinging hail squall to pass, they set off back for the launching slipway, heading into the wind and the sea.

They could see only two yards ahead and the tiny inflatable was constantly being filled by the seas. There was so much spray in the air that it was difficult even to breathe. Three times one side of the boat was lifted right out of the water and they thought that they must surely capsize. They only found their way back to the shore by catching sight of the reflective strips on the lifejacket of a lifeboatman on the shore. Keith Willacy had to muster all his skill to get the boat in, as he was driving virtually blind in these appalling conditions, but he got his boat, his crew and the survivor safely home.

LANCASHIRE LADS

A lifeboat coxswain is not a man you might expect to see among the potted plants if you walked into Ashton's Garden Centre in **Lytham.** Yet that's where Andrew Ashton has his day job. In case anybody should worry whether he can tell a fuchsia from a fender, be reassured, for Andrew is a qualified captain with a foreign-going master's ticket. Like all lifeboatmen, he has become accustomed to the unexpected. On one routine passage in 1989, taking the lifeboat to Holyhead for an overhaul, he was surprised to be called up by the coastguard and told of a timber-ship on fire in Liverpool Bay. The 500-ton *Nanna* was registered in Hamburg, like the *Mexico* whose plight had caused the terrible disaster at Lytham a century before.

As always, it is difficult to get the coxswain to admit to the dangers he faced. 'We altered course and set off at full speed through horrendous weather to get to the scene. When we arrived, two merchant ships were standing by but were unable to do anything.'

This is a point that many people miss. Large ships cannot nip in and out like a small lifeboat, which is designed with only one purpose in mind.

'By this time the ship was billowing smoke and it was getting hectic and very hot on board. The crew were reluctant to leave at first, but they realised they had to jump. They looked confused and exhausted more than frightened.'

As the lifeboat went in, the heavy swell tossed her 10 feet up the side of the ship, which was rolling heavily, but *Nanna*'s captain and seven crew were taken off safely. The **Hoylake** lifeboat was launched to stand by for nine hours while a fire tug fought the blaze and Andrew Ashton landed the German seamen in Liverpool, then turned back for Lytham, as it was now too late to reach the Holyhead boatyard, arriving after 11 hours at sea.

The next morning Andrew and the crew set out again and this time reached Holyhead without any interruption. Andrew's summary of the rescue was typically downbeat: 'Overall the operation went very smoothly. It was a different experience for us because we are used to rescuing small craft in the River Ribble.'

The lights, the fun-fairs, the landladies, the pier and the tower all add up to make **Blackpool** Europe's biggest resort. The town's civic pride is built on its ability to attract hundreds of thousands of holidaymakers, and

Blackpool seafront in January 1983, when three policemen died trying to save a man whose dog had jumped into the sea.

took a knock when British Rail withdrew direct trains from London in the 1980s. There had also been disquiet in the town when the RNLI withdrew the conventional lifeboat in 1975. Trials with an Atlantic 21 were not to everyone's satisfaction and two inflatable lifeboats now serve at Blackpool.

There are times when, off the promenade, no boat, big or small, can operate in conditions known locally as the 'edge'. Waves roll in at high tide, gaining power over the shallow beach, and rebound off the promenade wall, causing a cauldron of boiling foam. It was in these conditions that three police officers died in 1983 as, one after another, they went into the surf to try to help a man who had plunged in to save his dog.

Blackpool lifeboatmen know all about the 'edge' and know too that their inflatable inshore lifeboats, versatile as they are, have limitations placed on their use by the RNLI to protect the lifeboatmen. In January 1988, quite consciously, two of the RNLI's most experienced helmsmen broke those limitations off Blackpool to take both inshore lifeboats to sea when two separate boats were in trouble. Waves 10 feet high were pounding the beach and there was a dangerous undertow running at three knots, but Keith Horrocks and Philip Denham felt that they could get through.

One boat, *Dijon*, was firing flares, and the other, *Peebles*, had capsized. Keith Horrocks in the first inshore lifeboat reached the *Dijon* and told the occupant to head to sea and wait while he went to search for the *Peebles*. He found the bows of the boat sticking out of the water but no sign of life. Searching southwards the lifeboatmen found a person face down in the water. Sea conditions at the scene, typical of the notorious 'edge', were seven feet of curling broken surf with reflected waves, causing a confused cross-sea with steep peaks. There was no pattern to the waves, just a mass of churning water, and as the lifeboat slowed down to pick up the man, she was nearly overwhelmed. The crew reached over the side and grabbed the unconscious man, starting work immediately to try and revive him. They turned for the shore and the other inshore boat, having plucked a man from the *Dijon*, raced to join them.

Philip Denham and Terence Rogers, both qualified first-aiders, kept up resuscitation and heart massage until an ambulance crew arrived to take over. Although he was alive when landed, sadly the man died three hours later in hospital.

Meanwhile the lifeboats had to put out again to search for a second man from the *Dijon*, joined by **Fleetwood** and **Lytham** lifeboats and helicopters. As Blackpool's inshore lifeboats darted in and out of the surf for almost two hours, the wind increased, gusting up to force 9. Pieces of flotsam were seen and investigated and two lifejackets were recovered, but no survivor.

Unusually, the RNLI's report was quite dramatic: 'Sea conditions

Fleetwood lifeboat Lady of Lancashire *searching in rough seas.*

remained treacherous throughout the search and both helmsmen were acutely aware of the danger of being capsized bow over stern. Both boats shipped a lot of water and flying spray made conditions very difficult, with salt water and suspended sand affecting the eyes of all crew members.'

The tremendous skill and bravery of the helmsmen in handling the small inflatables was recognised by the award of Bronze Medals, a well-deserved boost to the pride of Blackpool lifeboat station.

The fishing port of **Fleetwood**, linked by tram to Blackpool, often sends its lifeboat to work with the Blackpool boats in searches off the beach. While the inshore lifeboats dodge in and out of the surf, the all-weather boat works in deeper water. Coxswain Ian Fairclough says that he would ideally like two big lifeboats, his old Waveney, *Lady of Lancashire*, ideal for work on the surfline as she was based on an American design for the wild Pacific coasts, and his present Tyne, with better crew protection and electronic gear for rescues out in the Irish Sea. Ian, however, already has his work cut out keeping one lifeboat at constant readiness.

Fleetwood's commercial lifeline, the River Wyre, dumps tons of silt in the lifeboat dock, which has an elaborate system of underwater air pipes to keep the silt moving. Every tide the pumps have to be activated, so Ian is often out at night, keeping the dock clear and the lifeboat ready.

One of the biggest employers in the town is the lozenge manufacturer Fisherman's Friend, still a family business. The famous sore throat remedy, used worldwide, was originally invented by local pharmacist James Lofthouse for the Fleetwood trawlermen, and was a natural product for a joint promotion with the RNLI. In 1990 the Lofthouse family agreed that one penny would be given for every packet sold over the next two years. The result was a magnificent donation of £200,000 to the RNLI, and in June 1993 Mrs Doreen Lofthouse, the managing director, named a new Mersey Class lifeboat *Fisherman's Friend* in Fleetwood. Ian Fairclough and his crew had worked hard to help arrange the ceremony, but his dream of two lifeboats at his station was not to be; *Fisherman's Friend* sailed off immediately after the ceremony for relief duties at Llandudno.

CUMBRIA

Up the coast in Cumbria, **Barrow** is best known as the town where Vickers build naval ships and submarines, a company town hit by successive defence cuts leading to massive lay-offs from the yard. There is now an imaginative Dock Museum, tracing the town's shipbuilding history, and it includes the former Barrow lifeboat *Herbert Leigh*. The lifeboat, which saved 71 lives from 1951 to 1982, was the gift of a Mr Leigh from Bolton whose business was Leigh's Paints. His nephew, Philip Leigh-Bramwell, took over as chairman of the firm and made a huge anonymous donation to buy Fleetwood's former lifeboat, *Lady of Lancashire*. Throughout her life at Fleetwood nobody knew who had given the boat, and it was only at the ceremony to name her replacement that Mr Leigh-Bramwell, a slight figure and a model of old-world courtesy, allowed his name to be announced as the benefactor.

His family's generosity extended further when his son Brian arranged to buy back the *Herbert Leigh* from the RNLI and present the boat for display in the Barrow museum. The family still shows a keen interest in the RNLI's work.

Coincidence followed the *Herbert Leigh* on her last passage, when she was taken from Barrow to Poole by sea. Stormbound in Holyhead, one of the crew wandered across to the harbour office to while away the afternoon with a chat. The man on duty turned out to be a former lightship keeper who had been rescued by the *Herbert Leigh* from the Morecambe Bay lightvessel in hurricane-force winds when he was seriously ill.

The Barrow lifeboat station is outside the town on Roa Island, the sixth site for lifeboats in the station's history. Roa Island is at the end of a mile-long causeway and comprises around 40 houses, a hotel and a cafe. Nowadays only Coxswain Alec Moore lives on the island; his is a lifeboat family and past crew lists are scattered with Moores as coxswains, mechanics and crew members. Alec used to work at Vickers before being made redundant and now works shifts for British Gas, only a mile and a half from the lifeboat station. The rest of the crew live at Rampside on the mainland and most work in Barrow, five miles away. A daytime call

The St Bees inshore lifeboat.

means a dash by car, trying not to break the speed limits. Even then, the lifeboat gets afloat within 20 minutes of the first alert.

A single-track railway line runs from Barrow right up the Cumbrian coast, through St Bees to Whitehaven, Workington and Carlisle, the only remnant of a network of lines linking West Cumbria's iron ore and coal mines to its ports. Now the main employer is British Nuclear Fuels at the Windscale nuclear power station, whose huge 1950s concrete towers can be seen from western Lakeland fells and all along the sandy coast to the sandstone headland of St Bees. A walk over the cliffs takes you to Fleswick Bay, a nesting site for hundreds of sea birds with a beach of almost surreal qualities, sea-smoothed beds of red rock scattered with rounded pebbles and indented with rock pools.

Fleswick Bay was no idyll for the crew of the fishing boat *Coeur de Lion* after she set out from Whitehaven one July morning in 1993, for the westerly winds forced her on to rocks 40 yards offshore and the heavy surf started rolling over her. When **St Bees** inshore lifeboat reached her, the *Coeur de Lion* had been pushed over and was listing heavily, and her crew of two were hanging on to the bow. The first rescue attempt ended in failure when both propellers on the lifeboat's outboard engines were damaged on the rocks. Lifeboatman Ian McDowell decided that the lifeboat would have to be run ashore and the propellers changed.

Approaching the beach, all four lifeboat crew jumped out to steady the

The Workington lifeboat is craned into the water.

boat but Alastair Graham fell backwards over a rock and the boat landed on top of him, injuring his leg. The boat was being tossed around in the surf, and both Ian McDowell and his son Paul were knocked about before it could be beached and the propellers changed.

While this was being done, Ian McDowell tied a rope around his waist and strode out through the surf to shout to the fishermen that the lifeboat would soon be coming. The boat was relaunched through the surf, oil and debris and Ian drove out, hitting numerous rocks and nudging the lifeboat's bow into the port side of the *Coeur de Lion*. He urged the fishermen to jump, and, after much hesitation, one man did, just as the lifeboat was hit by a large wave and pushed clear. Marcus Clarkson grabbed the helm and drove back in and the second man threw himself on to the lifeboat's canopy. Shortly after the lifeboat left, the fishing boat started breaking up on the rocks, becoming a total wreck.

Lifeboat inspector Guy Platten later summed up the rescue in his report: 'These men would certainly have perished had not the lifeboat managed to reach them just in time.'

The lifeboat up the coast at **Workington** is unique. Appropriately for a town whose steel works specialises in making railway lines, the lifeboat sits on a carriage that runs on rails to the quayside, where a crane lowers it into the water. The River Derwent is too shallow at low tide to provide an afloat berth, and although a launch from the beach is possible, the crane allows the bigger Tyne Class lifeboat *Sir John Fisher* to operate at Workington.

The statistics of the mechanism are impressive. The crane is over 50 feet long and 30 feet high; it can stretch to put the lifeboat 20 feet out from the quay; and the hoist has a design load of 26.5 tonnes. And the cost? A cool £1 million for the crane, carriage and boathouse. It's a price worth paying, however, for Workington gives all-weather cover to a huge area of the Irish Sea and all of the Solway Firth, with extra inshore cover from the lifeboats at Silloth and Kirkcudbright.

Silloth got its first lifeboat in 1860, to much celebration in the town. In spite of steady rain, large crowds turned out to gawp at the new lifeboat. A contemporary newspaper reported: 'The size and solidity of the boat and the strength of the carriage attracted general attention. Many persons appeared to have imagined that the boat was a light structure which might easily be carried on men's shoulders, like an Indian's canoe; but when they found that it required six stout horses to draw it and the broad-wheeled carriage on which it rested, their preconceived notions were entirely changed.' The 1860 lifeboat cost £135, had six oars and was 30 feet long.

Just over a century later Silloth got an inshore lifeboat and trials with a rigid inflatable received a much less flowery newspaper write-up. 'Silloth lifeboat station is on the crest of a wave. For it is the proud possessor of a new £20,000 inshore lifeboat. The semi-rigid inflatable has a 55 horsepower engine and a speed of 32 knots.'

"It's a small boat but its extra speed and acceleration will be a great help for emergencies," said lifeboat inspector Michael Vlasto.

MANX LIFEBOATS

The Isle of Man is famous for the TT motorbike races, its tailless cats, its horse-drawn trams and miniature railway.

There is a fairy bridge, which even be-suited businessmen will not cross without a greeting to the fairies, and the Tynwald, the oldest democratic parliament in the world. Yet the Island's celebration of being the birth-place of organised lifesaving at sea is muted; the most obvious evidence is in **Douglas** where the lifeboat is named *Sir William Hillary* in honour of the RNLI's founder, himself a Douglas lifeboatman, as we have already seen. Coxswain Robbie Curran carries on a long tradition of fishermen in the boat, and freely admits to a friendly rivalry between the island's sta-tions, a rivalry echoed between the fishing fleets of each port. The com-petition soon vanishes in emergencies, however, as it did on the first launch of the *Sir William Hillary* in March 1989.

The lifeboat spent 19 hours in very rough seas searching for a missing Belgian trawler and was joined by lifeboats from **Port St Mary, Barrow, Lytham, Fleetwood** and **Moelfre**. On a pitch black night with low cloud and gale-force southerly winds, the lifeboats ploughed through the waves to scour the Irish Sea for any sign of the trawler. The crews had to be out on deck, manning the searchlight and investigating every piece of flotsam, looking for tell-tale oil slicks from the trawler's fuel tanks. Robbie Curran changed the men on deck regularly to prevent prolonged exposure to the raw wind and spray – yet they had to be there, for this was a time when the high-tech electronics were overshadowed by the human eyeball look-ing for anything to give a clue about the missing boat. But there was noth-ing, even though the lifeboats put in a total of 67 hours of searching, helped by merchant ships, helicopters, aircraft and a warship. Only one body from the five-man crew was ever found.

The lifeboat stations at the northern and southern extremities of the Isle of Man are linked by one of the RNLI's most generous benefactors, Mrs Ann Ritchie, who provided four lifeboats in her lifetime and set up a trust fund to help the RNLI on the Island after her death.

Her first gift was the *James Ball Ritchie*, the **Ramsey** lifeboat, in 1970. She lived in Ramsey and used to call in at the lifeboathouse for a chat with Coxswain Jimmy Kinnin. In 1991 Ramsey received a new lifeboat, just after Mrs Ritchie's death; it was named *Ann and James Ritchie* in memory of her and her husband. It was in this boat one August night in 1992 that Jimmy Kinnin carried out a rescue within sight of Mrs Ritchie's old home.

A lone yachtsman was taking his boat from Fleetwood to Arran and, as the weather had deteriorated, he decided to shelter in Ramsey. As he approached the harbour his engine failed and the yacht was swept down towards the harbour wall. The yachtsman managed to get his anchor down but the yacht was rolling heavily, the mast almost touching the sea on each side. The lifeboat was called out and the crew found the boathouse doors being hit by the waves as they arrived.

Although the yacht was only yards away, she was so near the promenade wall that the lifeboat touched the bottom as Coxswain Kinnin circled to see how much space he had to work in. The answer was precious little. He would have to get the yacht's anchor up and start towing her at the same time or she would be smashed against the sea wall. The only way to do this was to get a rope around the anchor chain and pull like fury, but attaching the rope in the boiling seas would be no easy matter.

Five times the lifeboat edged in until the tow was fixed and the lifeboat surged ahead. At last the anchor pulled free and the yacht was dragged clear of the surf. The two boats went three-quarters of a mile to get into calmer water, then the lifeboat turned back and the coxswain nursed his catch back through the tricky harbour entrance. It was a rescue that Ann Ritchie would have been proud to see her boat perform.

Port St Mary, at the south of the Island, has Mrs Ritchie's other lifeboat, the *Gough Ritchie*, which made an equally spectacular rescue from another yacht, the *Melfort*, which had run aground just off Castletown. Like the yacht at Ramsey, she was only yards from the shore and coastguards on the breakwater fired rocket lines across and set up a breeches buoy, pulling a man to safety through the seas.

The *Gough Ritchie* had moored at the breakwater and the inflatable dinghy was launched and drove in as the yacht began to smash up on the rocks. The sea was breaking all around and filling the inflatable, and as one man struggled across the deck of the yacht, his legs got tangled in the wreckage and he was too weak to free himself. Lifeboatman William Halsall tried to pull him free, but a heavy sea lifted the inflatable away from the yacht and both men were swept into the water. The slack ropes of the breeches buoy tangled around William Halsall and as he fought to free himself the yachtsman slipped from his grasp and disappeared.

The inflatable's helmsman, Eric Quillin, had been half knocked out of his boat and now saw his crewman in trouble. He managed to drag him aboard, but the inflatable was now two-thirds full of water and hard to steer. Another wave hit her and she capsized, throwing both lifeboatmen into the water. Their boat was blown away from them and the men were swallowing seawater as the waves broke over their heads.

As their crewmates on the breakwater watched helplessly, the men were miraculously swept towards them and pulled out of the sea on to the breakwater. Then Coxswain Norman Quillin spotted a man hanging on to a lifebuoy being swept down the same way. He quickly grabbed a boathook and jumped on to the breakwater just as the man in the water was smashed against it, injuring his head. Norman Quillin hooked the man's jacket and hauled him high enough for the other lifeboatmen to pull him in.

The inflatable of Port St Mary's Gough Ritchie *reaches the yacht* Melfort, *while in the second photograph a man is pulled from the sea by lifeboatmen on the breakwater.*

The remaining yachtsman was now in dire straits. His boat was breaking up under his feet and rescue from the shore or by inflatable was impossible. The lifeboatmen urged him to jump into the sea and be swept down to the breakwater but, perhaps not surprisingly, he declined. As the tide was flooding there was now more water around the wreck, so Coxswain Quillin decided to take the *Gough Ritchie* in amongst the rocks. As he gingerly worked his way towards the yacht the lifeboat was banging on the rocks, but lifeboatman Derrick McCutcheon hurled a rope across, which the yachtsman tied around his shoulders. Slowly the lifeboat drove astern, out of danger, and pulled the man from the wreck, got him alongside, then safely aboard where he was treated for hypothermia, shock and minor injuries. Tragically the man who had earlier slipped from William Halsall's grasp drowned, and was brought in by helicopter.

Port Erin is just over a mile from Port St Mary as the crow flies, but over eight miles by sea around the Calf of Man, guarding the south-west approaches to the Island. The eight-knot Rother Class lifeboat *Osman Gabriel* was replaced in 1992 by a 32-knot Atlantic 21 inshore lifeboat and was sold to the Estonian lifeboat service. The Baltic state, independent again on the break-up of the USSR, was re-establishing its lifeboat service on voluntary principles. Throughout their years as part of the USSR, the Estonians maintained a skeleton lifesaving service, and delighted in receiving the RNLI's magazine 'Lifeboat'.

One of their first requests for overseas aid was for lifeboats, and the British ambassador in Tallin persuaded the Foreign Office to buy a lifeboat from the RNLI. Port Erin's *Osman Gabriel* was shipped to the Baltic and became the *Anita*, named after the ambassador's wife.

Peel, on the opposite coast to Douglas, had its lifeboat provided from a bequest left by the great-great-granddaughter of Sir William Hillary, Miss Ruby Clery. A very moving story emerged when that lifeboat was named. The tale starts with a ship's figurehead kept in the Peel lifeboathouse, which sits below Peel Castle. Affectionately known as 'George', the wooden figurehead came from the Norwegian barque *St George*, which was wrecked off Peel in 1889.

The ship was bound from Greenock to Montevideo, but was hit by a gale that carried away sails and masts. Out went the lifeboat. The contemporary account of the rescue takes up the story:

'Many people on shore felt that it was almost an impossibility for the lifeboat to get up to the vessel in the teeth of such a wind. But the gallant coxswain handled the boat splendidly and finally, after a prolonged battle with the elements lasting over two hours, he got sufficiently near to the distressed barque to hail those on board.'

Getting close enough to rescue people was more difficult, with broken rigging and spars floating around the ship adding to the hazards of the gale. The captain's dog had already jumped overboard and swam for the rocks, but it was hit by floating timber and drowned. A lifebuoy was sent across but got tangled with the wreckage. Then the rope that had been thrown from the ship snapped and injured one of the lifeboatmen. Time and again they tried to get another rope across and finally succeeded.

The first to be rescued was the captain's wife. Then came the ship's carpenter, his canvas bag lashed to his back. Thinking he was bringing his personal belongings, the lifeboatmen shouted out 'No clothes allowed', and told him to throw the bag away. But wrapped inside the bag was the captain's nine-month-old baby, and coming across in the lifebuoy the carpenter held his breath and stayed below the surface to save the child from a drenching.

The lifeboatmen were straining at the oars to keep the lifeboat clear of the *St George* as, one by one, 21 more people were hauled across, Captain Thorensen being the last to leave. As the lifeboat turned for home, leaving the *St George* a total wreck, she was greeted by a huge crowd on the breakwater. It must have pleased the pious Victorians to note that, 'To add to the thrilling character of the scene, a beautiful rainbow appeared in the western sky, just as the hapless mariners had reached a place of safety, after their perilous experiences in the open sea.'

Baby Sigrun Thorensen returned to Norway with her parents and grew up to have a daughter of her own, Karin. And on a grey afternoon in 1992, with 'George' the figurehead looking on, it was Karin who named the new Peel lifeboat *Ruby Clery*.

CHAPTER TWO

The North East – designed for danger

'His breast must have been protected all round with oak and three-ply bronze, who first launched his frail boat on the rough sea.'

Odes, *Horace*

JUST AS NOBODY can say for certain where and when the first lifeboat station was opened, it is impossible to be sure who invented the first lifeboat. In 1765 a Frenchman, Bernieres, drew up plans for a boat that was virtually unsinkable and almost impossible to capsize, but there is no evidence that it was ever used.

The strongest claims for the origins of the lifeboat undoubtedly lie in the North East of England, complicated by an argument 200 years old. Lionel Lukin, a London coachmaker, invented an 'unimmergible boat', which he patented in 1785. It was not specifically for lifesaving, and he had no luck when he tried to interest the Royal Navy in his ideas. His first boat was a converted Norway yawl to which he added a cork gunwale; it was given to a Ramsgate pilot for testing but seems to have been used for smuggling!

Undeterred, Lukin converted a second boat, which was named *Witch* because of her excellent sailing performance in bad weather. Then in 1786 Archdeacon Sharp of Bamburgh, Northumberland, sent Lukin a coble for conversion, and this was used as one of the first lifeboats, as part of an elaborate lifesaving organisation based at Bamburgh Castle.

A terrible tragedy in 1789 acted as a spur to lifeboat design. The ship *Adventure* was wrecked in the mouth of the River Tyne and hundreds of people lining the shore watched helplessly as the crew of the ship dropped from the rigging and drowned; conditions were so rough that no boat could be launched to save them. A group of local businessmen known as the Gentlemen of the Lawe House offered a prize of two guineas in a competition for the best lifeboat design.

Two Tyneside men who entered the competition came up with the best

A lifeboat going out to a wreck at Tynemouth in about 1870.

models. William Wouldhave, a house-painter and singing teacher, noticed that a woman drawing water from a well had a piece of broken wooden dish lying in the water, and that however the dish was turned over, it would right itself because of its shape. Wouldhave used this principle to make a model boat that was self-righting; he tested it in the tanks of a local brewery.

The competition judges were impressed with Wouldhave's ideas, but offered him only half the prize money. He is reported to have rejected the guinea and stormed off in disgust. Another of the competitors, Henry Greathead, was asked to build a full-size lifeboat and seems to have used some of Wouldhave's features, such as extra buoyancy, while

Henry Greathead and his lifeboat.

31

incorporating his own scheme of having a curved keel. He was to build another 30 lifeboats, and in 1802 was voted £1,200 by Parliament and 50 guineas by the Society of Arts.

While Greathead prospered, Lukin was furious, accusing Greathead of stealing his ideas; he said that the boats were 'to all the essential principles of safety, precisely according to my patent'. There was a vitriolic exchange of letters in *The Gentlemen's Magazine* about whether Lukin or Greathead could claim the title of inventor of the lifeboat. At least Lukin's tombstone describes him as 'the first who built a lifeboat . . . the original inventor of that principle of safety'.

Greathead's legacy is more tangible. In Redcar, Cleveland, the oldest lifeboat in the world, the *Zetland*, built by Greathead in 1800, is still preserved and on public display. Another Greathead boat can be seen in a shelter by a bus terminus in South Shields.

ENGINES TO THE RESCUE

Some 135 years after the wreck of the *Adventure*, another wreck in the North East proved a further turning point in lifeboat technology. This time it confirmed the value of engines in lifeboats, which were originally regarded with some suspicion. There were good reasons for this as there were considerable problems in keeping early internal combustion engines going as the lifeboat bucked and rolled in rough seas, subjecting the engine to angles it was never designed to meet. Indeed, when engines

The wreck of the Rohilla *off Whitby, with a lifeboat on the beach.*

were fitted in sailing lifeboats, coxswains were instructed that 'the motor is an auxiliary to the sails which latter are the principal motive power'.

The proof of motor power came in October 1914 when the steamer *Rohilla*, which had been designated as a hospital ship, was on her way from Queensferry to Dunkirk to evacuate the wounded. She had 229 people on board when she was driven ashore off Whitby in a gale and was smashed into two pieces by the sea.

Crowds gathered along the cliffs and the shoreline to watch the rescue attempts, and reporters and photographers were able to capture the events at first hand.

At daybreak the **Whitby** No 2 lifeboat, the lighter of the harbour's two boats, was hauled on skids to the scene of the wreck, being lifted over an eight-foot-high sea wall on the way. The lifeboat crew managed to row to the wreck and, threading their way between the rocks, took off 17 people. Having landed them, the boat went out again and, fighting through the waves, took off another 18. She was constantly bumping on the rocks and, after landing the second group of survivors, was too badly damaged to go out again.

The **Upgang** lifeboat was lowered down the cliff on ropes but could not get out in the tremendous seas. Meanwhile, the **Scarborough** and **Teesmouth** lifeboats had been called. The weather was too severe at Scarborough for any vessel to get out of the harbour, but there was some improvement in the late afternoon and the lifeboat set out, towed by a steam trawler.

They arrived in the dark and although they could not get near the wreck, they stayed all night in case the weather changed. At daybreak things were no better, so they returned to Scarborough.

At Teesmouth there was a motor lifeboat, which set out as the Scarborough lifeboat was returning. As she crossed the bar at the mouth of the River Tees, the lifeboat took a tremendous pounding, then fell into the trough of a mountainous wave and sprang such a serious leak that she could not go on and had to be towed back to Middlesbrough by a tug. That morning the Upgang and Whitby's heavier No 1 lifeboat tried again, but could not reach the *Rohilla*.

A telegram was sent to summon the **Tynemouth** motor lifeboat and at 4.30 on the Saturday afternoon she set out. Ahead lay a journey of 44 miles through the night and the storm and with no coast lights, as they had all been extinguished because of the war. The Tynemouth lifeboat arrived in Whitby harbour at 1 am on the Sunday morning, and at daybreak she set out to the rescue.

By now the survivors on the *Rohilla* had been stranded for two days and two nights, their broken vessel constantly battered by the storm. Some had tried to swim ashore and a few had made it while others perished. Fifty people remained aboard.

A reporter from the *Yorkshire Post* was there to capture the drama of the final rescue: 'The lifeboat, looking fearfully small and frail, throbbed her way towards the wreck. Nearer and nearer she got, and then, within 200 yards of the *Rohilla*, she turned seawards. Was she able to face the current running at four knots an hour and the curling seas, still fierce and strong, though of diminished size?

"She'll never get there," declared one of the watchers. But a burly fisherman remarked, "Just wait – she knows what she's about." Presently, she stopped dead and discharged over the boiling sea gallons and gallons of oil. It seemed that the ocean must laugh at these puny drops, yet the effect was remarkable; within a few minutes the oil spread over the surface of the water and the waves appeared suddenly to be flattened down as by a miracle. In the meantime the lifeboat turned about, raced at full speed past the stern of the wreck and then turned directly for the shore. The most dangerous moment came when she was inside the surf and broadside on to the waves; but guided with splendid skill and courage, she moved forward steadily, and a cheer of relief went out from the shore when she reached the lee of the wreck, immediately beneath the crowded bridge. A rope was let down to the lifeboat and immediately figures could be discerned scrambling down into the boat with a quickness and agility that seemed extraordinary in one presumed to be exhausted almost to death. In less than a quarter of an hour more than 40 men had been taken into the boat.

'It was then that two enormous waves were seen rolling up from the sea at tremendous speed. Twice the tough little craft disappeared for a moment beneath the spray, reappeared, tottered, and righted herself gamely. Indeed, not a man was lost, not a splinter broken. Closer still she hugged the vessel's side till every man aboard – fifty of them in all – had been hauled into the rescuing boat.'

The lifeboat had a dangerous return journey, being hit broadside by a huge wave, but made the harbour safely to be met by most of the townsfolk of Whitby. Perhaps the most significant part of the reporter's whole account – with the great benefit of hindsight – was the sentence, 'As the lifeboat slipped smoothly through the calm waters of the harbour the music of her engine was sweet to the ear'. For that rescue had done away for ever with any doubts about engines in lifeboats.

SELF-RIGHTING

The final great hurdle for lifeboat designers to overcome was to find a way of making a self-righting lifeboat that was not more prone to capsize in the first place. Richard Oakley solved the problem with an ingenious system of transferring water ballast through non-return valves from a tank in the bottom of the hull to one higher up and offset, creating a righting force. The first of his revolutionary new boats went to **Scarborough** in 1958, where she was immediately accepted by the crew.

In 1978 an exhibition was staged in the Science Museum in London to celebrate 20 years of modern self-righting lifeboats. Jimmy Savile, himself

Coxswain Bill Sheader of Scarborough and Jimmy Savile at the Science Museum in 1978.

an honorary member of the Beaumaris lifeboat crew, opened the exhibition and Scarborough lifeboat coxswain Bill Sheader was the other VIP guest.

After the opening, Sheader was whisked off to the BBC for a radio interview with disc jockey Brian Matthew. Having put Sheader at his ease, Matthew started to question him about a rescue in 1969 in his Oakley Class lifeboat, which had won him a Silver Medal for bravery. Never a man of many words, Sheader's replies were almost monosyllabic.

Had the rescue been at all difficult?

'Aye, a bit.'

Was it dangerous?

'Not really.'

What about the boat?

'She handled well.'

In exasperation, Matthew turned to the RNLI official accompanying Sheader. Could he give any more details of the rescue and explain how Sheader had won his medal? The story then came out.

The lifeboat crew were in the boathouse one Sunday morning, expecting trouble as a storm was brewing. Shortly after midday a report came through that a converted ship's lifeboat, *Sheena*, had capsized in the heavy surf in South Bay. Within minutes of being launched the lifeboat found the *Sheena* in the midst of rocky outcrops, boiling surf and very shallow water. With less than five feet of water under his lifeboat, Bill Sheader knew that if she capsized she could never right but would be jammed on the rocks.

The men had now been thrown out of the *Sheena* and when one of them was spotted in the surf, Sheader did not hesitate. He swung his lifeboat round, drove right alongside the man and shouted to the crew to grab him. Just as they leaned over the side, a wave filled the lifeboat and she hit the rocks just beneath her keel. Sheader coaxed the boat clear using his engines, while his crew struggled to pull the man to safety.

He was in poor condition and was taken straight ashore to a waiting ambulance.

Then the lifeboat set out again, as the second man had been spotted in the surf. Again Sheader went straight over the dangerous rock outcrops, again the lifeboat hit the bottom, again the crew pulled a man to safety. But this time thick seaweed had wrapped around the propellers and Sheader had to juggle with his controls to stop the engines stalling and the lifeboat becoming completely disabled. The second man was unconscious and, in spite of mouth-to-mouth resuscitation, died later in hospital.

The lifeboat then went out again to look for a third man, but after three hours, and in worsening conditions, the search had to be abandoned.

An RNLI report by an experienced lifeboat inspector, Leslie Hill, praised the crew for their teamwork in hazardous conditions in which, 'They took their lives in their own hands not once, but on three separate occasions. It proved their faith in Coxswain Sheader and in their lifeboat.'

Faith or not, Sheader could not be persuaded by one of Britain's most experienced broadcasters to tell the tale of this remarkable rescue; you can lead a brave man to a microphone but you can't make him talk!

MAN OVERBOARD!

Lifeboat design is one vital part of the safety chain. A lifeboatman's gear is another. Whitby lifeboatman Henry Freeman was the only one out of 13 to survive a capsize in 1861 because he was wearing a cork lifejacket. A century later Teesmouth Coxswain Billy Carter found himself washed right out of his lifeboat when a wave went straight through the wheelhouse. The crew found him in minutes thanks to the light on his lifejacket. And **Scarborough's** lifeboat crew found themselves hauling their second coxswain, John Trotter, out of the sea when he was swept overboard in September 1991.

The German coaster *Vineta* had broken down five miles off Scarborough and her anchor would not hold. She was drifting dangerously close to rocks and there was water in the engine room. Coxswain Stuart Ogden launched the lifeboat at 11.30 am to take over from the Whitby lifeboat, which had been standing by for several hours. 'Standing by' usually means tossing around in choppy seas, steaming slowly around, waiting. It's another lifeboat job, often with no result other than a disaster avoided.

A tug had been sent for but was not due until 7 pm, so the lifeboatmen

The Scarborough lifeboat stands by the coaster Vineta *during the September 1991 rescue.*

whiled away the hours, ready in case the coaster's position suddenly worsened. After four and a half hours it was agreed that Whitby should take over again, then the tug's arrival was brought forward, so the Scarborough crew picked up some portable radios for the *Vineta* to overcome communication problems, and set out again.

The seas around the ship were now very rough and as John Trotter went forward to the bow of the lifeboat to throw the radios to the ship, a big swell lifted the *Vineta* and the lifeboat fell off a sea under the ship. Coxswain Ogden had to drive astern quickly to avoid being trapped by the ship and John Trotter, already off balance, was pitched into the sea and swept away by the tide. The crew, trained for just this incident, reacted immediately and within minutes had got him back on board, bruised but otherwise unharmed. Safe on dry land, John Trotter said, 'I was only in the water five or ten minutes but it felt like a lifetime. The lads had it all under control though.'

Once in the sea, the killer is usually cold – hypothermia – not drowning. On every lifeboathouse wall is a chart that shows its effects. The stages are baldly described as 'sensations of cold; amnesia; unconsciousness; cardiac arrest'. In the North Sea in winter, survival times can be as low as a few minutes. So when **Hartlepool** lifeboatman Robbie Maiden found himself being plucked from the North Sea after 35 minutes in the cold February water, it was hardly surprising that he expressed his relief by telling the helicopter winchman, 'If you weren't so

Robbie Maiden (right) with brother Ian and father Robbie Senior.

ugly I could kiss you'. Chilled and with a broken thumb, Robbie was taken to hospital for a check-up, but was soon home to join his mum, dad (the former coxswain) and brother.

The afternoon had started routinely enough, in lifeboat terms.

A huge supertanker, the 97,000-ton *Freja Svea*, was anchored in Teesbay, but as a force-10 gale blew up, her anchors dragged and she started drifting towards the jagged rock scars that jut out along the beach at Redcar. The captain's call for help was answered first by the **Teesmouth** lifeboat.

The sea was very rough with 25-foot waves, and as the lifeboat came round the tanker one of the crew shouted, 'Watch out, there's a big one', and the stern was hit by a 40-foot wave.

The bow fell into a large trough and the lifeboat rolled over 90 degrees, the alarm bells ringing and the wheelhouse filling with smoke and steam. As coxswain Peter Race regained control, two more huge seas, close together, struck the lifeboat, which became airborne then dropped upright into the trough. Nobody was injured, though mechanic Rod Stott somehow managed to bend his seat.

One of the lifeboat's engines was faltering, so the boat stood by until a helicopter lifted off some of the tanker's crew, then put back to station for repairs. Meanwhile, in mid-afternoon, the Hartlepool lifeboat launched to take over. Darkness fell and the tanker ran aground on the sandy part of the beach, missing the rocks. After two hours standing by, the Hartlepool lifeboat was hit by one of the huge seas that had knocked down her Teesmouth neighbour. She started to climb the immense curling wave, but just before reaching the top was knocked back down into the trough and rolled right over. Just as coxswain Eric Reeve saw daylight through the wheelhouse windows, the lifeboat was capsized again, and again righted straight away.

Some of the crew had been thrown around, Ian Maiden knocking Thomas Price out of his chair, but one man, Robbie Maiden, was missing. Ironically he had been trying to get back to the safety of the wheelhouse fast before the wave struck and had unclipped his lifeline to move down the boat. As she rolled, he had grabbed the towing post but was washed away head over heels and surfaced 70 yards from the lifeboat, being bowled along by the wind and the waves. While his crewmates on the lifeboat did a head count, Robbie stayed remarkably calm, his presence of mind saving his life.

First he had to stop being tumbled along like spindrift. He jammed his legs down into the water, inflated his lifejacket, activated his light and tightened the securing straps. He then closed the Velcro strip on the jacket cuff around his wrists to stop the chilling sea water circulating around his body and pulled the jacket hood over his head and face to stop the spray and sleet blasting in his face. He also managed to get his back to the waves so that he would not have sea water forced into his mouth and nose.

Back on the lifeboat the desperate search began. Almost immediately the crew spotted a light, 20 yards astern. After two attempts to reach it, they realised it was not Robbie but a lifebuoy that had broken loose on the capsize. As the seconds ticked away, their chances of spotting a man between the huge waves and in the dark began to fade. Three white parachute flares were fired to light up the scene, and although Robbie saw the lifeboat pass within 20 yards of him, it plunged on past into the storm.

The lifeboat's main radios were out, but the portable VHF was still working and Ian Maiden set to, transmitting their plight. The Teesmouth crew heard the message and set out again on only one engine.

Meanwhile, the RAF rescue helicopter had landed on the shore and the crew were going for refreshments before returning to their station. Ian Maiden's timing was perfect, for if his voice had crackled through just seconds later, the helicopter might not have heard him. But luck was on Robbie's side as the airmen scrambled their helicopter within moments of brother Ian's radio call.

For Robbie, having already seen the lifeboat sail past him, worse was to come. He saw an aircraft fly over, waved his lifejacket light to attract attention but was missed again. By now he was beginning to get very cold, but he decided that the only thing to do was to think positively. Soon he saw the helicopter playing its searchlight over the lifeboat, then it turned and headed directly for him.

The helicopter crew had spotted him by the reflective tape sewn on to his lifejacket, which shone out in the beam of their searchlight. Down came the winchman and just after 7 o'clock in the evening Robbie was landed on the seafront, stripped of his wet clothing, wrapped up warmly and whisked off to hospital.

Robbie was later interviewed on television and said that he owed his life to his training and his equipment: 'I would have died without it'.

TRADITIONS AND INNOVATIONS

All along the North East coast, from the Humber to the Tweed, are traditional fishing communities, many now reduced to only one or two boats, some with no fishing left at all. The boats were designed for local conditions and the slight variations in the open, beach-launched cobles will identify their home village. As with boats, so with fishermen's sweaters. Each village had its own design of hand-knitted navy blue woollen sweater, the idea being that a drowned man could be recognised and returned to his home by the pattern on his sweater. Gold earrings were worn to provide money for a decent burial.

To call out the lifeboats in those days, you might have contacted Mr Ballard, the headmaster of the grammar school at Berwick-on-Tweed, the Reverend Dunscombe at the rectory in Amble, Mr Holliday at the colliery office in Ashington or, most appropriately, Captain Jacob Storm in Robin Hood's Bay. An important tradition was to have a lifeboat at each fishing village, manned by the fishermen largely for mutual protection.

Once there were lifeboats every few miles, but the advent of motor lifeboats started the slow process of station closures, as one new boat could cover the area of two or three old ones. In some places there were two or even three lifeboats, and often vessels were withdrawn, never to be replaced. In other places they were withdrawn, then decades later inshore lifeboats returned to re-open the stations.

In the First World War lifeboats often had to put to sea with scratch crews, as so many young men were away fighting. At **Berwick** in 1915 the lifeboat put out to stand by a stranded motor vessel with the honorary secretary and a soldier to make up the numbers. They stayed at sea through a whole November night in a biting gale and eventually rescued the crew of six. The return journey was described as one of the bitterest experiences that any man in the boat had endured, and when they finally got ashore the condition of every man was 'pitiable to see'. After this dramatic rescue, Berwick had a relatively quiet time and the lifeboat was replaced by an inshore boat in 1976, which in turn was ousted when an all-weather Mersey Class boat arrived in 1993.

Changes take some time to be accepted, particularly in tight-knit communities. The withdrawal of traditional all-weather lifeboats, slow and steady, and their replacement with fast inshore lifeboats with younger crews, is often greeted with scepticism by the older hands in the village. The only answer is to look at the records being built up by the new crews, impressive statements of their skills and the versatility of their boats.

At **Redcar** the Atlantic 21 often works with the lifeboat from Teesmouth, but when a middle-aged couple and their dog became trapped at the foot of high cliffs with the tide rushing in and threatening to sweep them away, only an inshore lifeboat could reach them. A 12-foot swell was breaking across the rocks all around them, and going in to the surf was very dangerous. Still the lifeboat could not get close enough and crew member Barry Wheater volunteered to swim ashore with a rope around his waist.

Derek Robinson also swam across and the two men gently guided the lifeboat, its engines tilted upwards to avoid the rocks, in to the shallow water. The seas were lifting the lifeboat and pounding her on the rocks and the helmsman, Peter Hodge, grabbed the two people and their dog, urged his crew to get back in to the lifeboat and told them to haul her clear. The anchor rope was cut and the lifeboat drove out through the surf to land the cold couple, a Mr and Mrs Darling. Their dog, Monty, sat on the deck looking nonchalant throughout!

Cullercoats also has an Atlantic 21 and a collection of strange tales. Lifeboats and helicopters often work together, so it was not surprising that the Cullercoats crew should find themselves involved with an RAF crewman, except that this time they were called out to rescue flying officer Mark Parsons. A helicopter had lowered the airman into a dinghy as part of a training mission, but the aircraft had suddenly developed a problem that prevented it from retrieving him. A puzzled Mark watched

Coxswain Robert Patton of Runswick.

as the helicopter abandoned him and, with no radio, he was left to sit and contemplate his fate.

The helicopter got straight on to the coastguard and within minutes Cullercoats lifeboat was on her way. Conditions were good and within five minutes of launching, the airman was safely aboard and on his way back to dry land. The coastguard Land-Rover was waiting for him and took him for a cup of tea at the coastguard station before his wife arrived to collect him. An RAF Boulmer spokesman, noting that he had been in no danger, admitted that 'There was a fair amount of merriment over what had happened. The poor guy had no idea what was going on, but he was very trusting. He'd guessed they had some sort of problem and hadn't just left him.'

The adjacent villages of **Staithes** and **Runswick** show just how much change there can be. A lifeboat was sent to Staithes in 1875 to help local fishing boats, which were at great risk when coming home in storms. A decline in fishing and a shortage of men led to closure in 1922, but a new harbour was built, the fishing revived and the lifeboat returned in 1928. A motor lifeboat was sent to Runswick in 1933, and by 1938 Staithes was closed again. Shortly before, in 1934, Runswick coxswain Robert Patton performed a supremely heroic rescue, one of the greatest individual acts of heroism in the RNLI's history.

A tug had been towing a steamer that had started to sink off Runswick, and although the tug managed to rescue seven men, one was still on board; he was disabled and could not get off.

With great difficulty in the heavy seas, Robert Patton drove the lifeboat, *The Always Ready*, alongside the sinking ship and shouted at the man to jump. Instead, however, he lowered himself over the side and hung there. Coxswain Patton grabbed him and ordered him to let go, but, petrified, he only clung on tighter.

Then the lifeboat was swept away from the steamer. As the two vessels parted, the coxswain had to take a split-second decision. He could let go, but the disabled man had no lifejacket and if he had fallen into the sea in the darkness he would almost certainly have drowned. So Robert Patton held on, was dragged overboard from his lifeboat and both men plummeted into the sea.

The lifeboat was lifted on a wave and started crashing back towards the steamer, with the two men in between. Summoning all his strength, Patton lifted the man out of the sea towards the outstretched arms of the lifeboat's crew, who hauled him to safety. But the lifeboat could not be stopped and the coxswain was hit by 20 tons of wood and metal and pinned against the steamer. Before his crew could get to him, he had been crushed twice more between the two boats. Soon afterwards the steamer sank; but for Robert Patton's heroism, the disabled man would certainly have died.

As soon as the lifeboat reached Runswick the coxswain was rushed to hospital. He had broken ribs, three fractures in his pelvis, fractured vertebrae and his abdomen had been severely crushed.

Two days later an RNLI official visited him in hospital. Patton said he knew of the risks but said, 'I could not let the poor lad go, as he might have been drowned'. Pneumonia set in and, nine days after the rescue, Robert Patton died. He was 46.

The shock in the 30 or so houses that form Runswick was intense and his immense personal bravery brought 4,000 people to his funeral. He was awarded the RNLI's Gold Medal posthumously, and the lifeboat's name was changed to *Robert Patton – The Always Ready*.

Runswick nowadays is almost a ghost village, many of the fishermen's cottages being used as holiday homes. The lifeboat was withdrawn in 1978 to be replaced by a fast Atlantic inshore boat at Staithes.

THE GRACE DARLING TRADITION

Individual bravery and dedication of a similar nature was a feature of the whole life of Margaret Brown of Cresswell, dubbed by the press 'the second Grace Darling'. **Cresswell** is a tiny village north of Newbiggin where, a century ago, 90 per cent of the villagers were named Brown and were 'renowned for their hardihood and giant stature'. Margaret, born in the 1850s, left school aged 13 to assist her father and brothers by digging bait, mending nets and helping to haul the fishing cobles up the beach when they came ashore. She saw her father and three brothers drown when their boat overturned in the surf only yards from the shore,

Launching the Cresswell lifeboat in 1935.

an accident that led to a lifeboat being sent to Cresswell.

Its first launch in anger came when a Swedish ship, the *Gustaf*, was being driven ashore in a gale and fired a gun as a distress signal. The Cresswell lifeboat had to be hauled half a mile along the beach to be launched, the women helping the men in this task. As the lifeboat put to sea the women saw that a small boat had got away from the *Gustaf* but had overturned. They waded straight out into the boiling surf and formed a human chain to bring the men ashore. Margaret Brown was farthest out, grabbing hold of the bedraggled sailors, often out of her depth and being swept off her feet.

Meanwhile, the lifeboat struggled to reach the ship but was driven back to the shore. The crew were exhausted and the coxswain wanted the rocket lifesaving apparatus from Newbiggin, five miles away. At once Margaret volunteered to take the message. With two other girls, Mary Brown and Isabella Armstrong, she set off, barefoot, to run along the coast. After two miles the track crossed the River Lyne but the plank bridge had been swept away by floods. Undaunted, Margaret plunged into the swollen river and was swept downstream, and only just managed to scramble ashore. She waded in again upstream and this time managed to grab the remaining planks of the bridge as she was swept past. Crossing the remains of the bridge on her hands and knees, she dropped into the water on the other side and was washed up on the opposite bank. Mary and Isabella followed.

The direct route was now over Newbiggin Moors, but they were too exhausted to battle against the gale and ran along the shore, their feet cut and bleeding, clothes torn and waves almost overwhelming them. At last they reached the outskirts of Newbiggin. Mary and Isabella were so shattered that they could not go on, so Margaret knocked at the door of the first house they reached and left them there. On she went, collapsing at the Newbiggin coastguard station, unable even to speak. The coastguard knew her and, realising why she had come, immediately sent the rocket apparatus to Cresswell. The lifeboat had relaunched and managed to take off the three women and seven men left on the *Gustaf*.

Margaret Brown married and became Mrs Armstrong, and was still helping to launch the lifeboat in her 70s, never missing a launch in 50 years. In the 1920s there was a special presentation to her of a gold badge, when either her shyness or the social etiquette of the time led to a member of the nobility, Lady Ravensworth, responding on Margaret's behalf. The contemporary account described her as '. . .the aged Countess of Ravensworth, who, with perfectly white hair and a Gainsborough hat, appeared a living representation of a bygone age.'

Newbiggin also has a history of brave women. In 1927 the local fishing fleet was in trouble at sea with most of the lifeboat crew on the fishing boats. A scratch crew was formed of miners coming off shift, and 25 women launched the lifeboat, then waded into the surf to relaunch her when she was thrown back on to the beach. During the war the women

Grace Darling.

had to pull the lifeboat up a cliff, over a moor and through sand dunes to launch her. The gale blasted sleet and sand into their faces, which were cut open and bleeding as the lifeboat rescued nine men from a Belgian ship.

Newbiggin is another station where an inshore lifeboat now copes with the work, attracting young people to the crew and using its superior speed to get to casualties much faster than the traditional lifeboat that she replaced.

The most famous sea heroine is Grace Darling. Her tomb in the beautiful Bamburgh churchyard overlooks the Farne Islands where she lived as a lighthouse-keeper's daughter. Local views of her famous rescue remain mixed; certainly her father, William, thought the rescue that he and Grace made from the *Forfarshire* commonplace enough, for he only gave it a brief report in his log, and Grace was not mentioned at all. But this slight young woman had spotted movement near the wreck, roused her father from sleep and set out with him in their small open boat to go to the rescue. Her courage caught the Victorian popular imagination and she was catapulted to fame overnight. She died young, some say because of the pressure of all the publicity. There is a small but fascinating museum in Bamburgh, which contains the boat she used and many pieces of the paraphernalia that her exploit generated.

Locals like **North Sunderland** lifeboat coxswain David Sheil take the Grace Darling tradition in their stride. He fishes the area and knows the Farnes, with their outcrops of rock and dangerous tides and currents, as well as anyone. There are 28 islands at low water, but only 14 when the tide comes up. With fishing in decline, the village has seen a total of 200 fishermen shrink to 30. Even so, over half the lifeboat crew are fishermen and they know that they may be looking after their own.

'In a small community like this, everybody sticks together,' says David. 'A lot of the time it's fishermen going to help other fishermen.'

The Northumbrian accents are strong and one of David Sheil's predecessors, Tommy Dawson, can remember them causing alarm on one rescue in the war. Five American airmen had ditched their Flying Fortress in the North Sea and were picked up by the lifeboat.

'They didn't know where they were,' recalls Tommy, 'and when they heard us talking, they thought we were Germans because they couldn't understand our dialect.'

FISHERMEN'S TALES

A few miles along the coast is the lovely village of **Craster**, with an inshore lifeboat that has helped plenty of fishermen. In one incident, in 1982, three men had left their fishing boat to row ashore and had been blown on to the rocks in their dinghy. The wind was force 7, on the margins for safety for the inflatable lifeboat, but the Craster men put out. The most senior man took the helm, using his extensive local knowledge to locate the men, and when a helicopter arrived overhead, it was decided that the lifeboat should take off the fishermen. It was a tricky job, but the men were safely landed.

Only 15 minutes after getting back to the lifeboat station, the boat was called out again to search for a man from a capsized dinghy. Again, the Craster men put out without hesitation, but it was soon established that the man had managed to get ashore.

Amble also has a small fishing fleet, and a double rescue in 1990 involved both a fishing boat and a yacht. Rodney Burge, now coxswain, was second coxswain at the time, but was in command as the boat headed out in hurricane-force conditions. The lifeboat was almost lifted out of the water by the steep breaking seas, and visibility was very poor. An RAF helicopter found the fishing coble in difficulty and hovered to guide the lifeboat in, but was diverted to another incident. The coble, of the traditional design, was an open boat with no shelter, and the four crew were desperately bailing out with buckets as they were tossed about in the storm. The violent movements made it very difficult to bring the lifeboat alongside safely, but Rodney Burge managed the manoeuvre and the fishermen scrambled on to the lifeboat.

Returning to harbour, a message came through that there was a yacht in difficulties, so the lifeboat diverted to investigate. The storm was blowing the anchored yacht over and she was in treacherously shallow water, but again Rodney Burge drew on his superb seamanship skills to get alongside and fix a tow. The yacht, her two

Sir Alec Rose boarding the Blyth lifeboat Shoreline *in 1979.*

crew and the four fishermen, were all taken safely to harbour.

Just down the coast at **Blyth**, the mixture of rescues is similar. Coxswain Charles Hatcher won a Bronze Medal for a winter rescue in which three fishermen had to slide down the side of their heaving rolling boat as it sank under them. In 1994, Coxswain Keith Barnard won a Thanks on Vellum for saving eight people from their dismasted yacht, which had been driven on to rocks.

An earlier visitor to Blyth would have been proud of him. Perhaps Britain's best-loved yachtsman, round the world veteran Sir Alec Rose had founded the Yachtsman's Lifeboat Association, which later became Shoreline. In recognition of all the support from members, Blyth's new lifeboat was named *Shoreline*, and as Sir Alec ended the ceremony with the traditional words 'May God bless her and all who sail in her', there was a special poignancy, for Sir Alec, of all people, knew what dangers the boat might face.

The RNLI committee of management representative at Blyth was Paulin Denham Christie, a manager from the Swan Hunter shipyard on the Tyne, who had himself once been the **Tynemouth** coxswain. One of his fond memories was to read of one of his rescues before it had happened!

Late one night the lifeboat was called. A trawler was on her way home from the fishing grounds and her chief engineer had fallen into her main engine and injured himself. The trawler would be four miles off the Tyne at 1 o'clock in the morning; the lifeboat was to meet her and take the engineer to hospital.

Having set out at midnight, the lifeboat got the message that the trawler, her engines playing up, would be delayed and the coastguard suggested that the crew return, as a meal had been laid on for them. A couple of hours later, after soup and sandwiches, they climbed down into the lifeboat and cast off again. As they moved off, the first edition of the morning paper was also tossed aboard. Right in the middle of the front page was a glowing report of the Tynemouth lifeboat taking off the seaman – a job they were just about to do!

A complex search for a fishing boat involved five North East lifeboats in 1987. The first alert came from the mother of one of the two men out on the Hartlepool boat *Sea Fox*. The boat was six hours overdue and the **Hartlepool** and **Teesmouth** lifeboats started to search her normal fishing grounds while coastguards scoured the beaches. The weather was worsening, so it was decided to launch the **Sunderland, Tynemouth and Blyth** lifeboats to extend the search. Coxswain Anthony Lee on the Sunderland boat was given a 10-mile stretch of coast, and posted two men on deck as lookouts. It was dark, wet and cold as rain and snow squalls blew through, and the lookouts had to be changed every 20 minutes.

The longer such a search goes on, the more hope fades, yet the Sunderland crew persevered through the night and after four hours were rewarded when, just before 2 am, they spotted a flicker of light two miles

The Sunderland lifeboat in 1990.

east of Seaham Harbour. Sure enough, there lay *Sea Fox*, at anchor, with a broken gearbox shaft. She was being tossed and blown around and the spray was starting to fill her. The fishermen were very cold but safe, and were quickly taken into the lifeboat, wrapped in blankets and put in the heated cabin. By 2.30 am they were safely ashore and in an ambulance, and five weary lifeboat crews were able to go home.

Fishing boats feature in the stories of virtually all the North East lifeboats. At **Tynemouth**, Coxswain Martin Kenny is unlikely to forget the rescue of three men from the fishing boat *La Morlaye* in April 1986, for he was lifted off his feet by a wave and swept over the stern of the lifeboat. *La Morlaye*'s nets had fouled her propeller out at sea and another fishing boat had tried to tow her home, but the rope had parted and she was swept in towards the shore.

John Hogg was in command of the lifeboat, with Martin Kenny as his second coxswain, and although he had to take his lifeboat into dangerously shallow waters and pounding surf, his first thought was to save the boat by towing her clear. It was during one of the attempts to get a line across that Martin Kenny was almost tipped into the surf. He had a rope in his hand and was standing at the stern of the lifeboat when the bow was hit by a large sea and reared up into the air. Martin was hurled backwards, lying horizontally across the rails. Instinct took over and he somehow managed to hang on as the sea swept over him, then hauled himself back on to the deck.

Coxswain John Hogg realised that time was running out and tried to

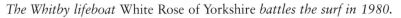

The Whitby lifeboat White Rose of Yorkshire *battles the surf in 1980.*

get a rope across using the rocket line, but this was swept out of the hands of the fishermen by the gale. Finally he had to do what he least wanted; take his lifeboat right into the surf to get alongside the fishing boat and take off the men. In spite of the risk of running aground, in he went and using superb seamanship got close enough to rescue the men. His gallantry and skill earned him a Silver Medal but, sadly, he died before it could be presented, and his widow travelled to London to receive it on his behalf.

Whitby has its own active fishing fleet, and because it is the only harbour between the Humber and the Tees with water at all states of the tide, it was traditionally an important trading port. It had one of the earliest lifeboat stations, and among its famous native mariners it counts Captain Cook. The lifeboat station record is impressive for both the inshore and all-weather lifeboats, the former having been used with great skill to rescue people from the base of the cliffs and from capsized boats. These rescues involve going into the surf, which is either threatening to sweep people away or has capsized their boat, and the lifeboatmen know that they are facing similar dangers of their own boat being overturned. Bronze Medals have been won by inshore lifeboatmen Mike Coates, Brian Hodgson, Nick Botham and John Pearson for overcoming those risks. The all-weather lifeboat has also seen many medal awards, to coxswains Eric Taylor, William Harland, Bobby Allen and Peter Thomson, usually for saving fishermen.

Down the coast at **Filey**, fishing is still from traditional cobles drawn up

The Filey inshore lifeboat assisting a local fishing coble.

The Flamborough lifeboat crew in 1993.

on the beach. Coxswain Graham Taylor can draw on a population of 6,000 for his crew and, in addition to three fishermen, can count on oil rig workers, joiners, teachers, a chef, a plumber, a policeman, a shop assistant, a wagon driver and a crane driver to turn up in emergencies. In 1993 he also had the town mayor, Colin Haddington, as a crew member. Ambulanceman Colin joined the crew at the age of 17, and his paramedic skills have often come in useful on the lifeboat.

In fact, many lifeboat crew members are trained in first aid, and the **Withernsea** crew once used their skills in a most unexpected way. They were travelling back in a minibus from a trip to the London Boat Show when a strange shape loomed up ahead on the motorway. It was the body of an aircraft; the British Midland flight that had just crashed at Kegworth trying to make an emergency landing at East Midlands Airport. The lifeboatmen were virtually the first on the scene and spent over three hours assisting in recovering the dead and injured people from the aircraft. While other emergency services received a welter of praise, the only recognition to the Withernsea men came from the RNLI.

Completing the picture on the Yorkshire coast are the lifeboats at **Flamborough, Bridlington** and **Humber**. Even in the small world of fishing and lifeboating, it is a strange coincidence that the three main characters at these stations, Les Robson of Flamborough, Fred Walkington of Bridlington and Brian Bevan of Humber, all went to school together; St George's in Bridlington has a lot to answer for! Les has recently had to cope with the difficult transition from being the coxswain of an Oakley Class lifeboat to becoming senior helmsman of an Atlantic 21, but views the change pragmatically: 'We're here to save lives. The inshore lifeboat is there for the same reason as the old boat.'

Under the beautiful chalk cliffs of Flamborough's south landing, the new lifeboat station is following the pattern of all those on the North East coast that have seen changes, and is building up its own record of service to add a new chapter to the station's long history.

HEROES OF THE HUMBER

On 15 February 1979, a forbiddingly dark and stormy day, the North Sea was whipped up by ferocious gales that drove a thick Arctic blizzard across a churning sea to blast the whole of the East Coast.

Off the Yorkshire coast the **Bridlington** lifeboat was battling towards the German ship *Sunnahav*, which was broken down and drifting towards Flamborough Head. Lifeboat inspector Tom Nutman was worried for her safety on launching and kept the Humber lifeboat on standby in case extra help was needed. Bridlington coxswain Fred Walkington found visibility down to 50 yards and was navigating blind, his radar knocked out of action. As the *Sunnahav* regained power and the lifeboat headed for home, he needed to find a landfall and spotted the cliffs near Filey. Then second coxswain Dennis Atkins suddenly saw only feet away the notorious rocks of Filey Brigg.

The coxswain flung the wheel over and as the lifeboat went beam on to the seas, she was knocked over to starboard so far that the capsize switches cut off the engines. They restarted at the touch of a button and the lifeboat made it back to Bridlington Harbour by 5 o'clock. Topping up with diesel was difficult as the fuel froze in the funnel, and after a change of clothes and a hot drink the crew had to rehouse the lifeboat, hauling her up the icy slip. They finally went home 13 hours after being called out.

With Bridlington out to the *Sunnahav*, Tom Nutman released the **Humber** boat to go south and take over the rescue of a Romanian cargo ship, the *Savinesti*, from the **Wells** crew, two of whom had suffered frostbite during their 11-hour service. The Humber's Arun lifeboat, with her enclosed cabin, at least kept the crew warm and dry, but a three-inch layer of ice soon built up and they had to go out on deck to chip it away from the radar scanner. In the atrocious conditions the electronic aids would scarcely function and basic seamanship was all that took the Humber men out to the *Savinesti*. By the time they arrived the weather had deteriorated from appalling to something even worse. The wind was hurricane force 12, the heavy swell had 40-foot breaking waves and the sandbanks were making the rollers run for several hundred feet. The heavy snow was endless and, with spume racing through the air, visibility was often down to zero.

A North Sea ferry, the *Norwave*, had tried to get a line across to the *Savinesti* to tow her, but failed. A tug, the *Lady Moira*, came out, but it was too dangerous for her skipper to risk putting men on deck. Eventually the *Savinesti* regained enough power to limp slowly towards the Humber, escorted by the lifeboat, *Norwave* and *Lady Moira*. By the time they reached the shelter of the estuary, the Humber lifeboat had been at sea for 17 hours.

Amazingly, the Humber men had been through an even worse ordeal six weeks earlier on New Year's Eve. The Dutch coaster *Diana V* was carrying a cargo of maize and it had shifted in heavy seas when she was 74 miles from Spurn Head. The lifeboat had gone 25 miles when suddenly she lost speed; an oil pipe had fractured and one engine was crippled. The **Cromer** lifeboat was on her way, so the Humber boat went back to Grimsby, brothers Bill and Ron Sayers stripping a pump ready for repair as they went. The pipe was picked up at Grimsby, fixed as the lifeboat went back down the Humber, and the rescue mission started all over again.

Out at sea, the *Diana V* had made some progress, but then she started leaking and a helicopter that had been sent out to help had to return to base because of the terrible weather. The lifeboat was the only hope and she had to punch into the 25-foot waves at full speed, taking a terrific pounding, at times taking off and crashing down into the next wave. One fall knocked out the electrics, but there was no time to fix them.

Reaching the *Diana V* the crew had to go out on deck with hand torches. Outside the cabin things were grim. Sea water was freezing on the deck, and the storm had ripped the liferaft and inflatable dinghy from their stowages, and they were hanging loose. The wind was gusting up to 56 knots.

The warship *Lindisfarne* lit up the *Diana V* with her powerful searchlight and the lifeboat moved in. *Diana V* was lifted on a wave, crashed down into the lifeboat and ripped away a strip of fendering. As the coaster dropped away, the lifeboat then found itself 10 feet above her deck. On the second approach, the lifeboat was hit by a sea and more fendering was lost. At one point Coxswain Brian Bevan's head was within a yard of the *Diana V*'s stern.

The third run was successful. A 12-year-old girl was dropped into the lifeboatmen's arms, a woman followed and four men jumped aboard, the lifeboatmen breaking their fall. Cold, wet and suffering from shock, the survivors were taken into the cabin while the captain, his crew safe, decided to try to save his ship. Seas were breaking right over her, but he bravely coaxed *Diana V* towards the Humber and safety. The lifeboat and warship escorted her and the lifeboatmen arrived home on New Year's Eve morning at 3.45.

The strain on the crew was huge. Brian Bevan said later, 'You seem to come back off a job absolutely dog tired. All you want to do is drop into your bed and within two minutes of being in bed you can't sleep. Everything is sort of wound up inside you. I think for 24 hours or so I was so mentally and physically wound up that I was miles away – even during the New Year celebrations. I am in a world of my own for 24 hours after a job like that.'

The February rescues brought Bronze Medals for Brian Bevan and Fred Walkington of Bridlington, and a Silver for David Cox of Wells. The *Diana V* incident won Brian Bevan a Silver. So what on earth do you have to do to win a Gold? Forty-eight hours before the *Savinesti* incident, Brian Bevan and his crew performed a classic rescue that did just that.

The Panamanian ship *Revi* had sent out a Mayday on the night of 13 February. She was slowly sinking 30 miles north-east of Spurn and although the captain was trying to make for the Humber, his ship was being overwhelmed by huge waves. It was bitterly cold with snow showers, and when the lifeboat arrived the captain asked for his crew to be taken off. With the whole ship awash it was too dangerous, so Brian Bevan asked the captain to steer south at slow speed to try and provide a lee.

Still the danger was immense. The listing ship was heaving erratically in the huge seas and the lifeboatmen had to go on to the foredeck, secured by their lifelines, to grab any survivors.

As the *Revi* tossed about unpredictably, one false move by the coxswain could leave his men crushed by the ship. The first run-in confirmed the peril. A sea lifted the *Revi*'s stern, which then started dropping towards the lifeboat. Quickly going astern, Coxswain Bevan avoided catastrophe, but he had to go in again and again, sometimes with the ship's hull towering 20 feet above his men. By the time they managed to pluck two men from the *Revi*, the ship was in dire straits. She was now flooding and listing over 45 degrees as the water and her cargo of silver sand shifted dangerously in the hold. The captain now had no choice. He could not possibly save her and he and the mate would have to abandon ship.

The *Revi* was slowly burying her bows into the water as if she had accepted her fate. Heavy seas continued to pound her, washing across the decks, and as the lifeboat come alongside her heaving deck, a large wave broke right across both vessels and pushed the lifeboat away. Again and again Brian Bevan fought to get in, and each time the seas forced the vessels apart. After 12 attempts he got close enough for the mate to jump six feet into the arms of the lifeboat crew. Only the captain now remained on board.

The *Revi*'s bows were now completely submerged and the stern loomed menacingly above the lifeboat. The captain was hanging on to the outside of the ship's rails, ready to jump. The coxswain made his run-in, but was defeated time and again by the seas and the danger to his own boat and crew. On the tenth run, the *Revi*'s stern suddenly rose into the air and crashed down towards the lifeboat's foredeck where the crew were lashed to the rails with no chance of escape. Bevan rammed the throttles full astern and the propellers churned, then bit, as tons of steel came thundering down, missing the lifeboat by inches.

Despite coming so close to disaster, the lifeboat had to go in again, but suddenly it looked too late. Three successive seas completely covered the *Revi*, and her captain was lost from view under the wall of green water. Surely no man could hold against the sheer weight of the sea. Yet as the water cleared, there he was, still clinging to the rails. Brian Bevan knew he would not get another chance. He drove in on a trough between two waves. The lifeboat ran straight into the ship, hitting it hard, and the captain jumped, almost fell, overboard but was just caught by the lifeboat crew. A few minutes later the *Revi* rolled over and sank.

CHAPTER THREE

The Second World War – under fire

'It drives on with a mercy which does not quail in the presence of death. It drives on as a proof, a symbol, a testimony that man was created in the image of God and that valour and virtue have not perished in the British race.'

Sir Winston Churchill, speaking of the lifeboat

THE SECOND WORLD War placed more demands on the RNLI than any other circumstance in its entire distinguished history. The seven months from September 1939 to April 1940 were the busiest in the Institution's 115-year existence, as Germany attempted to destroy the sea traffic of Great Britain.

The Eastbourne lifeboat rescues the captain of the steamer Barnhill, *on fire after an air attack in 1940.*

Later that same year lifeboats played a vital part in the Dunkirk evacuation – the Ramsgate crew alone rescued 2,800 servicemen. The Battle of Britain soon followed; lifeboats plucked hundreds of airmen from the English Channel during Germany's airborne onslaught on the ships and ports of the South Coast. Finally, throughout the war there were the countless rescues of sailors torpedoed, bombed or burned out of their ships and submarines.

Crews right round the British – and Irish – coasts all figure in this heroic history, but the main burden fell on the stations along the eastern and south-eastern seaboard. The south-eastern lifeboats were summoned to Dunkirk and it was from the south and east coasts, from Selsey to the Humber, that lifeboats most often went to the help of airmen.

No one should under-estimate the courage and commitment of these wartime crews. Added to the hazards of wartime rescues – the lurking mines, the risk of aerial bombardment, the total darkness in which night rescues were attempted – the RNLI faced other privations and frustrations. Crews often lost their youngest and fittest members to the navy; they were replaced by men in their 50s and 60s. In several cases fathers took the place of sons who had been called up. Fifty-five was the average age of the Mumbles crew in Wales, which rescued 42 men from a Canadian steamer in 1944; two of the lifeboatmen were in their 70s.

Although lifeboats were damaged and destroyed at an unprecedented rate, replacements were hard to find as boatyards were bombed and boat-builders were requisitioned by the navy. Crews also struggled against the restrictions placed on them by the navy. Up until the last six months of the war lifeboats were not allowed to put to sea without permission from the navy. In several cases this led to agonising delays, with lifeboatmen forced to stand by while men died.

Off the **Humber** one morning an RAF bomber in flames was spotted crashing into the sea. The coxswain rang up the local naval commander and asked for permission to launch. It was refused, as the lifeboat was wooden and the officer in charge would not risk her near the flames. He sent out two steel boats instead, and after another 20-minute delay, the crew were finally allowed to leave. By the time they reached the plane the flames had died down leaving nothing but wreckage. The plane's crew of nine were dead. The frustrated RNLI crew felt that if they chose to risk being burned alive, the decision should be left to them, and the coxswain rang the naval commander to tell him so. It was then agreed that only the coxswain had the right to decide whether the lifeboat should be launched.

The first in the long procession of war casualties rescued from the sea were brought ashore by the **Aldeburgh** lifeboat only seven days after war began. On a peaceful summer afternoon the Liverpool steamer *Magdapur* struck a mine off the Suffolk coast; she was the first ship to be sunk by one. The Aldeburgh crew saved 74, all smothered in black oil; five of the sailors had disappeared in the explosion and a dozen were badly wounded. After they had been landed, it took more than two hours to wash away the oil and blood in the lifeboat.

During the icy winter of 1939 to 1940, the arctic conditions added to the perils of the war. Ice had to be chipped away from returning lifeboats and oilskins froze to the lifeboatmen. The Wells crew suffered frostbite after their boat froze fast in the Ouse, where she was refuelling after a six-hour search for a missing vessel.

But the greatest challenge for the RNLI came in May 1940, when 19 lifeboats helped to bring off the defeated British Expeditionary Force stranded in Dunkirk. In nine days 330,000 British and French troops were rescued from the beleaguered port and the neighbouring beaches, under continuous shelling and bombing.

DUNKIRK

Events had moved with terrifying rapidity after the Axis invasion of Holland and Belgium on 10 May 1940. The French and British armies had advanced into Belgium to confront the Germans, but by the 15th the enemy had broken through the French line. By the 23rd enemy forces had divided the British and French, and were pushing the British towards the sea. Boulogne and Calais fell in quick succession, leaving the British no escape except through Dunkirk. Meanwhile, hundreds of enemy bombers swooped on Dunkirk and set the whole town ablaze. Only a narrow breakwater remained from which the British army could embark. There were also nine miles of sandy beaches, but even at high water ships could come no closer than half a mile from the shore. How could the thousands of waiting soldiers, many of them wounded, be ferried from the beach to the waiting ships? The solution to the problem was the launching of an armada of small boats, including the lifeboats, which could take the men from the shore in what the Admiralty described as 'The most extensive and difficult operation in naval history'.

The **Ramsgate** lifeboat was the first to reach Dunkirk. The scene was like something out of hell. Thick, acrid smoke from burning oil tanks hung over the town and the beaches were black with men waiting for rescue. Flames illuminated the shattered army and the many wrecked boats in the harbour. The noise was deafening – a whistle of shells from overhead, the scream of falling bombs, the staccato machine-gun fire and the angry buzz of dive-bombers.

The water was so shallow that the lifeboat could not get close to the beach. Instead, the eight wherries that she had towed from Dover were used to bring men from the shore to the lifeboat. Each wherry was rowed by naval men or lifeboat crew and could take eight soldiers from the beach. Once the lifeboat was loaded with up to 160 men, she put out to the larger vessels lying further off in the darkness and transferred the soldiers to them.

The lifeboat brought off about 800 men that night, Thursday 30 May, and as she took on board the last three boat-loads, an officer called out to her, 'I cannot see who you are. Are you a naval party?' He was answered, 'No, sir, we are members of the crew of the Ramsgate lifeboat.' He then called out, 'Thank you, and thank God for such men as you have this night proved yourself to be.'

As Friday dawned the shelling and bombing increased and the wind began to freshen. Boats were capsizing in the swell and it became impossible to row through the wreckage and the oil that clogged their oars. Instead, the lifeboat lay 80 yards off the shore and dropped the wherries down to the beach on ropes. By the afternoon only three of the wherries were left, the rest, broken and leaky, lay abandoned on the beach. The lifeboat now moved further east along the coast and went to the help of many small boats struggling out through the surf, towing some of them to the waiting destroyers.

During Friday night a piece of shell destroyed the last wherry, and early on Saturday morning the Ramsgate boat headed home. The crew were exhausted; they had rescued 2,800 men and had spent 30 hours working under fire. They had had no sleep for three days.

The **Margate** lifeboat reached the beaches at Nieuport, 15 miles east of Dunkirk, at midnight on the Thursday. The barge with her ran aground, but the lifeboat managed to edge her way slowly through the darkness to the shore. The crew heard a voice calling and they could just make out the silent black rows of waiting men. Eighty French soldiers forced their way through the surf, up to their armpits in the sea, until they reached the lifeboat. The crew had to haul the soaked men four feet over the boat's rail to pull them safely inside. The French soldiers were then ferried to the barge.

Next the lifeboat took off men from the Border Regiment. The load was so heavy that she was grounded and had to wait for the tide to turn and float her off. Day broke as the Borderers embarked aboard the barge, and all along the sands in both directions, as far as the lifeboatmen could see, more troops were waiting for rescue.

The coxswain soon lost count of the times the lifeboat plied between the shore and the destroyer, which was now receiving the rescued men. All this time planes were swooping low to machine-gun the boats and the patient troops, and bombs and shells were exploding on the sands. Finally, the gruelling work had to stop because of the rough weather. A treacherous surf was now pounding the shore, and knocking over the troops who were still wading out to the lifeboat. Laden with heavy equipment, men were unable to get up again, and were drowning close to the lifeboat, which could not get to them in the shallow water. By this time the lifeboat was the only small boat left afloat, and the coxswain decided that to remain longer was to tempt men to their deaths.

The lifeboat now made for Dunkirk, and on her way rescued two officers and 15 sailors who were desperately trying to row to one of the distant ships in a leaky old whaler. The men were the only survivors of a

The Margate lifeboat crew in 1940, Coxswain Edward Parker DSM in the centre.

party of 150 who had been working on the beaches for four days. The weather was now so bad that the lifeboat could do no more, so she set course for Margate. When she arrived there she had been out for nearly 24 hours and had brought off about 600 men. Coxswain Howard Knight of Ramsgate, and Coxswain Edward Parker of Margate, were both awarded the Distinguished Service Medal for their 'gallantry and determination'.

Some of the other lifeboat coxswains summoned by the RNLI met a rather different fate. The **Hythe** boat was the first to arrive at Dover after the Margate and Ramsgate crews had already set off for France. When her coxswain was given his orders, he refused to go. He said that it was impossible to run his 15-ton boat on the beach at Dunkirk, load her with troops and take them out to the ships. He could never get the boat off the shore without winches, and he would not attempt at Dunkirk what he knew he could not do at Hythe. The **Walmer** and **Dungeness** coxswains agreed with him, so the navy issued all three crews with rail warrants and packed them off home.

When the next seven lifeboats arrived at Dover the following morning they were taken from the RNLI crews and handed over to navy officers, who were not prepared to risk any more arguments. The lifeboatmen were surprised and indignant. They were eager to set off for Dunkirk, and they knew their boats far better than the sailors who were now in

The Eastbourne lifeboat shows the damage suffered during the Dunkirk evacuation.

charge of them; the navy stokers even had to be taught how to stop and start the lifeboats. But the navy would not listen to the protests of the RNLI crews.

Three weeks later the RNLI held an inquiry, which found that the Hythe coxswain had persuaded the Walmer and Dungeness crews not to take their boats to Dunkirk; he and the Hythe motor mechanic were dismissed. The latter highlighted the reluctance of some crews to take orders from the navy: 'If the order had come from the Institution to proceed to Dunkirk and do the best you can, there would have been no holding back,' he said.

When the Hythe coxswain heard of his dismissal, he swore that he would carry out rescues in his own fishing boat. Two months later he fulfilled his pledge by rescuing two British airmen from a crashed bomber.

Of the 19 lifeboats that went to Dunkirk, only the Hythe lifeboat failed to return; it was so badly damaged that it had to be abandoned. The others were riddled with machine-gun bullets – Eastbourne's had 500 bullet-holes in her – and some had damaged engines; a few were no longer seaworthy. No one knows how many thousands of men were rescued from Dunkirk by the lifeboats.

AIRMEN

The Battle of Britain, which followed later in 1940, was the next arduous test for the RNLI. Instead of the peacetime calls of 'fishing boat overdue' or 'trawler overtaken by bad weather', lifeboat crews responded to a different summons – 'bomber crashed into sea' or 'pilot seen to bale out'. The British planes were battling above the Channel with German squadrons, whose orders were to prepare for an invasion by destroying the South Coast ports, the south-eastern aerodromes and London itself.

During those summer weeks lifeboat stations were poised for action. At any moment the call might come: 'Expect air battle in this area within next hour. Arrange for lifeboat to stand by.' Later in the war, on nights when Bomber Command was making an attack on a German city, the **Sheringham** crew slept downstairs, fully dressed, with their boots standing next to them.

One September morning in 1940 the **Margate** lifeboat station received a message that an airman could be seen parachuting down into the sea. It was very misty, and the pilot had been in the sea for more than an hour when the lifeboat found him.

He was very badly burned, his skin hanging in shreds from his hands. He had decided that he was going to die, and had unscrewed the valve in his lifejacket, but the parachute billowing out around him would not let him drown. At last his rescuers arrived.

'I remember as in a dream hearing somebody shout; he seemed so far away and quite unconnected with me,' the pilot wrote later. 'Then willing arms dragged me over the side; my parachute was taken off; a brandy flask was pushed between my swollen lips; a voice said "OK Joe, it is one of ours and still kicking", and I was safe. I was neither relieved nor angry; I was past caring.'

The young pilot was called Richard Hope Hillary, and later the RNLI received a letter of thanks from his grateful father: 'It would surely have afforded my ancestor [Sir William Hillary] who founded the Lifeboat Service the liveliest satisfaction to know that his own kith and kin are numbered among those who have benefited by its wonderful work,' he wrote.

Richard Hope Hillary was a descendant of one of Sir William's brothers. He was a dashing figure, whose name was romantically linked with the actress Merle Oberon. After extensive plastic surgery he insisted on returning to the RAF. He was training as a night-fighter when, in January 1943, he was killed on active service; his ashes were scattered over the sea near the spot where he had been picked up by the Margate crew.

For sightings of airmen in the water, the lifeboat stations relied on the vigilance of people all along the coast. After a stormy night the landlord of a seafront pub at **Sheringham** was serving at the bar; the morning had been foggy, but suddenly the sun came out. As it did so the landlord glanced out of the window and saw a speck on the sea a mile away. He got out his telescope and saw that the speck was men, on what looked like a liferaft. Just then the second coxswain of the lifeboat came in for his lunchtime pint. He went off at once with the

A painting of the Wells lifeboat with a downed Lancaster bomber.

news and the lifeboat was launched. The crew found a rubber dinghy with six Polish airmen, who had come down in the gale the night before. Unseen in the fog, they had been tossed about in the sea for 17 hours, soaked, seasick and very weary.

Allied aircrews were not the only ones rescued by the RNLI.

Controversially, eight German airmen were also saved by lifeboat crews. When this became known, condemnation of the lifeboat service was loud and bitter, but the Institution stood by its founding pledge – to go to the help of all in peril at sea round the coast of the British Isles, regardless of race. In any case, during an air battle it was not possible to tell whether the dot hurtling down into the sea was a British or a German airman.

Every day of the war lifeboat crews braved the dangers of mines and bombs as well as stormy seas. All the crews were well aware of the risks. They sometimes had to stand by helplessly as the treacherous mines carried out their deadly work.

'Two Grimsby trawlers were blown up yesterday by enemy mines. One was blown to pieces and all hands killed. The other sank. . . Everything was over in three minutes,' wrote Coxswain Robert Cross of the **Humber.**

The Humber lifeboat was once searching for survivors from a wreck and asked the master of a passing ship if he had spotted anything. The answer was that he had just seen a German aeroplane drop two mines where the lifeboat was now standing.

One night the same crew went out in a blizzard to the aid of a ship that had drifted on to a sandbank. They knew that where the ship lay enemy aircraft had dropped a shower of mines just a few days before. The next morning they saw two ships blown to bits in the same water.

Sometimes lifeboats unwittingly blundered into English minefields. The **Skegness** lifeboat had travelled 50 miles by night searching for an aeroplane. As the tide ebbed the crew saw mines all around them, just on the surface of the low water. Very gingerly the coxswain managed to manoeuvre the lifeboat through them, then anchored until dawn came.

Bombardment was less insidious, but if planes first missed their target, they would return again and again until they succeeded. All one night the **Cromer** lifeboat laboured alongside a Liverpool steamer stranded on the Haisborough Sand. The crew knew that if the ship was still there at day-break she would be bombed by the German planes that had attacked her three times during the afternoon, without touching her. Tow-rope after tow-rope broke, and eventually the lifeboat took off the steamer's crew of 101 men. The following morning the bombers duly returned and destroyed the ship.

CONVOYS

In peacetime wrecks come singly. In wartime vessels move in big convoys and, when they are wrecked, as many as six may be wrecked at the same

Coxswain Henry Blogg of Cromer.

time. Lifeboats sometimes toiled for many hours going to ship after ship helpless in the same gale, or stranded on the same sandbank.

In August 1941 a convoy was sailing down that narrow waterway along the East Coast known as 'E-boat alley', after the German E-boats that would dash across from Holland to attack British ships. In the early morning the convoy was passing Haisborough Sands, a notorious sandbank nine miles long and a mile wide, when a gale blew up. Within a few minutes six ships had been swept on to the sandbank.

When the **Cromer** lifeboat arrived, five of the ships already looked like wrecks, and several sailors had been drowned trying to swim to the navy destroyers that were standing by. As the tide ebbed the water on the sands was becoming shallower, testing the skills of the lifeboatmen to the utmost.

First, Coxswain Henry Blogg chose a steamer whose decks were already under water. The crew were on top of the engine room, clinging to the funnel as their ship disintegrated beneath them. The sea had swept the decks clean, so there was nothing left to tie a rope around, yet the lifeboat had to make fast while she rescued the men.

Suddenly Blogg spotted a crack in the iron plates of the engine-room which he could use to hold his boat. He sailed her right over the bulwarks on to the flooded deck and drove her bow into the crack. At one point the breaking waters flooded into the lifeboat; the next moment, they flowed away, and the boat crashed on to the deck. Several times the sea washed the lifeboat out of her hold between the cracked plates, but Coxswain Blogg forced her back into the crack again. The crew quickly snatched the 16 men, one by one, from their precarious perch.

The Cromer crew then rescued 31 men from the second steamer, which was more than half submerged; the sailors jumped or slid down ropes into the waiting lifeboat. The 47 rescued men were transferred to a destroyer just as the second Cromer lifeboat arrived.

Coxswain Blogg next made for the third steamer, where only the bridge was still visible above the water. Again he sailed the lifeboat right on to the steamer's deck and held her there until the 19 survivors had jumped into her from the bridge. When he was able to look round once more, Blogg saw that the second Cromer lifeboat had rescued the crew of the fourth steamer, and that the lifeboat from **Great Yarmouth and Gorleston** was alongside the fifth. He at once headed for the sixth.

He drew alongside and waited while 22 men jumped into the lifeboat. However, by this time the water was so shallow that, as she moved away from the steamer, the lifeboat ran aground. For a few agonising minutes she was helpless, beached like a dying whale. If the next waves had broken on her, she would have capsized and everyone would have been washed away. Instead, the crest of the wave broke before it reached her, and she was lifted off the sands.

Between them the three lifeboats had rescued 119 men; Blogg's boat alone had rescued 88 of them. When he got it safely home, he found that she had been badly damaged by the ordeal she had endured. There were three large holes in the bow and over 20 feet of the fender had been ripped away.

For the RNLI the war ended on 8 May 1945, the last time that lifeboats went out to the aid of a casualty of war. This time their search was fruitless; all they found remaining of a torpedoed Norwegian mine-sweeper and its crew of 32 men were two cushions floating in the water.

During the war lifeboats saved nearly 10,000 lives. The crews had endured an unremitting trial of their skill and courage, and were depressed by the futility and waste of what they had seen.

'It has been sad work,' said Coxswain Robert Cross of the Humber. 'I shall never forget one Danish steamer that had been torpedoed. She went down in five minutes after we had taken off her crew. They stood in the lifeboat with their caps in their hands as she heeled over and sank. It was a pitiful sight to see such a beautiful ship go.'

The waste of war – Tynemouth lifeboat station, destroyed by a bomb in 1941.

CHAPTER FOUR

The East – exposed to peril

'The wind's in the east – I am always conscious of an uncomfortable sensation when the wind is blowing in the east.'

Bleak House, *Charles Dickens*

'SKEGNESS, IT'S SO bracing' boasted the advertisements aiming to attract the people of the East Midlands to the coast after the war. The posters showed a jolly fisherman skipping along the sands, and when lifeboat coxswain Ken Holland became town mayor, the local newspaper got him to do the same, to keep the tourists coming in.

Ken was succeeded by Paul Martin, himself a native of Leicester, and the station now has *Leicester Fox* as its inshore lifeboat. Remarkable as it may seem, large inland cities such as Leicester, Nottingham, Coventry, Birmingham and Wolverhampton are among the top fundraisers for the RNLI, with keen committee members, some of them sailors, and many supporters. The inshore lifeboat down the coast at **Happisburgh** also had Midlands links until recently, as it was funded by Leicester schools.

Unfortunately, the term 'Birmingham Navy' is used to describe people who set out in boats without learning anything about the sea, but many leisure sailors take their sport very seriously. Skegness lifeboat crew meet both types. Nothing incenses them more than going after children drifting out to sea in an inflatable toy boat, for every year young lives are lost from these. But people in real danger will find a sympathetic ear as they see the *Lincolnshire Poacher* (the Mersey Class lifeboat bought by Mr Geest of banana fame) or the *Leicester Fox* drawing alongside them.

Lifeboats are often called out to rescue people whose lack of preparedness to cope with a sea trip is quite startling. In June 1994 the **Lowestoft** crew launched to search for a former ship's lifeboat, *Markin IV*, which had failed to arrive at Wells at the expected time. A rescue helicopter finally located the boat, which was drifting two miles out from Lowestoft. When the lifeboat crew arrived they found that the boat's

Leicester schoolchildren hand over a new inshore lifeboat to the Happisburgh crew.

owner and only occupant, who was suffering from shock, had no sea or boat experience and suffered from diabetes and a heart condition. His craft had no radio and no lifesaving or navigational equipment. He was towed back to Lowestoft, where he was immediately taken to hospital by ambulance.

Shane Coleman, the second coxswain/mechanic of the Lowestoft lifeboat and skipper of the Lowestoft pilot boat, saved three men from a sinking tug – without using the lifeboat. It was a dark January night in 1990 and a force 10 storm was blowing. Shane was alone aboard the pilot boat, having just put a pilot aboard a 240-foot coaster. To his horror, shortly afterwards he saw the coaster collide with a 60-foot tug.

Shane at once headed for the tug, but by the time he reached her she had begun to sink; her wheelhouse was already only four feet above the water and her three crew could be seen standing on top of it, with flotsam from the tug floating round them. Shane knew that the pilot boat risked entanglement in the floating debris, yet there was no time to spare – the three survivors were about to be thrown into the icy winter sea without lifejackets.

Although the pilot boat's engines both failed as their propellers became fouled by debris, Shane managed to get the three men on to his boat. By this stage he feared that the powerless craft, and all her passengers, would

The Lowestoft lifeboat rescues two men from the ship Avenir.

be sucked under as the tug went down. He radioed for lifeboat assistance, and a few minutes later the tug sank. Fortunately, the pilot boat remained above the water, although her stern was pulled down by the lines attached to her propellers. Eleven minutes afterwards, the Lowestoft lifeboat arrived to take off the three survivors. Shane was later awarded the RNLI's Bronze Medal.

Shane Coleman is not the only lifeboatman to win a medal for a rescue without a lifeboat. At **Hunstanton** two lifeboatmen received Royal Humane Society awards for rescuing a windsurfer with the station's launching tractor. On a chilly December morning the station's tractor driver, John Connors, saw a white coastguard flare and rushed to the boathouse, followed by crew members Victor Dade and Alan Clarke. They could now see a surfer in trouble; his head was just visible in four-foot waves about 80 yards off the beach and the brisk wind was taking him out to sea.

The three men decided that the quickest way to help him was to unhitch the Atlantic 21 and use the tractor to get as near as possible to the surfer. John Connors drove the tractor out until its wheels were covered, with the two lifeboatmen perched on top in dry-suits. Alan Clarke then swam out to the casualty, and began to tow him ashore, helped by Victor Dade. Although the windsurfer was suffering from cramp and a nosebleed, he obstinately refused to let go of his board, so that had to be towed ashore with him.

A taxi is the strangest casualty ever assisted by the **West Mersea** lifeboat. The vehicle had broken down on the causeway to Mersea island and the driver radioed for help. The vehicle's lights were shining eerily under the water and helped the Atlantic 21 to find it quickly. The tide was

The West Mersea Atlantic 21 lifeboat Alexander Duckham.

already rising rapidly and the water had begun to lap at the shoes of the taxi driver and his passenger as they stood on the taxi's roof. They were taken aboard the lifeboat suffering from shock, but otherwise unhurt. In the RNLI's official report forms for each service carried out, there is a space to enter the Port of Registry of the casualty; the West Mersea honorary secretary duly completed it: 'DVLC Swansea'.

DOUBLE GOLD RESCUE

Only 30 Gold bravery medals – the ultimate accolade for outstanding bravery, and known as the 'lifeboatman's VC' – have been awarded by the RNLI this century. In the early 1900s two of the winners were Coxswain William Fleming of the **Gorleston** lifeboat, later renamed the **Great Yarmouth and Gorleston** lifeboat, and Coxswain Swan of the **Lowestoft** lifeboat, after a rescue lasting two nights and a day in a fierce north-east gale.

Shortly before midnight on Thursday 19 October 1922 the Gorleston pulling and sailing lifeboat launched in high seas to the SS *Hopelyn* of Newcastle, which had been wrecked on North Scroby Sands. Commander Carver, the Inspector of Lifeboats for the Eastern District at the time, takes up the story:

'On arrival at the scene of the wreck, he [Coxswain Fleming] was unable to do anything until daylight, owing to the darkness and terrific seas. At daylight he approached the wreck . . . no sign of life was visible and very heavy seas were sweeping right over.'

Concluding that there were no survivors, the Gorleston crew sadly left the desolate scene and returned to base, ten hours after they had first set out. However, an hour later the coastguard at Caister reported that a flag was being shown from the wreck, so the lifeboat immediately turned round and went back again.

The huge waves meant that she was still unable to get anywhere near the *Hopelyn*; to add to the danger, the ship was only about 30 yards away from an old wreck. The Gorleston lifeboat hit the sands heavily as it was trying to approach the ship, and was quite badly damaged.

Meanwhile, Commander Carver decided that the Lowestoft motor lifeboat would stand a better chance in such conditions, and the boat, with the lifeboat inspector on board, headed off for the wreck. On the way they met the battered Gorleston lifeboat limping home, and Coxswain Fleming agreed to return to the wreck with them. Again the intense darkness and tempestuous seas forced them back to Gorleston until daylight.

Very early on Saturday morning the Lowestoft lifeboat set out once more. Commander Carver describes the desperate state of the *Hopelyn* when the lifeboatmen first glimpsed her through the grey dawn:

'We . . . found only the bridge, funnel and fiddley casing above water. The fore and after decks were completely submerged, and the hull of the vessel was split down . . . with jagged edges of plates projecting, leaving barely the length of the lifeboat in which to come alongside.'

As the lifeboat struggled to come alongside the ship, a huge wave hit it

Twin brothers – Coxswains Tony Hawkins of Dover (left) and Richard Hawkins of Great Yarmouth and Gorleston.

and almost smashed it on to the 1,301 ton *Hopelyn*'s afterdeck. With her engines at full throttle, the lifeboat managed to hold its position, and within 30 seconds the ship's 24 grateful crew members and one black kitten had managed to slither down ropes or jump into the waiting boat. Just as the lifeboat forged clear of the partly submerged wreck, it was completely buried by a terrific wave. Fortunately no one was washed out, and the lifeboat returned safely to Gorleston.

Coxswain Fleming and Coxswain Swan, of the Lowestoft lifeboat, each received Gold Medals for their determination and bravery, and the Lowestoft and Gorleston crews were awarded Bronze Medals. In fact, Great Yarmouth and Gorleston station, as it has been known since 1926, has one of the finest medal records in the RNLI. Forty-five medals have been awarded to date, including 21 Silver.

The present coxswain/mechanic, Richard Hawkins, is the twin brother of the Dover coxswain, Tony Hawkins. Richard is a Bronze Medallist, and has also been commended for rescuing a 22-stone yacht skipper who had been taken ill aboard his boat during a force 8 gale in August 1990. When the lifeboat reached the yacht she was pitching and rolling heavily. Visibility was poor in the heavy spray, and an RAF rescue helicopter at the scene could not get near enough to the yacht to lift the skipper off; he would have to be moved to the lifeboat and winched aboard from there.

On the lifeboat's third attempt to approach the yacht, David Mason, the second coxswain, managed to leap aboard the boat and assess the situation. He found the skipper, who had been suffering from chest pains, weak and unsteady. Just as the lifeboat drew near enough to receive him, his legs gave way, and it was not until the sixth attempt to grab him that he was brought safely on board the lifeboat. He was finally winched up to the helicopter after five unsuccessful efforts to land a winchman and a stretcher on the lifeboat's deck.

SHOCK

Lifeboat crews can never afford to underestimate the dire effects of shock and exhaustion on casualties' usual good judgement. Even experienced sailors can start to behave in bizarre and unexpected ways if they have been battling with the elements for some hours, and maybe even staring death in the face, before the lifeboat arrives.

As the **Walton and Frinton** crew have found, one of the problems can be that survivors refuse to leave their boat. Shortly after 1.30 am on a July morning in 1990, the lifeboat left to find a 32-foot yacht that had gone aground on the Gunfleet Sand. The yacht was in very shallow water, but the second coxswain used a grapnel to secure the two boats together. The yacht was pounding against the sandbank, and it was essential that her crew should be taken off immediately. But shock and disorientation had clouded their judgement and they were so reluctant to leave that they had to be virtually manhandled aboard the lifeboat.

The yacht's skipper was the last to leave; when he did, it was discovered that his lifeline was still attached to a shroud. The lifeboat crew had quickly to push him back aboard to prevent him from being crushed between the boats, and he was then taken off at the second attempt.

By the time the lifeboat reached Walton, the survivors were suffering from seasickness as well as cold and shock. Fortunately, they were met by the station's honorary secretary, Philip Oxley, who took them home with him, and comforted them with hot baths, food and drinks.

Walton and Frinton is one of the lifeboats that can be called out to East Coast ferries in difficulties. Along with other emergency services, the local lifeboats take part in regular exercises planning a large-scale evacuation from a ferry.

All the emergency services were alerted when a fire broke out in the engine room of the passenger and cargo ship *Nordic Ferry* on her way to Felixstowe. Although the fire was soon extinguished, the **Walton and Frinton, Harwich** and **Aldeburgh** lifeboats were all asked to stand by the ferry while the electrical system and engine were tested. They remained until the master of the ferry asked them to withdraw to Harwich Harbour, as their presence was causing alarm among the passengers!

The **Harwich** crew once spotted a former trawler on fire as they were on their way back from a publicity visit at the East Coast Boat Show. They asked the coastguards to alert local fire services before they sprang into action with their own extinguishers and fire hose. Heavy acrid smoke was pouring from several openings and the fire seemed to be about to break through the deck, but Captain Rod Shaw, the station's honorary secretary, and other crew members boarded the burning vessel and set to work.

Marie Celeste-like, there was no trace of any crew. It turned out that there was no one on board, as the trawler was being converted into a pleasure craft; as the smoke cleared, the crew saw a horrific cocktail of highly inflammable material below decks. Pressurised containers of acetylene, oxygen, propane and butane gas were nestling alongside petrol and diesel fuel. Boxes of polystyrene and cork tiles had produced most of the smoke. The Harwich crew continued damping down the fire until a fire service dory arrived to take over.

GALES AND BLIZZARDS

All lifeboat crews have experience of grappling with the very worst weather conditions. The busiest day in the history of the **Cleethorpes** lifeboat, 30 July 1989, when they rescued 36 people from canoes, rafts and a yacht, coincided with winds gusting up to force 10. Their hectic day started at 10.23 am with a search for five missing canoeists who had been last heard of on their way from Grimsby to Spurn Point.

Despite the high winds and waves of up to ten feet, which continually filled the D-Class inflatable, and the extremely poor visibility, the

The Cleethorpes inshore lifeboat sets out on a search on a bitterly cold night in February 1990.

canoeists were found within 20 minutes. One of the canoes had capsized, shooting its occupant into the water; the rest had been rafted together for safety. All five people were soon aboard the lifeboat, which was now weighed down by eight passengers and still full of water, so the canoeists were soon transferred to a pilot launch and taken ashore at Grimsby docks.

But there was no break for the lifeboat crew. There was no time to go ashore before they were away to a yacht with a broken mast off Spurn Point. After towing the yacht and its crew back to Grimsby, the Cleethorpes crew had barely hung up their wet-suits when it was time to set off again – this time to stand by a charity raft race.

Unluckily, the weather deteriorated again only half an hour into the race, when the wind picked up from force 4 to a squally force 7. The first two rafts reached the finish safely, but the third was swamped and its four occupants were thrown into the water, where they were soon picked up by the lifeboat. The Cleethorpes crew alerted the coastguard that more help was desperately needed, but as they returned to the beach with their four rafters, the crew found another four in the water without lifejackets, clinging to their raft.

Returning once more, the crew picked up another four casualties, including one who was in such a bad way that one of the crew had to get into the water to help him into the lifeboat. After rescuing another 17 rafting casualties, the Cleethorpes crew were finally able to take their boots off at 6.45 pm. They had been working nearly flat out for more than eight hours.

That might be enough to make some people think twice about carrying on, but not Dave Steenvorden, who won a Bronze Medal that day. He went on to join the Humber lifeboat crew, one of the busiest in the country.

High winds and driving snow form some of the grimmest conditions for lifeboats. The **Southwold** Atlantic 21 and her crew survived a bitterly cold January rescue in 1981, involving a fishing boat that had broken down three-quarters of a mile east of Southwold harbour piers. The helmsman, Roger Trigg, suffered the most.

'I did not expect to be out so long; I just put on a dry-suit over a jersey and did not take a hat as I normally do,' he recalls. 'We were out about three or four hours in the snow and I was absolutely frozen at the end of it. I really missed my hat; you lose a great deal of heat through your head.'

Added to the biting cold, the seas were so high that, after one failed attempt to get the fishermen off their boat, Roger decided that they would have to tow the fishing boat back to harbour. He takes up the story himself:

'During our sweep round, one of my crew, Nick Westwood, had found the towline from the fishing boat floating – I don't know how, but he found it. So I said, "Make it fast. We'll try to get them out of here, the boat and the people", because I did not think we should have enough time to make another sweep round to get the people off.'

At this point the Atlantic 21 was repeatedly hit by a series of 15-foot waves.

'We couldn't see the first sea, but we could hear it coming,' says Roger Trigg. 'I told the boys to hang on. It hit us . . . and we were up there, vertical. Nick Westwood tried to get to the bow to keep it down. Then we heard the second sea coming, and we could see it too, about 12 feet behind the first one.

'We were still up vertical, the Atlantic pointing skywards, and the sea was actually breaking higher than that. The crew were all washed down and hanging in the roll bar, even those who had been seated. Just as they were trying to scramble back the third sea hit us. I shouted, "We're going over this time!" We were looking up at the sea. It was higher than the Atlantic . . . we could hear it coming down. Then it went silent for something like five to ten seconds. There was water pressure in my ears and I assumed we were upside down. . . I shall always remember one of the crew saying as he got washed by me, "It's good here, isn't it?" It seemed an eternity, but going through my mind was, how do we get to the beach quick?'

To the crew's amazement the lifeboat had not capsized; the waves had gone right over her and washed through her, but she then emerged safely once more.

'To our astonishment we still had the trawler and the blokes and everything on the towline behind us! Which quite surprised us. We didn't even realise we were still towing them.'

Roger Trigg later received a Bronze Medal for his courage. One of Roger's crew during this rescue, Jonathan Adnams, is now senior helmsman of the Southwold boat. He is a member of the brewing family and his father, John Adnams, is the station's honorary secretary. In 1990 Jonathan received an award for the best Atlantic 21 rescue of the previous year.

In gale force winds the lifeboat took a fishing vessel and its four crew in tow. The fishing boat began to surf on the choppy waves set up in the wake of the Atlantic 21, threatening to crash into the lifeboat. The tow line also snatched repeatedly, making Jonathan Adnams so anxious about possible damage to the lifeboat that he asked the Lowestoft all-weather lifeboat to take over the tow. On the return journey the sea was so rough that the lifeboat had to be restricted to half its normal speed.

Such hardships are faced by the crews of all inshore lifeboats, which are gaining more female members. At **Burnham** you might think that Yvonne James would have learned enough about the cold and wet from husband John, who was in the crew for ten years, to be put off. However, when

Yvonne James, crew member at Burnham on Crouch.

John stepped down from the crew, Yvonne joined. The standard question 'What does your wife think of you being on a lifeboat crew?' was reversed, and John declared, 'I'm right behind her'. As for Yvonne, she regards herself as 'Just one of the chaps'.

FROSTBITE

It is hard to imagine setting off in a 37-foot boat when the breaking seas are 40 feet high. Harder still to think of standing for 11 hours up to your waist in icy sea water while the air, at four degrees below zero, gradually numbs, then freezes, your face and fingers until the skin is painful to the touch. But the **Wells** lifeboat crew endured these conditions when they went to the rescue of a Romanian cargo ship during a blizzard.

Coxswain David Cox knew the risks before they set out; he waited for his most experienced crew, all fishermen, before he launched. The stricken vessel was the *Savinesti*, which had engine failure, an incident already encountered in the chapter on the North East. As the lifeboat entered the open sea she was hit by the full force of the wind, and was continually filling with water from the massive waves that were washing right over her. She soon lost her radar, MF radio and echo sounder, and it took the crew three hours to find the *Savinesti*.

As the storm intensified to hurricane force 12, the lifeboat stood by the cargo ship until she was relieved by the **Humber** lifeboat two hours later. On the return journey, snow was blowing directly into the cockpit, and one crew member had the task of keeping the screen and compass glass clear. It took the lifeboat two hours to negotiate the final seven miles home; visibility was so poor that a local fishing boat had to act as a pilot to guide the lifeboat over the bar and into the harbour.

By the time the lifeboat finally berthed, the crew were rigid with cold and unable to walk. They had to be helped ashore and into dry clothes before being driven to their homes. Two men had frostbite and lost the feeling in their fingers for three weeks. Wells itself was cut off by snow for the next three days.

Graham Walker, who is now the coxswain, said that the cold was so intensely painful that he would have been relieved if the lifeboat had capsized and never come up again. The sea was warmer than the biting cold of the blizzard.

'It was like somebody throwing bath water over you,' he recalls.

On reaching the quay, the lifeboatmen saw that well-wishers had lined up bottles of brandy and rum for them; but all Graham wanted was a cup of tea. Graham was one of the men with frostbite, but he still insists that 'I wouldn't have missed it for anything.'

In the roughest weather conditions they had ever faced, the **Cromer** crew rescued a 30-foot yacht with a faulty gearbox and her five crew in October 1993. The heavy seas lashed the boathouse doors as the lifeboat launched down the slipway. As she slid into the water, she

The Cromer lifeboat crew watch the rig supply vessel St Mark *sink. Her ten crew were all saved.*

The Cromer lifeboats rescue three divers, exhausted but safe.

was completely buried by the waves and disappeared from view.

When the crew spotted the yacht, she was being violently tossed around in the sea, while the skipper was hanging on as well as he could. By this time the waves were as high as a bus, and Coxswain Richard Davies decided that it was too dangerous to approach the yacht without damaging her. He told the skipper to hold his course with the lifeboat, but as daylight faded, a towline was passed to the yacht.

During the tow a giant wave broke right over the casualty, leaving the skipper's head only just visible above the water.

Another time the yacht broached completely, bringing it and the lifeboat stern to stern.

The skipper was nervous about bringing the yacht into harbour at Great Yarmouth, so the second coxswain, William Davies, leapt across in the darkness and took the helm. The appalling weather made it impossible for the lifeboat to return to Cromer to rehouse for another five days.

The coxswain, Richard Davies, who has been on the crew for more than 30 years, was later awarded the Bronze Medal for this rescue. Richard is continuing the proud traditions of his uncle, Henry Blogg, who was coxswain for 38 years and was awarded the Gold Medal a record three times. The name 'Davies' also occurs many times in the RNLI's annals; Cromer is a small, tight-knit community, and many of the station's volunteers and crew members are related to each other.

Unlike many other coastal communities, where lifeboat crews now include teachers, doctors and estate agents, the Cromer crew still earn their living in a traditional industry: all but one of them are crab fishers. Richard's wife runs a fish shop and his son, John, another crew member, is also a crabman.

Cromer enjoys some friendly rivalry with neighbouring **Sheringham**, particularly when the talk turns to crabs.

Sheringham also has its famous lifeboat families, the Wests being given nicknames to distinguish the individual members. 'Downtide' West was coxswain in the days of rowing lifeboats, and 'Joyful' West was coxswain of the Oakley Class lifeboat, which was replaced by an Atlantic 75.

Once a lifeboatman, always a lifeboatman, no matter where you happen to be or whatever you happen to be doing, as David Williams, one of the Sheringham crew, found when he was holidaying in Minorca. David was strolling along the beach with his wife Audrey and two young children, Robert and Caroline, when he spotted a man trapped between the rocks in high waves. He immediately dashed to the rescue and received several bad cuts as he too was battered against the rocks. David found the man unconscious under the water, so he carried out artificial respiration before dragging the 13-stone casualty, a Mr Alan Redhead from Leeds, on to the beach. Meanwhile, Robert and Caroline raced for a mile across the soft, sinking sand of the beach to fetch a doctor. Thanks to David and his two children, Alan Redhead afterwards made a full recovery.

BEYOND THE LIMITS

Southend has two inshore lifeboats stationed at the end of the famous 1 ¼-mile pier, and another on the shore. When the miniature railway is running, lifeboatmen responding to a 'shout' jump on to a train to complete the final leg of their race to the lifeboat. The station's busiest day ever must be 7 August 1971, when a heavy squall and thunderstorm almost wiped out a regatta. Ninety yachts capsized, and the two lifeboats helped to rescue 26 people.

Lifeboats are not infallible and, very occasionally, the lifeboat itself has to be rescued. During a force 8 gale in October 1989, Southend's Atlantic 21 got into difficulties when its engines failed as it was trying to help a sand barge in the Thames Estuary. The scything winds were blowing the lifeboat into dangerously shallow waters and, after much agonising, the honorary secretary of Southend lifeboat station decided to launch Southend's D-Class inflatable.

The wind was now gusting at force 10, and the weather was far beyond the small inflatable's usual limits, but she made good speed, despite the total darkness, and stood by the Atlantic 21 while two exhausted crew members were lifted into a rescue helicopter. The helmsman, Paul Gilson, was then able to tow the Atlantic 21 into shallower water, where she could be secured and later recovered.

Aldeburgh's inflatable lifeboat has also braved weather conditions far beyond its normal limitations. At low water on 17 August 1977 the 42-foot all-weather lifeboat, on its way to help a yacht in distress, was unable to clear the beach. At once the 16-foot inflatable set out, undeterred by the force 7 winds and heavy surf. When she reached the yacht, the *Spreety*, the crew took off the owner's young son so that he could be winched into a rescue helicopter. The inflatable stood by the yacht until the arrival of the all-weather lifeboat, which had managed to use a heavy wave to lift her off the beach.

A few years before, the all-weather lifeboat herself was saved by John Sharman, the 16-year-old son of the motor mechanic. The lifeboat was being prepared for service when a link of the securing chain suddenly

The Aldeburgh inshore lifeboat in heavy surf off the beach.

parted and, entirely unmanned, the boat launched herself into the water. John Sharman managed to hang on to the boat, swing himself aboard and steer her seawards before bringing her back to safety.

Lifeboats have to rely on the brute strength of their crews to effect a rescue. In October 1982 the **Mablethorpe** inflatable lifeboat had to take off two injured men from a grounded barge. In heavy surf the lifeboat was struggling to keep alongside the barge so that the injured men could come aboard. Eventually, Wayne Docking, a very strong and powerfully built young man, held the lifeboat against a tyre fender while John Mayfield, another crew member, jumped on to the barge, taking the painter with him. He made the line fast to the barge and it was then tied to the lifeboat's grab handle.

Quickly he then started to check the two injured men. Unfortunately, as the lifeboat pitched and tossed in the six-foot breaking surf, the grab handle and the tow line were ripped away, and Wayne Docking once more used all his strength to keep the inflatable next to the barge.

Meanwhile, John Mayfield had been thrown into the sea as the barge rolled heavily in a particularly large swell. He scrambled back on to the inflatable, then on to the barge, where the skipper, who appeared to have a broken arm, was now unconscious. John Mayfield handed the injured men to Wayne Docking, while a third lifeboatman held the inflatable steady. As soon as the lifeboat was beached, the two bargees were taken ashore to an ambulance.

A £2 LIFESAVER

One of the most terrifying experiences for a crew member is falling overboard in darkness. This is exactly what happened to Thomas Ridley, a member of the **Clacton** crew. The Clacton Atlantic 21 had been launched to help a yacht that had gone aground. In Force 8 winds and a rough sea the lifeboat towed the yacht safely back to the marina at Wallasea, with one of the lifeboatmen aboard to assist the inexperienced crew.

However, on the way back to Clacton an enormous wave broke from the darkness and buried the bow. Seconds later the helmsman, David Wells, realised that lifeboatman Thomas Ridley had been washed overboard. The helmsman immediately turned the lifeboat and retraced his course. He and Terence Bolingbroke, the other crew member, had only a few seconds left if they were to stand any chance of finding their colleague in the pitch black.

Suddenly Terence saw a flash of light ahead; it was the retro-reflective tape on Ridley's lifejacket winking in the glow from the lifeboat's navigation lights. They found Thomas Ridley 50 yards away, and had to leave the controls to heave him aboard. Fortunately, he was only bruised from his ordeal, and was soon fit enough to go out with the lifeboat again. £2-worth of reflective tape on a £160 jacket had saved his life.

CHAPTER FIVE

The South East – hurricane!

'And they round the headland and battle their way
Through the mountainous waves and the
blinding spray
As the lifeboat shudders and heaves and groans
As she turns their stomachs and rattles their bones
While they look for a sign in the hell ahead –
And the rocks prepare to receive their dead.'

The Lifeboat Men, *William Douglas-Home*.

HAYLING ISLAND IS one of the busiest lifeboat stations along the south coast. It serves Chichester Harbour, a magnet for sailors, and the shallow waters make it seem deceptively safe, but when a storm whips up, the short, sharp waves can quickly overwhelm boats and people. The most dangerous times of the year are early summer and the months of September and October, according to Rod James, helmsman of Hayling Island's 21-foot rigid inflatable.

'The equinoctial gales can run through the channel very fast.

The wind can rise from force 3/4 to force 7/8 within an hour and it catches people out,' he explains. 'A lovely day's sail can become a disaster within moments.'

The fate of the 75-foot yacht *Donald Searle* in October 1992 shows how things can suddenly go terribly wrong.

'It should never have happened,' recalls Rod. 'It was a huge boat, capable of sailing anywhere in the world in any conditions.'

Yet a series of events almost led to tragedy. As the *Donald Searle* was crossing the bar at Chichester Harbour, its engines overheated and it began to have problems with its anchors. Soon it was being hurled about in 20- to 30-foot waves, which threatened to drive it on to the sands.

When the coastguard received a Mayday call from the yacht, Hayling Island's lifeboat had already gone to the rescue of a board sailor in difficulties inside Chichester Harbour. But other Hayling Island crew members were monitoring transmissions from the stricken yacht.

Immediately, lifeboatman Frank Dunster, who was then helmsman of the Hayling Island lifeboat, decided to launch his own 28-foot single-engined inflatable, *Hayling Rescue*, which was kept at a nearby marina.

Rod James, Frank Dunster and the crews that took part in the Donald Searle *rescue, Hayling Island.*

He took the helm with two lifeboat station volunteers, Evan Lamperd and Damien Taylor, as crew. When he reached the scene he could see the sea picking up the ketch and hurling her perilously close to an old submerged ship, the *Target Wreck*. He realised that the all-weather **Bembridge** lifeboat, which was already on its way, would have difficulty getting alongside the yacht. He had to act at once, before the ketch was smashed against the wreck.

After radioing for helicopter assistance, Helmsman Dunster headed for the ketch. On his second approach the yacht was thrust almost vertical by a huge wave, but the rescuers managed to haul the first of her 17 crew aboard the inflatable. As Frank went in again, the yacht reared up on the crest of another enormous wave, threatening to crush the *Hayling Rescue* as she came down. Despite the danger, Frank edged closer and a woman jumped from the yacht; she fell between the two boats, but was instantly pulled on board by Damien Taylor and Evan Lamperd.

At this point Frank Dunster decided to head for home. He knew the helicopter and the Bembridge lifeboat would soon arrive, and the treacherous seas were putting his own boat at risk of capsizing at any moment.

'There is one sea which I always fear,' admits Frank Dunster. 'The 12 to 16-foot solid wall of water, which, because of the shallows, is becoming unstable with the top four feet curling nastily and then breaking. There isn't time to move clear of it. You have got to face it head on. Will the boat go through it? And if the boat does go up it, will that unstable four feet at the top push the bow over?'

Loaded down with its five passengers, the *Hayling Rescue* eventually reached the Hayling Island lifeboat station safely. Meanwhile, Hayling Island's inshore lifeboat was picking its way towards the yacht through waves the height of a double-decker. Suddenly, one particularly large wave stood the lifeboat on end and both engines stalled. Rod James was convinced that the lifeboat was going to somersault and capsize.

'I was having to hang on to the steering wheel to stop myself falling out and I took a deep breath in anticipation of the boat turning over, with me underneath.'

Just in time the crew restarted the engines and regained control. To the relief of the anxious observers on the shore, the lifeboat was once more upright and continuing southwards.

'After that, I felt a great sense of elation. I thought, "We've got away with it – now let's get on with it".'

The lifeboat and the rescue helicopter reached the ketch together.

'Once you're on the scene, you're too busy to worry about the sea – you just have to get on with it,' said Rod.

He says the worst moment was when he had to decide whether to take the crew off the yacht. 'The people on board were comparatively safe at that moment, yet once you take them off into a vulnerable 21-foot inflatable, they're in great danger.'

In the end, Rod made the difficult decision to get the *Donald Searle*'s crew on to the lifeboat. He knew that, if the ketch foundered, there would suddenly be 18 people in the water, where it would be much more difficult to rescue them. He drew alongside the yacht five times, each time removing one of the crew. After each rescue he had to pull the lifeboat smartly away before it was crushed by the yacht as it ploughed up and down in the waves.

'The boat was falling off the waves on top of us. Fortunately, as it did so it pushed us away and only damaged the navigation lights,' explains Rod.

On the sixth approach, two more survivors jumped into the lifeboat, while crew member Christopher Reed boarded the yacht so that he could grab the hi-line being winched down from the helicopter.

'Chris stepped on the boat and disappeared into the air as the boat moved in the other direction,' Rod remembers.

Wedging himself tightly between a cabin and a guardrail, Christopher Reed grasped the line as it came towards him. Soon the helicopter winchman was being lowered on to the yacht; Rod James could now return to Hayling Island, knowing that the remaining eight survivors would soon be winched to safety. In fact the Bembridge lifeboat succeeded in taking off one of the crew left on the yacht.

For their bravery and skill, Rod James and Frank Dunster were both awarded the RNLI's Silver Medal. Rod, a deputy headmaster, is the first helmsman of an inshore lifeboat ever to win two Silver Medals. He won

Hayling Island deputy headmaster Rod James is the first helmsman of an inshore lifeboat ever to win two Silver Medals.

his first for a rescue in 1981, when he saved a 17-year-old boy, a former pupil, who had been clinging on to a groyne for 20 minutes to stop himself being swept away by the huge waves. Rod jumped overboard from the lifeboat and swam through the very rough seas to reach the boy.

'By the time I reached him he had given up hope and thought he was going to die,' Rod said. 'He had let go of the groyne and I just managed to grab him in time. He was very badly cut and bruised and had inhaled a lot of water, so he couldn't have lasted much longer.

'When he saw me, he said "Gosh, I've never been so glad to see a teacher before", except his language was rather more colourful than that – he hadn't been one of our most co-operative pupils.'

Another much-decorated lifeboatman is Dave Kennet of the **Yarmouth,** Isle of Wight, lifeboat. In 1975 he won a Silver Medal for gallantry for rescuing a yacht's crew of five in a storm and torrential rain.

In 1990 Dave went on to receive a Bronze Medal for rescuing two members of the crew from the *Al Kwather 1* during a severe gale. The vessel, a 495-ton car ferry, was rolling and pitching violently in the hurricane-force winds, with her cargo of cars loose on deck. She was unable to head for shelter because of the danger to the crew from the cars hurtling round the deck.

Thirty-foot waves picked up the **Swanage** lifeboat that was standing by the *Al Kwather 1*, and carried her for some distance before the coxswain could regain control. To relieve the Swanage boat and her buffeted crew, the Yarmouth lifeboat launched at 3.10 pm that afternoon. They stood by

The Yarmouth lifeboat assisting the yacht Valdemar *in 1992.*

the stricken vessel until Dave Kennet decided to make for Swanage, as the cargo ship was not in immediate danger. The crew also needed a chance to recuperate in case they needed to carry out a rescue later that night. Sure enough, shortly after midnight, the Swanage and Yarmouth lifeboats were both called out again; the *Al Kwather 1* now had engine problems and wanted her crew to be taken off.

The Yarmouth boat arrived first, and saw the cargo ship heaving violently. As Dave Kennet edged the lifeboat gingerly up to the ship's stern, the crew could hear her cargo shifting as she rolled. Both boats collided as the lifeboat was swept up and down the ship's side by the waves.

At last one of the ship's crew managed to clamber into the cargo net that had been rigged over a stern door, and virtually rolled on to the lifeboat. But the second sailor to leave the ship caught his foot in the net and plunged down below the lifeboat's deck. At considerable risk to themselves, two crew members hauled him aboard the lifeboat. The ship's remaining crew were eventually taken off by a rescue helicopter.

BOXING DAY RESCUE

Lifeboat crews get no rest, even at Christmas. On Boxing Day 1985, Ron Cannon, coxswain of the **Ramsgate** lifeboat, had gone down to the

The Ramsgate lifeboat loaded down with 68 people from the burning ferry Sally Star *in 1994.*

harbour to check the lifeboat's moorings, as the weather had blown up to a storm force 10. Then came a garbled Mayday message from a French fishing boat that had run aground trying to get into the harbour. By now the storm was so violent that the windows on the pier lookout, 30 feet high, were smashed by waves.

The lifeboat drove out of the harbour into tremendous seas, and although the trawler was only two miles away, she could not even be picked up on the radar. The Frenchmen spoke no English but indicated that they would not leave their boat, which was only one year old. In any case, getting them off would have been perilous and standing by meant risking going aground.

Ron Cannon decided to try a tow. A heavy rope was attached, and now Coxswain Cannon needed all his skill to coax the heavy trawler into open seas without the boat dragging his lifeboat on to her side. His crew stood by the rope with axes, ready to cut it at a moment's notice. Twice the seas flung the lifeboat into the air, breaking the tow, but the lifeboatmen patiently went back in and eventually started to pull the trawler clear of the shallows. Out in deeper water the tow was slipped and the trawler, now with full power, was escorted to the relative safety of Ramsgate harbour, though even here the pier had been structurally damaged and nine boats had sunk at their moorings.

HURRICANE!

Perhaps the worst storm ever to hit the south this century was the hurricane of October 1987. In the early hours of the morning, winds of over 100 mph left a trail of destruction along the south and south-east coasts. Yet, as Robin Castle, the coxswain/mechanic of the **Sheerness** life-

The Dover lifeboat in storm-force conditions.

boat recalls, 'We had nothing to tell us there was going to be a wind at all.

At eight o'clock that evening it was a beautiful night – there wasn't a breath of wind at Sheerness. Yet from about midnight onwards they upgraded the gale warning to a hurricane warning within two hours, and within another hour, that was it – it was on top of us.'

The strain on crews negotiating the violent winds and waves was immense. The 40-year-old acting coxswain of the **Dover** lifeboat, Roy Couzens, suffered a heart attack while going to the aid of a Bahamian cargo vessel, *Sumnia*. Braving waves as high as a house, the lifeboat still succeeded in rescuing three survivors from the ship, which was dragging along the breakwaters outside Dover Harbour.

One man was spotted in the water in the middle of an oil slick only because his hand was sticking out. With great difficulty the lifeboatmen got him on to the deck, apparently lifeless. While the official report records that they applied resuscitation, the crew will tell you that this was of an unconventional nature. In a hurricane it is clearly impossible to bend over to give mouth-to-mouth resuscitation. One of the crew gave the survivor the benefit of a size 10 sea-boot on his back, causing the man to vomit oil and seawater, after which he started breathing again.

After the lifeboat landed the three survivors, Roy Couzens recalls, 'It was pretty obvious that the crew themselves were very badly shaken. We were only alongside for about five minutes before we went out a second time. There was a sort of driving force, no one even questioned that we might go out again.'

In spite of their exertions, one man from the *Sumnia* died and this worried Roy Couzens.

'When I was in hospital, lying three beds down from me was the third survivor we picked up. I could not wait to speak to him.

In my own mind I wanted to know whether, if I had gone out there 20 minutes earlier, we might actually have got everybody. He reassured me, actually.'

At the height of the hurricane, the Sheerness lifeboat was also under way. Red flares had been spotted off the Isle of Grain and, despite wind speeds of 90 knots, the lifeboatmen set off to investigate.

The crew were already on the lifeboat, shifting it to a safer berth just minutes before a huge dock crane was blown off its rails and crashed down, blocking the entrance. Even their journey down to the boathouse was fraught with difficulty. The road to the docks was strewn with trees and overturned lorries and trailers, so the crew members had to run the last mile to the boat.

Once the lifeboat reached the mouth of the river, it was pitching and rolling violently in the 25-foot waves. Coxswain Robin Castle recalls, 'I knew it was going to be a bit bad, but I've never heard the crew so quiet. They never said a word, nothing at all. One of the crew was on the shore and all he could see of the lifeboat was the blue flashing light on top of the mast.'

The lifeboat fought her way round to find a small fishing boat with two people aboard being swamped by the waves. They had been out since the previous evening, and when the weather hit them it was too late for them to escape. The boat owner was so desperate that he was singing hymns. The fishing boat was in shallow water and the coxswain had to take a calculated risk.

'It was a case of either standing off and seeing these two guys get washed away, or run in and try and grab them and run back out again. You can't watch two people drown and not do anything.'

Cautiously Robin Castle edged his lifeboat across the shallows, drew alongside and the two survivors were quickly pulled on board. Cold, wet and exhausted, they were taken below, strapped in and given a hot drink.

Coxswain Castle now tried to manoeuvre the boat out of the shallow area – but the water was a metre lower than usual as the gale pushed it away from the sandbank. As they edged out of the gulley, the wind caught the bow and the lifeboat went aground.

For more than 30 minutes the crew tried to free their boat. Dennis Bailey and crew member Richard Rogers donned dry-suits and jumped into the water, attached to a lifeline. They were trying to float the spare anchor seaward so that the lifeboat could be pulled off. But the heavy spray made breathing very difficult, and Richard Rogers was pulled underwater when the lifeline became trapped in the anchor.

Eventually the storm abated and, after ten hours' anxious waiting, the crew managed to refloat the lifeboat on the next tide. They returned home to Sheerness a gruelling 13 hours after they had first set out. Even for Robin Castle, an experienced coxswain and seaman all his life, it takes a while to recover from such a rescue.

'I went home, sat down and started having the shakes. A couple of large brandies helped and I reflected on it, then I thought, I was out in that. It didn't put me off though.'

Always in the back of his mind are the crew and their families. 'Nobody's ever said anything about it, but I suppose all the wives in one way look to the coxswain, he's the bloke that's going to take the boat out and bring their husbands or boyfriends back. That night the honorary secretary went round all the crew houses when we were out and said, "Don't worry, they'll be back later on tonight", and reassured them that way.'

Robin has no trouble finding volunteers. On his crew are a carpet fitter, three steel-workers, an ambulanceman, shop owners, service engineers and a salesman. Training usually starts in the inshore lifeboat.

'We put them through a six-month ordeal of training before they can go afloat. You can normally tell which ones are going to come out right. They are the ones that put themselves out, ask questions. Some realise they are not going to make it and drop out early, and a few you have to tell.'

One quality they all share is humanity. One call was to a raft drifting in the Medway. A tramp had made the raft and piled all his possessions – which amounted to very little – on board. He had no paddles or oars and was content to go where the tides took him. The crew gently guided him ashore into the care of the police, who told them to break up the raft to prevent the man setting out again.

'It was sad, really, it was all he had got, just a few bits of timber lashed together and a pair of shoes he had made himself.'

CHILDREN

Much more tragic is the experience of bringing a body ashore, especially if it is a child.

'We had a 13-year-old who had gone swimming and banged his head. He was floating underwater and by the time we found him, it was too late. That was the worst bit. We took him back and covered him up and when the policeman came he uncovered him and didn't even bother to put the blanket back. That really upset a couple of the lads.'

Even on routine jobs the crew take special care of children, realising what a traumatic experience it can be to have a boat sinking under you and then to be dragged on to a lifeboat by a bunch of strangers. The lifeboat even carries a glove puppet. One of the crew often goes below with it and sits there making faces.

'It brings them out of themselves, and after we've given them a packet of sweets, they come off smiling,' says Robin Castle.

A six-year-old child was one of those rescued by the crew of the **Shoreham Harbour** lifeboat in January 1980. The boat set out at 8.40 am after a distress call from the *Athina B*, a 3,500-ton Greek freighter laden with pumice from the Azores and bound for Shoreham. With only a mile and a half to go before she reached the safety of Shoreham Harbour, the ship had got into difficulties; she was wallowing like a wounded whale in the very rough sea, and waves were continuously breaking over her starboard side.

'*Athina B* was in the heaviest surf I have ever experienced,' recalls

Coxswain Kenneth Voice. 'Anyone connected with the sea knows that once you get into surf your boat acts quite differently. . . You can't steer the same and you haven't got the same power. You are in the lap of the gods, make no mistake about it.'

When they reached the *Athina B* Coxswain Voice ordered the lifeboat's bows to be heavily fendered to protect them in case the boat collided with the huge freighter. The lifeboat was plunging 15 feet down the freighter's side before the massive waves caught her each time and forced her up again. Despite the violent motion, the lifeboat crew managed to snatch the captain's wife, young daughter and six-year-old child from the *Athina B*'s side deck. The lifeboatmen could not persuade anyone else to leave, so the lifeboat moved off.

By now the wind had increased to storm force 10- and 20-foot waves were lashing the lifeboat. After radio discussions with the *Athina B*, it was agreed that the lifeboat should make another attempt to take off the remaining woman and anyone else who wanted to leave the ship.

The coxswain brought the lifeboat alongside the ship's port side, but a tremendous wave lifted her and brought her crashing down on to the ship's gunwale. She managed to pull clear, and made an approach further down the *Athina B*. This time the second woman was taken safely aboard the lifeboat. She was suffering from shock, seasickness and hypothermia, so the crew's first-aider, Motor Mechanic Jack Silverson, tended her while the lifeboat made for Shoreham. There they were met by an ambulance.

After landing the four survivors, the lifeboat returned to the stricken vessel again. Coxswain Voice told the *Athina B*'s crew to be ready on deck, wearing their lifejackets. The lifeboat was pitching and tossing in the waves, but Coxswain Voice managed to hold her steady while 11 of the freighter's crew jumped into the waiting arms of the lifeboat crew.

The master of the *Athina B* insisted that the remaining crew would stay aboard, so the lifeboat once more returned home. After landing the survivors she immediately went to stand by the freighter, but as the vessel was out of immediate danger it was decided that the lifeboat should return to station and stand by there.

At 20.45 the *Athina B* put out a Mayday distress call – she had now run out of fuel and was rapidly being swamped by waves and spray. The Shoreham crew immediately set off again, for the fourth time, and 20 minutes later the **Newhaven** lifeboat followed. She had only just left harbour when a large wave hit her, spinning her round 90 degrees. Then another wave struck her, almost capsizing her. One crew member was washed overboard, but was pulled back aboard, still attached to his lifeline. The second coxswain, Alan Boyle, had to be given first aid for a head wound.

Meanwhile, the *Athina B* had run aground about 250 yards off the beach. As Coxswain Voice tried to bring the Shoreham lifeboat alongside, she was caught by a breaker, which smashed her against the freighter.

The Athina B *ashore on Brighton beach in 1980.*

Fortunately there was no damage, and while the lifeboat was being tossed up and down the freighter's side, ten of the crew threw themselves and their suitcases at the lifeboat's deck, where the lifeboat crew were ready to catch them.

Suddenly another man was seen standing on the ship's bridge. He was eventually persuaded to come down, but mistimed his jump, landing in the water. Two lifeboatmen quickly hauled him out before he was crushed between the two boats. At 22.45 the lifeboat entered Shoreham Harbour for the last time that day; she had rescued 26 people. The Newhaven lifeboat was able to return home as soon as she was informed that the Shoreham boat had saved everyone from the *Athina B*.

Kenneth Voice received a Silver Medal for his part in the rescue, but he insists that it was a team effort.

'It's the crew who are up on the open deck. I am full of praise for my crew,' he said. 'I never forget . . . that it takes seven or eight chaps to pull off what we did that day on the boat. You don't do it on your own.'

Selsey coxswain Mike Grant also won a Silver Medal for a rescue from a freighter in terrible conditions on 10 January 1979. The Panamanian-registered *Cape Coast* was taking in water in a force 11 storm, and when the lifeboat arrived she found the freighter's decks being swept by heavy waves. The anchors were dragging and two liferafts that the crew had inflated were blowing around like kites. The lifeboat stood by all night and when, in the light of morning, the storm had abated to a mere force 9, it was judged safe enough to take them off.

The lifeboat drove in three times so that the 20 people could be snatched, one at a time, from the pilot ladder. The *Cape Coast* was pitching and tossing and the lifeboat was smashed into her side several times by heavy seas. Mike Grant had put out heavy rope fenders, but even these were destroyed.

'*Cape Coast* was an old ship and you can imagine tearing up the side of a ship with a load of rivets sticking out; it was going to do a lot of damage,' Mike remembers. 'She rolled down on top of us at one stage, and it was a bit frightening at the time. In fact she bent our aerials. We went full astern and away for another attempt.'

INSHORE LIFEBOAT PERILS

The **Brighton** lifeboat crew's foray into a force 9 gale and 15-foot waves nearly led to disaster on 26 August 1986 when their Atlantic 21 capsized only 20 feet from the people they were trying to save. The boat was heading for two survivors from a yacht who were in the water when a steep sea lifted her bow almost vertically into the air. At the same moment the wind caught the underside of the hull and the lifeboat capsized.

She landed upside down, though completely level, and Helmsman Alan Young and crew member Stan Todd found themselves underneath the

Brighton's Atlantic 21 lifeboat off the Marina.

boat. The third lifeboatman, Roger Cohen, was thrown clear and managed to hold the port lifelines as his two crewmates emerged from beneath the hull. Alan Young found the air bottle release for the righting bag as the other two hung on to the port safety line.

The lifeboat quickly righted itself, but just as they were clambering aboard, another breaking wave lifted the boat for 25 yards before turning her upside down again. This time Young and Cohen were thrown into the water, and Cohen, who was too far away for Todd to reach him with the quoit line, had to be left to drift safely ashore. The lifeboat was knocked over once more by another rogue wave before Stan Todd managed to bring her safely ashore. Fortunately, within minutes of the lifeboat being beached, the three survivors from the yacht were also washed ashore about 75 yards further along the beach.

As well as foul weather, darkness is another hazard faced by lifeboat crews. All-weather lifeboats have their own powerful headlights, which are often used to illuminate the scene of a rescue, but the smaller inshore lifeboats are not so fortunate.

The **Bembridge**, Isle of Wight, inflatable lifeboat carried out a difficult rescue in total darkness in August 1993. The crew were summoned in response to a distress call from a yacht, the *Bari*, which had been holed when it grounded on the rocky Bembridge Ledge and was taking on water.

To make its approach the lifeboat had been using the yacht's navigation lights, which were still switched on. However, just as the lifeboat drew near the yacht to take off the three crew, the survivors put them out. In the pitch black Helmsman Alan Attrill had to manoeuvre the lifeboat alongside the yacht in only three feet of water. With difficulty he held the boat steady while the yachtsmen scrambled aboard. Shortly afterwards the yacht was swept further into the rocks and sank.

One of the calls most dreaded by all lifeboat coxswains must be the cry 'Man overboard!'. Searching for someone in rough seas, often in pitch darkness, is a nerve-racking experience. All crews receive training in the best procedures to follow when this happens, but nothing can prepare them for the agonising uncertainty of a frantic search for a fellow lifeboatman.

The **Walmer** crew is one of those that has had the daunting task of finding a colleague who has fallen overboard. On 18 July 1991 the Walmer inshore lifeboat had been summoned to a Belgian yacht that had run aground during a force 9 gale. It was being heavily battered by the waves and was taking on water; the three crew were in imminent danger, so Helmsman Duane Brown decided to take them off.

The first survivor was already aboard the lifeboat when an enormous wave knocked crew member John Collins into the water, just as he was reaching over to help the second Belgian. He clung on to the lifeboat and lifeboatman Shaun East rushed forward to grab him, pushing him down when it looked as though he was going to be crushed between the two boats. Meanwhile, Helmsman Brown had to swing the lifeboat round sharply.

John Collins was helped on board, bruised and shaken; Shaun East had sprained his wrist. They then brought the two remaining survivors on to the inshore boat, before transferring them to Ramsgate's all-weather lifeboat. Luckily, neither John Collins nor Shaun East suffered any lasting ill-effects.

COMBINED EFFORT

While outstanding acts of individual heroism often feature in lifeboat rescues, co-operation also has an important part to play. Lifeboat crews and other RNLI personnel have to learn to work closely together, particularly when they are searching for casualties over a wide area.

One search for five missing anglers in April 1991 involving all seven lifeboat stations from **Dover** to **Newhaven**, lasted 21 hours and covered an area of 3,400 square miles. The Dover lifeboat was the first to launch, in a north-easterly gale of force 7 to 9; the crew had been asked to find an angling dinghy that had been seen signalling for help.

It was extremely cold, and by the time the **Dungeness** lifeboat joined the search just after midnight, the wind had worsened to force 11. After a hazardous launch by tractor into huge waves, the all-weather boat headed for the search area.

At **Littlestone** the honorary secretary had picked up news of the rescue bid on his radio, and he immediately offered the services of the station's inshore lifeboat, which launched soon after the Dungeness lifeboat. By 1 am the three boats were joined by a rescue helicopter.

Meanwhile, another craft was reported missing; the hunt was now on for two dinghies and five people. Conditions were now so bad that, at 3 am, the Littlestone lifeboat had to return to station to refuel and change crew. The men were exhausted after the continual buffeting in the unprotected inshore lifeboat.

At last, nearly seven hours after they had first set out, the Dungeness crew spotted the first casualty; it was a small boat with three men aboard. They were all suffering from exposure, exhaustion and hypothermia, and they were taken to Dungeness boathouse and airlifted to hospital by helicopter.

After only a 30-minute break, the Dungeness lifeboat launched again to search for the second missing vessel, a small cabin cruiser with two anglers aboard. Early in the morning the Dover lifeboat and the **Rye** inflatable began to comb the whole area, the Dover lifeboat extending the search far out into the channel. At 8.15 am the original Littlestone crew took over again, and searched until they were ordered ashore by the coastguard because of the bad weather.

The **Eastbourne** crew, who were on a routine Sunday morning exercise, also became involved and hunted for six hours, until the missing boat was

The Newhaven lifeboat in action. On this occasion it took six men off the listing freighter Georgious *before escorting her to safety.*

eventually spotted. By this time the **Newhaven** lifeboat had also joined the search. It was the rescue helicopter that finally found the capsized vessel, shortly after 4 pm. The **Hastings** lifeboat, which had launched in the morning, took the cruiser in tow but, sadly, the helicopter crew soon noticed two bodies in the water nearby.

The bodies of the missing anglers were eventually recovered by the helicopter.

WHY DO THEY DO IT?

Why does anyone take on the heavy responsibility and considerable personal risks involved in being a lifeboat coxswain? For Robert Wilkie, coxswain of the **Calshot** lifeboat on the Hampshire coast, the answer is simple; when he was a boy, his life was saved by the Dunbar coxswain.

'We had built a canoe, a friend and I – a framework canvas canoe. We decided to go from Belhaven beach to Dunbar harbour, but unfortunately we got caught a mile off Dunbar harbour – we sank,' recalls Coxswain Wilkie. 'My legs had got trapped in the canoe and we couldn't swim in because of the rocks.'

In vain they tried to attract the attention of people on land. 'We were waving at people along the coastal walk, and they were waving back.

The Calshot lifeboat assisting the yacht Software Mistress *in 1992.*

Then the daughter of the chap we were with realised we were in trouble and ran down to the harbour. The coxswain came out and picked us up in his own fishing boat and took us to hospital. I've always felt I owed the RNLI something.'

His own experience makes him fairly tolerant towards inexperienced and even foolish would-be seafarers who get into difficulties, although one incident continues to amaze him.

'It was a lovely sunny day – everybody was out. Then this fog came in without any warning. It was a pea-souper. . . We were standing by a yacht that had missed the Beaulieu River entrance. While we were waiting, this gin palace draws up.

'The skipper says, "Is this the Hamble River?" "No," we says. "No. Your compass should have told you that."

'Then we looked up on his boat – there must have been £2,000 worth of radar and electronic kit on his boat. We discovered later he didn't know how to work his radar. He had to follow us up to Hythe marina.'

Would-be seafarers trying to negotiate the Channel in anything from tyre rafts to baths are the main problem for Dennis Bailey, the second coxswain of the **Dover** lifeboat. One incident that is now part of the station's folklore is the crew's encounter with a man trying to paddle his way to France in an empty chest freezer with the lid taken off.

Another time the Dover lifeboat was called out to six surfboarders

The Dover lifeboat taking passengers from the disabled hovercraft The Princess Margaret *in 1985.*

making for Calais in dense fog. The crew finally caught up with them six miles from Dunkirk, in imminent danger of being flattened.

'You have hovercraft, jetfoils doing 38 knots, coming in there, and the surfboards aren't showing up on radar,' explained Dennis Bailey. 'When we eventually found them, they said "We're keeping the sun over our shoulder. We can't be far from Calais now". If they'd carried on, they'd have ended up in Denmark.'

Film stuntmen have a reputation for being able to take care of themselves, but even they are fallible, as the crew of the **Eastbourne** inshore lifeboat discovered when they were called out to a stunt crew involved in a James Bond film. As part of the stunt, a Land-Rover had to be catapulted from the clifftop into the water, and a coastguard officer, Graham Russell, was present to check on safety.

He was just clearing the cliff edge so that the film crew could begin shooting when he was told that a 17-foot dory, which had been fetching equipment from beneath the rocks, had capsized, pitching its three occupants into the sea. Peering over the cliff edge, Graham Russell could see the three men clinging to the upturned boat as it was driven towards the foot of the cliffs.

A few minutes later the Eastbourne's inflatable was launched. After some skilful navigation through the rocks and heavy surf, the RNLI crew found the stuntmen – bruised, but otherwise unharmed.

FIRST AID

Many lives are saved by crew members' prompt use of the latest first aid techniques. Generally each crew includes someone who is a first aid specialist, but everyone on board has been trained in resuscitation methods and the treatment of cardiac arrests, hypothermia, seasickness and other conditions affecting casualties, and sometimes RNLI crews.

First aid at sea is hampered by the motion of the lifeboat, which can make mouth-to-mouth respiration impossible, for instance. Extreme cold aboard an exposed inflatable makes the treatment of hypothermia very difficult, while the high cabin temperature (up to 40 degrees C) on a larger lifeboat can cause heat stress.

An inflatable lifeboat provides little scope for complicated medical manoeuvres, as any helmsman would be the first to admit.

'You are very, very limited to how much you can do,' says Alan Clarke, helmsman of the **Hunstanton** Atlantic 21. 'Obviously, if you have recovered someone unconscious, or something like that, you have to get some air into him, do a bit of resuscitation. In most circumstances, broken bones have to wait until you get ashore.'

For Rod James, helmsman at **Hayling Island,** the main issue is whether to risk transferring a casualty to an Atlantic 21.

'In most cases we leave them on the boat and tow the boat in,' he explains. 'They are on a 30-foot or 40-foot yacht perhaps, and to put them on to our 21-footer is a shock to them – and then charging 30 knots across the sea would be worse.'

Nevertheless, many people owe their lives to the medical skills of Atlantic 21 crews. The Hayling Island crew rescued a man they had found floating on his back in the sea with his arms outstretched, apparently unconscious, having been knocked overboard from a yacht. Once he had been hauled aboard the lifeboat, Rod James discovered that the survivor was actually breathing, but was barely conscious. He encouraged the man to talk, so that he could monitor his level of consciousness.

As Rod was giving him first aid, a huge wave stood the lifeboat vertically on her stern and filled her with water. Rod managed to grab the survivor, who had been swept between the engines, and he was soon airlifted to hospital; he was able to return home the next day.

The **Portsmouth** crew once saved a man who had spent more than an hour clinging to an upturned dinghy on a bitterly cold April day. He was unconscious by the time three lifeboatmen had managed to hoist him into the lifeboat; he was not breathing and he had no detectable pulse. Cardiac massage and resuscitation were started immediately, and he was transferred to a helicopter, where the air crew continued the resuscitation attempts. By the time he arrived at a hospital, he was breathing again.

An elderly man was revived by two members of the **Margate** crew after he fell from some rocks near the Winter Gardens. Without waiting for the lifeboat to be launched, Coxswain Peter Barker and crew member Clive

Simpson ran from the lifeboat house across the beach and waded in to save the man, who was lying face downwards in a gully. Although there was no sign of life when they carried him from the water, they started artificial respiration and he began to revive. Afterwards he made a complete recovery in hospital.

The crew of the **Whitstable** lifeboat claim to provide a complete 999 service; they can offer not only first aid but also have a policeman, a fireman, an ambulanceman – and an undertaker – on the crew! The first aid expertise of crew member Brian Hadler came in handy when the lifeboat went to the aid of the catamaran *Rumpleteazer*, which had broken her steering gear on passage from London to the West Country.

The lifeboat arrived after the catamaran had started taking on water, and the Atlantic 21 was lashed alongside the casualty, providing power and steerage. Both boats then headed back to Herne Bay, where the exhausted crew of the *Rumpleteazer* were taken aboard the lifeboat; the skipper was also suffering from hypothermia, and crew member Hadler tended him carefully until the lifeboat arrived back at Whitstable.

A DARING DOCTOR

Lifeboat crews are not immune to the conditions that often affect casualties. In the course of difficult rescues, crew members have suffered seasickness, heart attacks, hypothermia and broken bones.

Hastings's honorary medical advisor, Dr Peter Davy, was awarded a Silver Medal and entered in the British Medical Association's Book of Gallantry for attending injured sailors after he had broken seven ribs during a rescue attempt.

On 23 December 1974 the Hastings crew, with Dr Davy on board, set off for the Argentinian warship *Candido de Lasala*; there had been an explosion on board and medical help was urgently needed. Shortly after the lifeboat had launched it was joined by a rescue helicopter, and Dr Davy was asked to transfer to the helicopter so that he could reach the injured men more quickly.

Dr Peter Davy of Hastings receives his Bronze Medal from RNLI President the Duke of Kent.

One of the helicopter crewmen was lowered safely into the lifeboat. Just as he was putting Peter Davy into a harness, ready to be winched up to the helicopter, the helicopter lost contact with the lifeboat. Both men were dragged off the deck and smashed into the lifeboat stern before being swept into the water.

Peter Davy was quickly plucked out of the sea and taken on to the Argentinian ship, where he tended the injured sailors. Although he himself was in considerable pain, he then accompanied the sickest man to hospital aboard the helicopter. When they arrived it was only after ensuring that the injured man was being cared for that Dr Davy let a colleague examine him, when he was found to have broken his ribs. Today Dr Davy is the chairman of the Hastings station; his connection with the RNLI now goes back more than 20 years.

LONG SERVICE – RNLI VETERANS

Dr Peter Davy is only one of the many long-serving volunteers drawn to the RNLI. The late Ken Derham, a cafe proprietor in Christchurch on the Hampshire coast, was a keen volunteer at the **Mudeford** station for more than 30 years, as well as winning a Silver Medal for a single-handed rescue. Before the RNLI stationed an inflatable lifeboat at Mudeford in 1963, Ken Derham had more than once rescued swimmers and others in trouble in his 11-foot rowing boat; his cafe right at the harbour entrance provided an ideal vantage point to spot anyone in trouble.

On Easter Monday 1959 a 30-foot fishing boat, returning from a pleasure trip with three passengers on board, capsized at the mouth of the harbour, and a worker at the cafe saw the passengers struggling in the water about 250 yards from the shore. Ken Derham immediately informed the coastguard and, although he was still recovering from a major operation, set out in his own boat to help.

There was heavy surf on the beach, and Ken had to stand and row to get the boat launched. The sea was so rough that he knew he did not stand much of a chance of returning safely. After a time he found two people clinging to wreckage just ahead of him. One was a 19-year-old youth, the owner of the capsized boat. The other was a 15-year-old girl who was completely exhausted; her father had already drowned. Ken had to leave his oars to pull the girl into his dinghy, hoping that it would not capsize in the seven-foot waves. The 19-year-old held on to the dinghy as Ken rowed back to shore through the heavy swell.

As soon as the Mudeford station opened, Ken Derham became its first honorary secretary.

Another long-serving volunteer is Alan Coster, the **Lymington** harbourmaster, who was a member of the Lymington crew for 28 years. In 1980 Helmsman Coster won a Bronze Medal for rescuing two men from a fishing boat that was sinking at the entrance to Lymington River.

In near-gale-force winds, Alan managed to bring Lymington's inflatable

The Mudeford lifeboat with the appropriately named burning speedboat Hot Banana.

lifeboat to within ten feet of the fishing vessel, which was dangerously close to the sedge and mudbanks of the river estuary. As he tried to get alongside the boat to bring off the crew, a huge wave picked up the lifeboat and spun her round, forcing her down to the sea bottom. The engines stalled temporarily, and Helmsman Coster decided it was too risky to approach any closer; oyster-trawling gear was streaming out for 80 feet behind the stricken vessel, threatening to entangle the lifeboat.

Alan Coster guides HRH Princess Anne at the helm, with son Peter Phillips behind, on the Lymington Atlantic 21 lifeboat.

As the trawler was sinking fast, he decided to swim the 20 yards to the boat and guide the two men through the marshes to a rendezvous further up river, where it would be safe for the survivors to board the lifeboat. He reached the boat just as it sank, the two crew jumping over the side on to the sedge. With his expert knowledge of the marshes, Alan Coster was able to help the two exhausted survivors, who were suffering from exposure, through the treacherous terrain. One minute the three would be walking on mud and sedge; the next they would be almost up to their necks in the icy water of a gully. After 25 minutes they reached the lifeboat, and the two men were brought back to Lymington and taken to hospital.

One of the longest-serving families in the RNLI must be the Tarts of the **Dungeness** lifeboat. Ben Tart was on the crew of the lifeboat for 37 years, ten as coxswain, while his wife Doris was a lifeboat launcher for 44 years. Before a tractor and carriage launch was introduced in 1985, lifeboats at Dungeness had to be hauled manually into the sea by volunteers like Mrs Tart heaving on ropes.

In small fishing communities most of the able-bodied men were needed to crew the lifeboat, leaving only a few men and the women to launch her. In Newbiggin the cry used to be: 'Every man to the boat and every woman to the rope'. The women of Dungeness have continued the long and honourable tradition almost right up to the present day; ladies like Mrs Joan Bates, who served for 37 years, and Mrs Serena Fair, who was a launcher for more than 50 years. The worst launch she recalls was in

Women helping to rehouse the Dungeness lifeboat in the 1950s.

1929 when her husband, Edwin, was in the crew. The storm was so severe that a man in the stern of the lifeboat could not be seen from the bow. In those days there was no radio, so the launchers, cold, soaked and exhausted, used to huddle around the stove, awaiting the return of the lifeboat and the important job of recovery.

'I never expected to see them again, sometimes,' said Mrs Fair. 'But I never missed a launch.'

To meet the returning lifeboat the heavy greased wooden skids ('the woods') were laid across the beach, then the boat was hauled up with a capstan pushed around by men and women alike; there was no electric winch in those days. It took two hours to heave the boat up.

'It was never a woman's job,' says Ben Tart. 'It was too hard.

But there was no one else to do it.'

Among all the terrible tempests that have battered this bleak, isolated belt of land, the one of 11 February 1974 stood out in Doris Tart's mind. In the middle of the storm, the Dungeness lifeboat had to launch into hurricane-force winds to take a seriously injured man off the MV *Merc Texco*.

'The only night I was really worried was the night of the *Merc Texco*,' Doris admitted. She was twice blown off her bicycle on her way down to the lifeboat house to launch the boat, and during the launch the lifeboat was swept broadside on to the huge breakers. As the launchers dashed down the beach to haul her up for another attempt, Ben Tart gripped the wheel and made a snap decision. As the lifeboat started lifting on the next wave, he drove her out backwards, stern first.

Somebody watching the launch thought that the lifeboat would overturn and reported this to the press, so there was little rest for Joan Bates, when she returned to the house and the telephone after helping with the launch. She and her husband, Mick, who was honorary secretary, were inundated with phone calls asking if the boat had in fact capsized.

When the lifeboat returned, Doris thought it was too rough for the boat to come ashore. The men who waded into the sea to connect the winch wire were secured with a rope so that the other launchers could hold on to them should they be swept off their feet.

The gallantry of the Dungeness launchers continues. In October 1992 a massive wave swept under the lifeboat and jammed it into the launching carriage. It was freed and recovered by the tractor, but the carriage was being rapidly submerged by the incoming tide. The crew and the shore-helpers at once waded into the rough sea and battled against the waves to lift the carriage free.

BLUE PETER TO THE RESCUE

Littlehampton is one of the stations that has a boat funded by the Blue Peter appeal of 1993. Appropriately, one of the many rescues carried out

The first Blue Peter *lifeboats with Valerie Singleton, Christopher Trace and John Noakes aboard.*

by the Littlehampton crew that year was that of a little girl, Katie Hazael, who got into difficulties while swimming off the West Pier. Her friend, Abigail Martin, takes up the story:

'It was just a normal sort of July evening, a bit choppy, but we didn't think anything of it.'

'After a while we realised we were going too near the breakwater,' explains Katie, 'so we tried to swim back but the current was too strong. When we actually got to the breakwater, we just had to hang on until the waves died down a bit. But they were really, really strong waves and it was then we realised we were in trouble. The waves kept bashing us against the breakwaters, which had barnacles on.'

The girls were screaming for help, but their friends on the shore thought they were only calling and waving, and waved back.

'We were screaming to the shore. We were so scared – we thought we were going to drown,' says Katie.

After a while, by moving from breakwater to breakwater, Abigail managed to battle her way to the beach and raise the alarm. Meanwhile, Katie was hanging on for dear life.

'I knew that if I let go, I'd be taken out to sea and I'd drown, so I just held on. I didn't care how much it hurt.'

But soon, to her relief, she saw the lifeboat coming towards her. 'When the lifeboat arrived, I felt so safe because they looked so big and I knew they'd be able to save me.'

The waves were so rough that the helmsman couldn't bring the inflatable in close enough, so crew member Steve Tester dived in and swam towards Katie.

'As soon as I was there, she just jumped on me and clung on,' he recalls. 'I didn't have to coax her off at all. She was quite happy to see me, I think.'

CHAPTER SIX

Animal rescues –
tails from the deep

'The more I see of men, the better I like dogs.'

Madame Roland

RESCUES ARE NOT confined to people; RNLI crews have also saved recalcitrant goats, over-enthusiastic dogs, trapped horses and one endangered dolphin.

Dogs on coastal walks have an alarming habit of failing to spot the cliff edge and tumbling over the precipice. Brandy, a two-year-old collie on holiday with his owners near Swanage, was too busy chasing rabbits to notice a 100-foot cliff at Anvil Point and plunged dramatically out of sight. His anxious owners could not see him, but after about 15 minutes his terrified yaps were heard from the foot of the cliff.

The sea was too rough for the **Swanage** lifeboat crew to attempt a rescue the next day, but Brandy was sustained with opened tins of corned beef thrown from the cliff. When the weather improved on the following day, the Swanage crew was able to grab Brandy from his precarious perch, completely unharmed after his two-day ordeal.

'I am amazed at all the trouble they went to for a dog,' said Ted Bradley, Brandy's owner, after the rescue. 'If it was a human in the same position they couldn't have done more.'

The crew of **Walmer's** D-Class inflatable lifeboat feared the worst when they heard that a dog had fallen 150 feet over a cliff three miles from their station. But when they arrived at the scene, they were amazed to find the dog crouching on a ledge six feet above the water, apparently unharmed. Crew member Derek Brown was then landed despite a heavy swell. High waves breaking against the cliff at high water spring tide forced the boat away from the foot of the cliff, but Derek tucked the dog firmly under his arm and swam the short

Walmer lifeboatman Derek Brown's lifeline becomes a lead for rescued dog Molly.

distance to the inflatable, where they were both hauled aboard. Molly, a crossbreed, was soon reunited with her grateful owner.

Five goats on the Isle of Inchkeith in the Forth Estuary were determined not to be rescued. Tiffany, Timothy, Chocolate Drop, Snuffles and Gem were stranded on the island when the animal sanctuary where they lived was moved to the mainland; the sanctuary trustee had been unable to capture them and was forced to leave them behind.

The goats grew to enjoy their lonely existence, unaware that uninvited visitors were roaming the island on shooting forays.

The animal sanctuary was so concerned that, in January 1992, a group of volunteers was dispatched aboard the *Spirit of Fife* ferry to attempt a rescue. After a long chase, three of the goats were rounded up, but, desperate to evade capture, the other two plunged into the sea and swam out to a rock, well out of reach.

As the waves lashed the rock, it became obvious that drastic action was needed to save the animals from drowning. The ferry captain quickly contacted **Queensferry**'s inshore lifeboat, which launched to the rescue. The crew succeeded in cajoling one goat aboard; the other had to be towed along behind the Atlantic 21. Once back on the island, the two ungrateful animals immediately made off again.

For one of the most difficult animal rescues in the RNLI's history, nine members of **West Kirby's** lifeboat crew and the station's honorary secretary were awarded the RSPCA's Bronze Medal in 1988. One April afternoon crew member Malcolm Jones was perturbed to see two horses being ridden towards a dangerous gutter in the River Dee estuary off

West Kirby, and the animals and their riders were soon trapped in the soft mud for which the area is notorious. With only three hours left until high water, Ron Jones, the station honorary secretary, decided to launch the lifeboat, which was carried across to the casualties.

By this time the tide was inexorably approaching the horses. Their riders were quickly helped to firmer ground, but the animals could not be freed. As the tide advanced, they continued to sink into the soft mud and became very distressed. Eventually a vet was called in case one of the horses, which was very tightly stuck in the mud, had to be put down. Using an improvised sling, lifeboatmen managed to free one of the horses. The other remained trapped as crew members struggled in water up to their waists to free it, while holding its head above the water. In the nick of time, only 20 minutes before high water threatened to engulf it completely, the second animal was finally released and led to safety.

Although both animals were very tired after their two-and-a-half-hour ordeal, neither had been permanently injured.

The West Kirby crew is the only one to have rescued an animal inland. On a bitterly cold January day in 1991, the crew members took their inflatable 14 miles by road to rescue a boy and his dog from a lake in a Liverpool park. Thirteen-year-old Fred Allen and his dog Buster had fallen through ice into a lake 50 feet deep in the centre of Liverpool. They had managed to struggle on to an island, but police and firemen were unable to reach them and, as dusk fell, the temperature swiftly plunged to minus 4 degrees C.

After their trip through the Mersey Tunnel, the crew arrived at the park; it took eight lifeboatmen to lift the inflatable over the park railings. Two of the crew used their wellies to break the ice as the boat slowly made its way to the island, and soon the boy and his dog were safely on

Thirteen-year-old Fred Allen and Buster, rescued from an icy Liverpool park lake by the West Kirby inshore lifeboat.

board. Fred was taken to hospital suffering from hypothermia, but was later allowed home.

'This was an unusual call,' admitted Ron Jones, the station's honorary secretary. 'We're not called an inshore lifeboat for nothing!'

Mumbles lifeboatmen took part in another unusual rescue when they rescued a well-known local seal that was trapped in a fishing net. The old seal, which sometimes has to be shooed off the lifeboat slip before a launch, was spotted by Alan Jones, the Mumbles coxswain. Its claws had become entangled in a net near the lifeboat station, so the coxswain and a few of the crew put out in their D-Class inflatable and cut it free. Their swift action almost certainly saved the animal's life.

'He's quite a character down here and the crew wanted to do what they could to help,' explained Captain Roy Griffiths, the station's honorary secretary.

Crewmembers at **Amble** in Northumberland found themselves acting as nursemaids to a dolphin in 1989. The lifeboat *Margaret Graham* had been launched as safety back-up to some navy divers who were about to explode a wartime mine. After dropping the divers at the site of the mine, the lifeboat set off to find a local bottle-nosed dolphin and try to keep him safe while the 500-pound mine was detonated. The *Margaret Graham* soon managed to attract the dolphin's attention, and kept him and throngs of spectators entertained until the explosion was over.

The strangest animals rescued at sea were two deer rescued by the **Bridlington** crew. The deer had taken to the water after they were chased from a nearby park by dogs. Using their inflatable, the lifeboatmen managed to turn the deer back to the shore, where they were soon rounded up and taken back to the park. The park wardens were extremely grateful, as the animals were worth £500 each!

Another deer rescue, this time by the Tynemouth inshore lifeboat in 1965.

CHAPTER SEVEN

The South West –
air and sea rescue

`Roll on, through deep and dark blue Ocean – roll!
Ten thousand fleets sweep over thee in vain;
Man marks the earth with ruin – his control
Stops with the shore.'

Childe Harold's Pilgrimage, *Lord Byron*

MAURICE HUTCHENS IS a brave man. For 33 years, 12 as coxswain, he served on the **Sennen Cove** lifeboat, less than a mile from Land's End, and faced the Atlantic storms with a stoic determination. Yet when he had to attend a lunch in a top London hotel as a guest of honour and receive a medal from the President of Iceland, Maurice got cold feet and had to be gently frogmarched back into the banqueting room when he tried to escape before the presentation.

The Icelandic award came for one of the most remarkable combined rescues ever performed by a lifeboat and a helicopter. Radio links between the two broke down and, in the darkness and maelstrom, the lifeboat coxswain and helicopter pilot relied on their raw skill and instinct to pluck 11 Icelandic seamen to safety.

It was on 19 September 1981 that the Icelandic coaster *Tungufoss* sent out a Mayday. She was sinking off Land's End, buffeted by a force 9 gale and very heavy seas. Sennen Cove is a station where, in severe storm, the coxswain must stand at the top of the slipway watching the waves, waiting for a momentary lull for a safe launch; as soon as the lifeboat hits the water, there is a sharp turn to be made to avoid a treacherous outcrop of rocks. Coxswain Hutchens knew the risks well and, as he set out in the 37-foot lifeboat, she rolled violently.

Arriving at the scene he found a Royal Navy helicopter from Culdrose was already at work. The *Tungufoss* was listing over to 45 degrees, making rescue very treacherous, and although the helicopter winchman had pulled three men to safety, he had been smashed into the *Tungufoss* and was injured. Now it was the turn of the lifeboat.

The *Tungufoss* crew had thrown their liferafts over the side of the ship

111

and, one by one, three men jumped into them. The men left on the ship paid out the ropes to let the liferafts drift down towards the lifeboat, where the survivors were hauled aboard. As the fourth and fifth men tried the same manoeuvre, everything went horribly wrong. They slid down the rope towards the liferaft but lost their grip and dropped into the sea. Around the *Tungufoss* the water was in turmoil and the men were sucked away in the darkness. The coaster's lights were out and as the lifeboatmen scoured the sea, the 26-year-old helicopter pilot trained his spotlight on the men, pinpointing them as the lifeboat raced towards them.

The Icelanders, hardy, disciplined seamen, had prepared for their rescue and were fully kitted out in warm clothing and lifejackets. However, the clothing was waterlogged and the extra weight made it hard to get them over the side of the lifeboat, but they were saved just as the *Tungufoss* slowly started to go down. There were still three men on her.

Hutchens recalls: 'The trouble was we were running out of time. We could see the ship going down as well as increasing her list; she was disappearing. It was pretty horrific to see this vessel going out of sight with the people still there.'

He drove the lifeboat straight in towards the stern of the ship and two men slid down the cabin top, which was now vertical. With the lifeboat ranging up and down in the waves and the ship sinking, some damage was inevitable, and huge gouges were made in the lifeboat's planks, forcing Hutchens to back off for another run in.

The last man on the *Tungufoss* was the skipper, now up to his knees in water as his ship literally sank under his feet. The two rescuers, Hutchens and Houghton, unable to communicate, both made desperate last bids to save him. Hutchens knew that the *Tungufoss* would suck the man under – and maybe the lifeboat too – as she sank. Undeterred, he steamed in over the top of the sinking ship.

'I thought at least we would be in there, in the turmoil, so that if he came off we could have a stab at getting him.'

But the helicopter beat him to it. Flying as low as he dared, Houghton dropped his lifting strop and aimed for the skipper, going so close that the strop hit him in the mouth. Grabbing the strop, the Icelander was whisked up into the helicopter as the *Tungufoss* settled and sank. A few seconds later and the captain would have gone down with his ship.

For the crews of the lifeboat and the helicopter it was a remarkable achievement. 'We had no communication whatsoever,' marvels Hutchens. 'We had such . . . I don't know what it was . . . an understanding. It was nothing conscious on my part, I can assure you. He was right there. That boy flying the helicopter was above us all the time. Nick Houghton is a very skilful pilot. And, of course, at the end of the day we were very pleased to come back from *Tungufoss* with seven men on board. It made us feel good. That is what it is all about.'

In London, after the Icelandic President had given out the official tributes, the towering skipper of the *Tungufoss* stopped Maurice Hutchens in

Hallur Helgason, saved from the Icelandic coaster Tungufoss *by men of the Sennen Cove lifeboat, is greeted at the airport by his wife and son Halli.*

the hotel corridor. He handed over eight bulky woollen seamen's jumpers.

'For your crew,' he said. 'Thank you.'

ALL AT SEA

Imagine, if you can, a wall of water 50 feet high racing towards you. It hits your boat, washes you overboard and, when you struggle to the surface, you find the boat is upside down. Yet for Mike Hicks, a crew member on the **Salcombe** lifeboat in April 1983, there was worse to come.

'I could not believe what I was seeing,' he recalls. 'I could see the starboard propeller turning high in the air. The vessel was bow-under and turning to starboard. . . Finally, the lifeboat came upright, flopped round low in the water, and lifted to its usual position . . . then it set off away from me!'

Sunday lunch that stormy day had been interrupted for the lifeboat crew by a distress call. The shallow, rocky waters off the Devon cliffs

Coxswain `Griff' Griffiths of the Salcombe lifeboat is interviewed straight after coming ashore from a lifeboat capsize in 1983. Frank Smith looks on.

The Salcombe lifeboat locates a missing diver.

were no place to go in a force 9 gale, but four divers were missing after their inflatable boat had capsized, and now Coxswain 'Griff' Griffiths spotted the dark shadow of the inflatable and was heading for it at full speed.

Suddenly crew member Brian Cater saw the rogue wave, shouted 'Look out! Big one coming!' and, as it hit, Hicks was sent spinning over the guardrail, hanging on for a few grim seconds until the force of the water loosened his grip.

A second huge wave hit the lifeboat and rolled her over. In the wheel-house everything went black. Washed around by the turbulent water, the lifeboatmen clung on to anything they could find. Frank Smith remembers seeing the coxswain's face underwater. David Lamble found himself pinned under the lifeboat by his lifejacket. Even in this predicament, Lamble remembered to unclip his safety line, but he still has no idea why he tucked it carefully into his pocket!

'I tried to dive clear and, as the boat righted, something hard hit me in the chest. I grabbed hold of it,' Lamble explains.

When the boat came up, Lamble found himself clinging to the mast! After two attempts, Hicks was picked up and the lifeboatmen continued the search for the divers. Eventually, two divers were washed ashore, alive but severely shaken, and two were picked up by helicopter. The Salcombe lifeboat returned safely.

But tragedy is never far away at sea. After a life spent saving others, Griff retired as coxswain on Christmas Day, 1984. Only ten months later he became entangled in his own fishing lines, fell overboard and drowned.

Frank Smith is now coxswain at Salcombe. He became a national figure after appearing in the central TV series *Lifeboat*, a 'fly on the wall' documentary that followed the lives of the Salcombe crew for a year. Watched every week by millions, Frank was chased down Salcombe's main street by holidaymakers eager for his autograph.

He found fame a far worse ordeal than the remarkable rescue of the coaster *Janet C* in January 1992, which earned him a Bronze Medal. Their 27-ton lifeboat was dwarfed by the 1,200-ton coaster, yet the crew struggled for over three hours to save the vessel from hitting the cliffs. The perils faced by the Salcombe lifeboat that night bore an uncanny resemblance to the dangers that finally overwhelmed the Penlee crew in December 1981, when all the men were lost.

THE PENLEE DISASTER

The **Penlee** lifeboat disaster, just six nights before Christmas 1981, evoked a massive outpouring of public sympathy and created myths and problems on a scale never seen before by a lifeboat community. The tragedy itself, the disaster fund and the media attention all caused controversy. In the middle of it all, eight families in the tiny village of Mousehole had to try and cope with their devastating losses.

The bald facts of that terrible night were summarised in the report of the formal investigation: 'On the night of 19th December 1981 the motor vessel *Union Star* was driven aground in a severe storm on the rocks near Tater du lighthouse on the south coast of Cornwall and wrecked with the loss of those on board her. In the most valiant attempts to rescue and take those on the *Union Star* to safety, the RNLB *Solomon Browne* from Penlee was lost with her entire crew.'

But the questions were endless. Why had the young captain of the *Union Star*, Henry Morton, made an unauthorised stop on his voyage to pick up his wife and stepchildren? Had he realised how serious his situation was as he and his engineer struggled to get the engine restarted? Should he have asked for help earlier? Did he know how quickly his ship was approaching the treacherous cliffs? Could the salvage tug nearby, which offered assistance, have helped?

Then there were allegations, later withdrawn, against the coastguard's handling of the incident, questions regarding liaison with the lifeboat authorities and the coxswain before the lifeboat launched, long technical debates about how water got into the *Union Star*'s fuel supply and stopped the engine. Perhaps with hindsight the most important question was one that was never asked: if the lifeboat had been launched earlier, might there have been eight survivors with eight heroic lifeboatmen returning to Mousehole firesides? Because before the lifeboat was smashed into tiny pieces on the Cornish rocks, Coxswain Trevelyan Richards had done what a powerful twin-engined search and rescue helicopter could not; he had rescued four people from the *Union Star*.

The helicopter, with its highly experienced pilot, was beaten by the hurricane-force winds and spray from the huge seas. As the *Union Star* rose and fell 30 to 40 feet on the swell, and air turbulence buffeted the helicopter, the ship's mast at one point came within six feet of the rotor blades. Even in this madness the helicopter crew pressed on, but each time a line got near the ship it missed, slipped from the crew's grasp or got tangled in the rigging.

Only after the helicopter had tried did the lifeboat start her rescue attempts. Time was desperately short as the *Union Star* lost one anchor and dragged towards the cliffs as the other failed to hold.

Coxswain Trevelyan Richards was an experienced fisherman, tall, round-faced, quiet and careful. He had won an RNLI bravery medal in 1975 for a service in January of that year to a fishing boat that sank in hurricane-force winds; only five bodies were found. When the call came to go to the *Union Star* he chose his crew with care, for there were more than he needed in the boathouse. He turned down Neil Brockman, whose father Nigel was already on board, refusing to take two men from the same family. The station chairman, Dr Dennis Leslie, also stepped forward, but Trevelyan gently told him he was too old. Dr Leslie later became a mainstay of support to the bereaved families.

The crew chosen, the lifeboat was lowered just out of the boathouse to the top of the slipway. Heavy seas were breaking right across the slip and the coxswain chose his moment, gave the order for launch and, at 12 minutes past eight, the Penlee lifeboat hit the water. Reaching the *Union Star*, Trevelyan Richards drove his lifeboat in again and again, hitting the ship and trying to get the people to come out on deck to be rescued.

Even when the ship was right in the broken surf, just yards from the base of the cliffs, the lifeboat kept going in. At 21 minutes past nine, the Penlee lifeboat radioed the coastguard: 'We got four off at the moment, male and female. There's two left on board. . .' Then there was a bang, the message was cut short and nothing further was ever heard from the *Solomon Browne*.

Exactly what happened next will never be known. The lifeboat may have been going in again and was swept right over the ship into the cliffs; the ship may have capsized on top of her. Whatever, the *Solomon Browne* was smashed to pieces. The helicopter set out again to search and lifeboats from **Lizard**, **Sennen** and **St Marys** joined in, but by dawn the awful truth was apparent; there were no survivors from either the ship or the lifeboat. Some bodies were never recovered. Others had been cruelly broken and bruised by the sea. And while the country woke to the news of the loss of a lifeboat crew, the families of the dead on the *Union Star* were largely ignored.

A disaster appeal for the lifeboat families was launched immediately by the local council. This too caused problems – it grew huge, reaching £3 million. Then a government official raised the question of tax, causing outrage throughout the grieving nation. A new lifeboat crew had already started to train on the relief lifeboat supplied by the RNLI, and they refused to carry on their training missions until the tax issue was resolved. The media wrongly reported this as a strike, but so great was the out-pouring of fury that Lord Goodman stepped in and resolved the issue – no tax would be paid.

Cranks caused more problems. A 'bounty-hunter' descended on Mousehole, trying to befriend one of the widows. A press photographer burst in on one of the families on Christmas Day, hoping to get a picture of the Christmas dinner with no father at the table. The local media behaved with great sensitivity, but some London television crews caused offence with their intrusion at the funerals.

Later, Trevelyan's elderly mother Mary travelled to London with another mother, Pat Smith, and two of the widows, Janet Madron and Jackie Blewett, to receive posthumous medals. Inside the Royal Festival Hall a throng of photographers pressed forward as the women fought back their tears. Then one stepped just too far forward and found his lens blocked by a lifeboatman's cap. He turned to protest, but was advised by the RNLI's press officer to withdraw – for his own safety!

Shortly after the disaster the RNLI headquarters received a mysterious telephone call. The caller claimed to be speaking on behalf of a wealthy benefactor who was concerned that the people of Mousehole would be wondering whether they would get a new lifeboat. He wanted a senior official to travel to Cambridge where he would be met and interviewed by the benefactor. No name was given.

This call was one of hundreds being received by the RNLI, yet somehow it rang true and the Deputy Director followed the instructions. He was taken to the Newmarket home of reclusive millionaire Sir David Robinson who duly bought the new lifeboat *Mabel Alice*, named after his wife. Sir David went on to buy two more lifeboats in his lifetime, and left money for a further two in his will.

He also had the last laugh on the press. His wish was to be buried at sea, but in complete privacy. Any recluse excites the media and the word got out that the burial would be from a lifeboat. The press, assuming Penlee would be the place, descended on Cornwall. But they had reckoned without Sir David's modesty, wishing to avoid both attention and a waste of money. Rather than incur a costly road journey from Newmarket to Cornwall, he had asked to be buried from the nearest convenient lifeboat, and while the press fretted in Cornwall, Sir David was being taken out on the Gorleston lifeboat for a committal performed by lifeboat inspector Dick Perks.

The arrival of the *Mabel Alice* in Newlyn was another trial for the community. The crew had already met problems on the passage. One evening they went for a drink in a rugby club, wearing their Penlee RNLI sweaters. A drunk rugby player staggered up to coxswain Kenny Thomas,

The crew of the new Penlee lifeboat Mabel Alice *pay tribute off Mousehole to the lost lifeboat crew that had gone before them.*

a fisherman whose build would fit him for the second row of any scrum, and accused the crew of being publicity-seekers. Thomas used a few words of seamanlike language to tell the rugby player how his anatomy might be rearranged if he persisted; the man wisely slunk back to his pint.

The arrival at Newlyn, another media jamboree, was preceded by a gesture from Kenny Thomas and the new crew. Unannounced, they sailed straight past Newlyn to the tiny harbour at Mousehole, brought the *Mabel Alice*'s bow to face the village and cut the engines for their own silent tribute to the crew that had gone before them.

Today the coxswain of the Penlee lifeboat is Neil Brockman, the 17-year-old turned away in 1981 by Trevelyan Richards. He was on the new crew under Kenny Thomas before taking over as coxswain in 1993. Like most people in Mousehole, Neil has learned to keep his thoughts private. Publicly he shrugs off the emotional side and gets on with the job.

'I think about Dad a lot, but on the boat there is so much to do and the adrenalin is pumping. You just concentrate on the job in hand. When we go out it is because there is somebody in a worse position than you and they need help,' he said. 'This is a close community and most people make their living from the sea. The dangers are known. There are deaths among fishermen each year. The disaster didn't stop lifeboat volunteers coming forward.'

ISLES OF SCILLY

Helicopters often grab the headlines with spectacular rescues, the immediacy of the story and the ability to carry a camera crew adding to their newsworthiness. As lifeboats are still battling through a storm, perhaps towing a boat back to port, the helicopter lands the survivors, who are interviewed and their story broadcast before the lifeboat has got home. Yet helicopters are vulnerable themselves. In 1983 the regular Penzance to Isles of Scilly flight took off in thick fog and, after a routine sea crossing, the pilot made a fatal error of judgement, bringing his machine down in the sea just short of the island.

The helicopter filled with water and sank; only six people – two children, two women and the two pilots – managed to scramble out before she sank in 20 fathoms of water. Among those travelling that day was Mrs Langley-Williams, chairman of the St Marys Ladies Lifeboat Guild and a stalwart RNLI fundraiser. As she surfaced, she found two children in the sea, their mother and father lost. Then came two big bangs, the lifeboat maroons. Comforting the children, Mrs Langley-Williams said, 'Don't worry now, loves. Matt's coming to get us'. And sure enough, through the fog came the orange and blue hull of the **St Marys** lifeboat, Coxswain Matt Lethbridge's instinct leading him straight to the bedraggled survivors.

Matt Lethbridge was a veteran lifeboatman who hated leaving the Isles of Scilly, and had to be persuaded to go to London for a discussion on lifeboats working with helicopters. One of his earliest experiences with helicopters had been when the giant tanker *Torrey Canyon* had run aground in 1967. She was the biggest tanker afloat at the time and had changed course to avoid some fishing boats and hit a reef near the Seven Stones lighthouse.

The St Marys lifeboat had been the first to reach her. The first thoughts were to refloat the tanker, so the crew stayed on board. Then, with the weather worsening, the lifeboat took 14 men off and stood by all day and all night. The following morning it was decided to take off more of the crew.

'There was quite a bit of rise and fall, about 15 feet I should say, and as she came up on the big ones, just level with the deck, men were jumping off on to our rope box,' recalls Matt. 'Well, eventually it always happens. You get someone who doesn't know whether he wants to go or not. The ninth man changed his mind at the last minute and then found it was too late. Of course, he came over and he went down between us and the *Torrey Canyon*. As soon as I saw him, my heart just went, because he might have been killed. I thought "This is it".

'I shouted to the bowman to let the line go and rammed her astern. But the next wave threw her against the *Torrey Canyon* and we heard the belting go with a crash. Then the boys shouted "He's all right!". We got him on board but no more of the men would come off. They said, "No fear. We'll have a helicopter".'

The helicopters of the time, single-engined Whirlwinds, had very lim-

Coxswain Matt Lethbridge, exhausted after 20 hours at sea searching for yachts in the Fastnet Race of 1979.

ited capacity, and two were needed to take off nine men, leaving only the captain and five crew on the *Torrey Canyon*. To protect them the St Marys and Penlee boats kept up a constant vigil until the next day.

In a very practical example of co-operation, the lifeboat was able to offer the helicopter some help. While a lifeboat can stand by a ship for many hours, even a modern helicopter is limited to six or seven hours in the air. With the *Torrey Canyon*, lifeboat and helicopter crews were working flat out.

Matt remembers: 'One chopper told us that they had come away without any breakfast. We used to carry a tin of biscuits and chocolate. "Come over and we'll send you some up," we said. So we sent up this tin of biscuits. And then we were there for about 30 hours without any grub! You can't get better co-operation than that, can you?'

What Lethbridge did not know when he set out for that discussion in London was that he was being set up to appear on the television programme *This is Your Life*. As a man to illustrate traditions in the lifeboat service, none better could have been chosen.

Matt Junior, as he was known to distinguish him from his father, had won three Silver bravery medals. His grandfather and father had also been coxswains; at one time his father was coxswain, uncle was second coxswain, he was bowman and his two brothers and a cousin were on the crew.

He realised what a strain it put on the families. 'It is the women, waiting at home, that have the worst of it. Out on the water we have worries, of course we do, but we are on the spot and we can tackle them. We know what is happening. It's not nearly as bad as having to wait. It's definitely the women who have the worst of it.'

While most lifeboatmen would agree with that, many have haunting memories of their own. Matt won his third medal for going out one appalling night to a French trawler, but the mission ended in failure.

'I think about it time and time again. You are always thinking if only this and if only that . . . but we had no time. From the moment the Mayday was picked up there was no waste of time at all.'

The trawler was smashed to pieces and all her crew lost.

Barry Bennett took over as coxswain in 1991. He, too, has had his problems among the rocky bays that he, as a fisherman, knows well. In September 1993 two yachts were in trouble as the tail end of Hurricane Floyd blew into Port Cressa Bay. Normally a safe anchorage, the bay was the worst place to be that evening as the force 9 gale blew straight in and the water, always shallow, was falling as low tide approached. There was a 15-foot ground swell with 20-foot breakers funnelling into the bay – not the best place to be in a 25-foot yacht.

Barry Bennett was worried as he took his 52-foot lifeboat into the shallow bay, watched by hundreds of locals and holidaymakers clustered anxiously on the shore.

'The yacht was being tossed about like a cork,' he recalled later. 'The bay's very rocky and there was only about three feet of water before our propellers touched the bottom.'

He had little room for manoeuvre and no room for mistakes; the seas were pushing him off course as he repeatedly tried to get close enough to the yacht to pass a line. Twice contact was made, but as more huge breakers rolled in Bennett had to pull the lifeboat clear for his own safety. Then a wave knocked the yacht flat and snapped her mast. Miraculously she stayed afloat, though she was rapidly filling with water. Barry Bennett realised that there was now no hope of saving the boat. But he would have to go in and get the man.

The lifeboatmen clipped on their safety lines and, with seawater rushing around their thighs, waited in the bow for a chance to grab the survivor. A first careful approach had to be abandoned, but during the second attempt the man jumped, just reaching the outstretched arms of the lifeboatmen who hauled him on to the deck. Ninety seconds later the yacht was engulfed and disappeared under the waves.

'I can never thank the lifeboatmen enough,' said 46-year-old yachtsman Roger Adcock afterwards. 'There's no way I could have survived without them. I would just have been another statistic.'

DUMB SURVIVORS

Not all survivors are as grateful to their rescuers. Steve Vince, coxswain/mechanic of the **Poole** lifeboat, reckons that he can always tell if a yachtsman has caused his own problems by his reaction to the lifeboat crew.

'If it's a genuine accident, they're delighted to be rescued. They'll ask you to have a drink when you've got them back. Otherwise, they'll be really embarrassed and the last thing they want is for you to take them into their yacht club.'

The skipper of one catamaran refused to utter a single word to the **Weymouth** lifeboat crew throughout an extremely hazardous rescue in a force 10 gale on 16 October 1987. He initially refused lifeboat assistance, even though the yacht, *Sunbeam Chaser*, had engine and steering problems. As the storm intensified, he finally appealed for help and the Weymouth lifeboat battled its way towards him. During the journey the waves washed the VHF aerial away, the starboard spray rail was damaged and the inflatable Y boat was torn loose and had to be lashed down. Two buoys and a boathook were swept overboard.

After three hours the lifeboat reached the catamaran. The boat was corkscrewing wildly and its crew had finally mutinied; against the wishes of the skipper, those on board asked the lifeboatmen to take them off. Meanwhile, the skipper stared fixedly ahead, unwilling even to acknowledge the presence of the lifeboat. Despite Coxswain Derek Sargent's appeals through a loudhailer, the man totally ignored the lifeboatmen, who had to carry out the rescue without his

The Weymouth lifeboat with a sinking fishing boat off Portland Bill.

co-operation. Several times the lifeboat nearly hit the catamaran.

Up to their waists in water, the lifeboatmen clipped themselves to a safety wire as the lifeboat drew alongside the catamaran, which veered away violently whenever the lifeboat drew close. After 20 minutes the crew had managed to grab the *Sunbeam Chaser*'s passengers. However, the taciturn skipper continued to ignore the lifeboat, making it plain by his silence that he wanted to stay with the catamaran.

The coxswain decided to protect him by escorting him to Weymouth. However, the stubborn sailor would not follow the lifeboat, nor did he acknowledge radio warnings that his boat was too near the Shambles. As a result he almost wrecked his boat. When the shelter of Weymouth Bay was reached, seamen from HMS *Birmingham* boarded the catamaran to bring the boat into Weymouth. It was reckoned that the skipper would find it difficult to ignore the Royal Navy!

ROCKY RESCUES

Calls to windsurfers now almost equal services to pleasure boats in some areas. The coasts of North Devon and Cornwall, where the beaches take the full force of the Atlantic rollers, used to be notorious for shipwrecks, but their heavy surf now makes them popular with young board sailors.

At **Appledore**, a picturesque Devon fishing village with steep cobbled streets of colour-washed cottages, the windsurfing enthusiasts will also brave the freezing waters of midwinter. In December 1985 Appledore's

Appledore's Tyne Class lifeboat George Gibson.

Atlantic 21 was called out to a board sailor in difficulties in a gale. Speed was essential in order to reach the windsurfer before he was swept on to the rocks. The sea was choppy and the lifeboat reached the sailboard in waves 20-feet high; the inflatable soared through the air as she left the crest of each wave.

The crew could now see the windsurfer clinging to his board, about to be smashed against Asp Rock by the wind and sea.

An RAF helicopter had already tried to winch the man to safety, but he had refused help. During a slight lull in the storm, Helmsman John Pavitt brought the lifeboat next to the man and crew members Roy Tucker and Michael Weeks hauled him aboard. He had become entangled in his own harness, which was still attached to the sailboard.

By this stage the waves were so high that John Pavitt could no longer see any navigational marks; during the return journey he had to follow the mast of Appledore's all-weather lifeboat, which had also launched.

With two lifeboats to crew, it can be difficult to get the right volunteers. Michael Bowden, who is coxswain of Appledore's all-weather lifeboat, says that a lot of the young men are too involved with the amusement arcades to show much interest in the lifeboat.

'When I first joined, half the village used to come down when the lifeboat went out,' he said. 'That's changed. The last time we had a recruitment drive, most of the young lads coming up to the right age didn't want to know.'

For those who do join a crew, the challenge and variety of the call-outs usually outweigh the disadvantages of making the commitment. Along the coast at **Bude**, in North Cornwall, young crew member Simon Chadwick had not bargained on going for a climb when the lifeboat was summoned to help a yacht aground on rocks at Crackington Haven in

June 1991. It was his first call-out as a lifeboatman and he felt excited as the inshore lifeboat headed out.

When they reached the yacht it was being pounded by the surf and they could see someone halfway up the nearby cliff. The helmsman, Martin Woodrow, was reluctant to force the boat through surf and rocks to the beach, so Simon volunteered to swim ashore to investigate. He could find no one aboard the yacht; after scouring the beach, he climbed 80 feet up the cliff to reach the person there.

He found the skipper and sole occupant of the yacht, a 70-year-old man who was completely exhausted and unable to move up or down the crumbling cliff face. Simon was very relieved to see an RAF helicopter arrive. He shielded the old man with his own body from the flying debris whipped up by the draught from the helicopter's rotor blades, and helped him into the strop so that he could be winched up. The helicopter took the man straight to Barnstaple hospital, where he soon recovered. But Simon's mission was not yet over. He returned to the yacht, collected the survivor's personal belongings and then swam back out to the lifeboat.

On one occasion the **Newquay** crew had to deal with an angler who had fallen from rocks into the sea. When the lifeboat was called, honorary secretary Mike Morris had the difficult decision of whether to launch the inshore lifeboat, as the conditions were almost beyond its limits. The boat did go and had dangerous breaking surf to negotiate as the crew searched the area under the cliffs, lit by flares, below the coastguard cliff rescue team.

An unusual assignment for the Bude lifeboat, getting bride Kath Harris to the church on time when the town flooded in 1993!

Minehead's Atlantic 21 lifeboat heads seawards.

Helmsman David Snell caught sight of the man in the water 50 yards from the cliff face amidst outcrops of rock. Steering in on the surf, David made a calculated turn by the man and the crew grabbed him as the lifeboat headed back out to sea. He was in a very poor shape and they began first aid straight away. As he slipped into unconsciousness and his pulse began to fade, the lifeboat raced back to the harbour where a waiting ambulance crew took over.

A Devon helmsman also found himself on an unexpected climb after the **Minehead** crew received word that a man had been seen in distress on Culver Cliff, near the resort. He had been spotted about 50 feet up, standing on a small overhanging rock and waving his towel, while his transistor radio, which had fallen a few feet further down the cliff, continued to blare out pop music.

When the crew reached the scene the radio was still playing, and David James, the acting helmsman, scaled the cliff face of loose chalk and grass to reach the man. Although the casualty appeared uninjured, he refused to climb down, so David James had to scramble down for the anchor line, which he then took up the cliff. One end of the rope was secured under a rock and the stranded man was lowered down to the beach. David then retrieved the radio – still playing!

Cornish villages, with their steep cobbled streets, whitewashed cottages and air of competing for the best-kept village award provide some of the most picturesque settings for lifeboat stations. At **Port Isaac**, before room was found for the lifeboat station on the tiny quay, the lifeboat had to be brought on a carriage several hundred yards down through precipitous, winding lanes before it could be launched.

As the lifeboat descended, a few people went ahead to steer the carriage; the rest hauled on ropes behind to stop the boat running away down the slope. In some places there were only a few inches between the sides of the boat and the houses, and one can still see the marks scored by the ropes on the walls.

St Ives, in North Cornwall, has a new boathouse with a romantic his-

In 1927 the Port Isaac lifeboat is hauled through the narrow streets to be launched. Note how the ropes have scored into the walls over the years.

Forty years later in 1967, the new Port Isaac inflatable lifeboat braves surf and rocks where no other lifeboat could go.

tory. The boathouse, which has been named 'Penza', was chiefly funded by a bequest from Mrs Eugenie Boucher. Her father was a surgeon in the White Russian army, and they had to flee their home town of Penza in Russia during the Russian Revolution.

Typically, the crew has a long connection with one family. The second coxswain is Tommy Cocking; his father, also Tommy, was coxswain, and his father, grandfather and great uncle all served in the boat. It was grandfather Thomas Cocking at the helm in 1938 when the lifeboat capsized, fortunately without loss of any of the crew, but a year later, in another capsize, all but one were drowned, including Thomas Cocking, his brother John and his son-in-law.

Today's coxswain, Eric Ward, holds two medals for gallantry, but is better known in some circles for his skills as an artist. His lifeboat is named *Princess Royal*, and during the winter of 1994 she was kept company, afloat in St Ives Bay, by the lifeboat *Her Majesty the Queen*, as harbour works prevented her 'daughter' from launching at low tide.

A few miles up the coast, **St Agnes** was one of the first stations to receive a lifeboat funded by a Blue Peter appeal. Since *Blue Peter IV* arrived in 1966, 127 lives have been saved by the St Agnes boat. The second Blue Peter boat had to be taken out of service because it had been so badly battered, as the inflatable lifeboat often has to launch right into the surf. The crew, which includes 19-year-old Natasha Mikail, have to cling on for safety as the boat crashes against the waves. St Agnes now has a new D-Class lifeboat, one of the fruits of Blue Peter's 1993 appeal.

'LIKE AN INSECT IN A PLOUGHED FIELD. . .'

Further north on the Atlantic coast, **Padstow** is a quiet little town whose tranquillity belies the savage storms that sometimes hit this exposed western shoreline. In hurricane-force winds on 15 December 1979, during the worst storm within living memory, the Padstow lifeboat ventured out to a Greek freighter, the *Skopelos Sky*, which was listing dangerously in mountainous waves.

'Before we went down the slipway we had seen the sea. We had listened to the wind all night and it was frightening,' Coxswain Trevor England admitted later. 'We never, ever expected to launch in conditions like that, and if we had not had a self-righting lifeboat, I don't know that we would have launched that morning. I thought that no way were we going to get away for any length of time in that sea without the boat turning over.'

Anxious watchers on the shore shared Trevor England's fears. 'When the radio announced a ship in distress and the Padstow lifeboat had been called out . . . I gave you small chance of returning,' one onlooker, a retired air force officer, told Trevor afterwards. 'From my house I overlook Constantine Bay, Trevose Head, and I have never seen such seas in Cornwall or in over 40 years of flying over most oceans in all parts of the world,' explained Air Commodore Clouston.

William Wouldhave working on his model of one of the first lifeboats.

A Victorian lifeboat returns to the quay.

The D Class inflatable lifeboat from St Ives station.

Another inflatable, Bangor's Atlantic 21 lifeboat.

St Ives's Mersey Class lifeboat The Princess Royal.

Valentia's Arun Class lifeboat
Margaret Frances Love.

The future - the 25-knot
Severn and Trent Class
lifeboats.

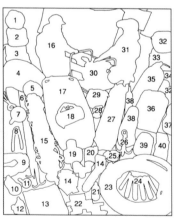

1 Drogue tripping line; 2 Drogue line; 3 Arun/Tyne mooring line; 4 Drogue; 5 Fire
hose and diffuser; 6 Single and double boat hooks; 7 Loudhailer; 8 Wire cutters; 9
Atlantic drogue; 10 High-powered torch; 11 D Class compass; 12 Lifebuoy light; 13
Guernsey (woollen); 14 Drinkpack (Ovaltine, coffee, cup soup); 15 Scrambling net;
16 All-weather lifeboatman wearing Musto jacket and trousers, seaboots,
RNLI/crewsaver lifejacket and bump cap; 17 Basket stretcher; 18 Speedline rocket
kit; 19 Self-heating Hot Cans; 20 Teapot; 21 Brandy; 22 Sweet pack; 23 Breeches
buoy; 24 Pyrotechnics (l to r): red pinpoint flare, red parachute flare, illuminating
parachute flare; 25 Ear defenders; 26 Grapnel; 27 RNLI version Neil Robertson
stretcher; 28 Spotlight; 29 Searchlight; 30 Salvage pump; 31 Inshore lifeboatman
wearing diagonal-zip dry-suit, lifejacket, helmet and visor; 32 Veering line; 33
Mooring line; 34 Plaited towline; 35 Fender; 36 First aid backpack; 37 Coir fender;
38 Entonox Peacemaker kit (and cylinder); 39 Ambulance pouch; 40 Fracture straps

*Wells lifeboat station, with Coxswain Graham Walker. Mersey Class lifeboat (22): 1 Coxswain/Mechanic: responsibl[e]
for all decisions once the lifeboat is at sea, and for the safety of the boat and its crew. At Wells the coxswain is als[o]
the full-time mechanic, and has to make sure that the boat is in good working order, replace any damaged equipmen[t]
and run the engine at least once a week so that the lifeboat is ready for an emergency; 2 Second Coxswain; 3 Assistan[t]
Mechanic; 4 Crew members, D Class inflatable lifeboat (23); 5 Helmsman and crew; 6 Station honorary secretar[y]
and his wife: he is responsible for the general administration of the station and deciding whether the lifeboat shoul[d]
be launched; 7 Deputy launching authorities; 8 Honorary medical adviser; 9 Honorary treasurer; 10 HM Coastguar[d]
sector officers and auxiliaries, who receive radio messages and 999 calls, and are responsible for co-ordinating th[e]
activities of the other three main search and rescue organisations (the RNLI, the Royal Navy and the Royal Air Force[)]
11 Branch chairman; 12 Ex-coxswain; 13 Branch committee members; 14 Deputy head launcher; 15 Tractor driver[;]
16 Assistant tractor driver; 17 Launchers; 18 Shore helpers; 19 Ladies lifeboat guild members; 20 Local voluntar[y]
lifeguards; 21 Sea King helicopter, RAF Leconfield; 22 Mersey class lifeboat; 23 D class inflatable lifeboat; 24 Tal[u]
MBH launching tractor; 25 Lifeboat house.*

Right: Coxswain Brian Bevan of the Humber lifeboat, holder of four gallantry medals.

Below: Yarmouth Arun class lifeboat, Joy and John Wade.

Bottom: The Sheerness lifeboat Helen Turnbull *sets out on a rescue mission.*

Above left: Padstow's lifeboat launches down the slipway.

Above right: The Hastings lifeboat launching off the beach.

Below: The St Marys lifeboat, under Coxswain Barry Bennett, rescues yachtsman Roger Adcock seconds before his yacht sinks.

Bottom: With Coxswain Hewitt Clark at the helm, the Lerwick lifeboat takes the crew off the sinking fishing boat Boy Andrew.

Above: In very rough seas in June 1994 the Alderney lifeboat prepares to tow the dismasted yacht Eclat, saving the two adults and two children by putting two lifeboatmen on to the yacht to take charge.

Below: The Baltimore lifeboat in action, rescuing from the water three men who had abandoned their ship Dina 15 minutes before she sank on 12 March 1994.

Dwarfed by the freighter Skopelos Sky *and huge seas, the Padstow lifeboat stands by in hurricane-force winds.*

When the lifeboat reached the freighter, she was several times completely lost to sight in huge waves by watchers on the cliffs only a quarter of a mile away.

'I felt like an insect in a ploughed field,' Coxswain England said later.

Dwarfed by the 2,800-ton freighter, the lifeboat stood by while three men were airlifted to a rescue helicopter. After the high winds had cannoned the winchman into the freighter's superstructure three times, the helicopter pilot suggested that the lifeboat should take off the rest of the crew. Trevor England managed to bring the lifeboat next to the *Skopelos Sky* five times, but as the sailors were high on the after deck of the ship, where they had been waiting for the helicopter to lift them off, it was too far for them to jump into the lifeboat.

One of the worst moments for the lifeboatmen came when they saw the freighter's stern looming above them, threatening to crush the lifeboat.

'She was coming down on top of us . . . but we couldn't get away from her,' said Trevor England. 'My eyes were just glued to that great lump of steel coming down on top of us and the three blokes up on deck who were looking back at you with frightened looks saying, "Well, are you doing what you are supposed to be doing back there?" Because they are relying on you.'

After a few terrifying moments when the lifeboat crew on deck didn't know whether to freeze or try to run clear, the *Skopelos Sky* rolled off the lifeboat again. The boat continued to stand by and pass information between the freighter and the helicopter, which was unable to communicate with the stricken vessel. After six hours the final man was lifted to safety from the freighter and the lifeboat was able to return to base.

In a letter to Trevor England, Air Commodore Clouston expressed the views of many who were deeply impressed by the heroism and skill of the Padstow crew: 'The fact that you and your crew launched, gave assistance and returned safely speaks volumes for your capability as seamen . . . this was the most outstanding act of unselfish courage and seamanship that I have known in my lifetime.'

One of the most tragic tasks for any crew must be recovering the lifeless bodies of fellow crew members. The saddest occasion Alan Tarby, the current Padstow coxswain, can remember is picking up the body of one of his own crew, one of five fishermen who had been overwhelmed by stormy weather.

'Two never turned up, but we found their boat, and the day before Christmas the lifeboat picked up one of the lads. It was terrible.'

'The hardest thing I've ever done is searching for a missing diver who was a crewman,' says Steve Vince, coxswain/mechanic at **Poole**. After looking all night, Steve eventually had to take the painful decision to call off the search. Twenty-six-year-old Peter Benson's body was found later that day, and Steve had to go and break the news to the dead man's young wife.

LOCAL KNOWLEDGE

A lifeboat crew's local knowledge can make the difference between life and death for a sailor who has been reported missing at sea. Their understanding of local currents and tides means that coxswains often head unerringly for the right spot when they are searching for survivors.

Torbay coxswain Dave Hurford used his extensive local experience to find a 21-year-old fisherman whose trawler mysteriously sank off the Devon coast in March 1992, leaving him in the freezing sea for nearly an hour. The Torbay lifeboatmen had no idea of the trawler's exact position, yet they arrived just in time to save Richard Mead's life. He was not wearing a lifejacket, but they saw his red jumper as waves washed over his body, and Nigel Crang and Ray Foster dived in and rescued him. Nigel held his face above the water while Ray, who is a doctor, immediately gave him the kiss of life.

'Another few seconds and he would have had it,' said Nigel afterwards. 'He was already turning blue and his lungs were filling with water.'

Ray Foster then used the breathing equipment aboard the lifeboat to resuscitate Richard Mead, before they were both airlifted to Torbay hospital by an RAF helicopter.

A similarly dramatic call was received by the **Ilfracombe** crew on a stormy September day in 1983. A man aboard the yacht *Liberty* had radioed the coastguard that his skipper appeared to be dead, and he himself had no experience of boats. The yacht was dragging her anchor close to the Rapparee Rocks, just outside the entrance to the outer harbour. By the time the lifeboat arrived, 20-foot waves were throwing the *Liberty* ever nearer to the Rapparee Rocks and the sheer cliffs beyond, now only about 20 yards away.

The cliffs and a series of Dan buoys marking lobster cages made it impossible for Coxswain David Clemence to get alongside the yacht and put a crew member aboard. The yacht was now sounding on the sea bed in the trough of each wave, and the man on the yacht's deck was preparing to try and swim ashore. David Clemence told him to stay on board while he tried to pass a line across. The coxswain had to use his engines to edge closer to the yacht, while the wind, waves and tide were pushing both boats towards the rocks.

As the lifeboat and yacht pitched and tossed, lifeboatman Wayland Smith threw a rope across and the lifeboat towed the yacht out of immediate danger. On the way back to Ilfracombe, the yacht's anchor became entangled in buoys and a crewman had to jump across and saw through the anchor cable. As he did so the yacht was again driven by the seas to within 20 yards of jagged rocks, but the lifeboat managed to drag her clear and into the safety of Ilfracombe harbour. An ambulanceman confirmed that the skipper was dead, and the sole survivor was landed, distraught but safe.

MARITIME MARATHONS

All crews dread long services where they are at sea for hours on end, usually freezing cold, completely drenched and bone-tired. But what makes it all worthwhile are the lives they have saved.

The **Lizard** lifeboat was out for 12 hours in winds of up to force 11 looking for a yacht in trouble about 40 miles south-east of the station. The yacht *Heptarchy* had been taking part in a race from Helford to the French coast when disaster struck on 30 May 1993. A fishing net fouled her bow and propeller and she was then caught in the storm and knocked down by the high winds.

The lifeboat crew reached her after three hours and saw the substantial 56-foot yacht dwarfed by the huge buffeting waves. 'We were never so pleased to see another boat,' recalled the *Heptarchy*'s skipper, Chris Tyler, describing the moment when they first saw the lifeboat battling towards them. 'The crew were superb.'

It took the coxswain nearly an hour to manoeuvre the lifeboat into a suitable position to pass a towline. When this was achieved, the lifeboat towed the yacht for around six hours until they reached the shelter of the Helford River. The crew arrived home nearly two hours later.

In the words of the Lizard honorary secretary's report: 'Eight exhausted men disembarked after some 12 hours service in conditions so violent they could neither eat, drink nor perform the needs of nature. . . [We are] proud of a superb lifeboat . . . ten lives were saved this morning.'

The **Falmouth, Penlee** and **Plymouth** lifeboats took part in another marathon rescue in February 1985, lasting nearly 24 hours in all. The drama began when the Falmouth crew set off at 4 am in a ferocious force 11 gale to answer a call from a fishing vessel, the *St Simeon*, which was sinking 19 miles south-east of Lizard Point.

Plunging violently in the 50-foot waves, the lifeboat took nearly three

The French fishing boat St Simeon *in the foreground is escorted by the Falmouth lifeboat.*

hours to reach the trawler, which was almost completely swamped by the sea. A salvage pump had been lowered by a naval helicopter, and the *St Simeon* was eventually able to get her engines going again. The lifeboat began to escort her towards Plymouth.

The Falmouth lifeboat had already been at sea for nearly ten hours when she was relieved by the Penlee lifeboat. The tenacious French skipper was determined to save his vessel by continuing on to Plymouth, so the Falmouth crew took over the escort duties for four hours, until they were relieved by a French fishing boat.

All went well until the salvage pump stopped working. At this point the Plymouth lifeboat was dispatched to take a new pump to the *St Simeon*. Unfortunately, during a turbulent journey the sea engulfed the well of the lifeboat and washed out the pump's handle. The increasingly desperate French skipper insisted that another pump should be airlifted to him, but, as the coastguards soon discovered, there were no more available.

The outlook for the French boat and her crew was hopeless. Waves up to 50 feet high were breaking over the vessel and she was drifting. Two hours after the Plymouth lifeboat arrived, the skipper finally accepted that he and his crew would have to abandon ship. The fishermen were already exhausted after their arduous voyage, so Plymouth Coxswain John Dare decided it would be too risky to expect them to jump into the lifeboat. Instead, he asked the men to take to their liferaft.

After five attempts the men in the raft managed to grab a line thrown to them by the lifeboat crew, just as a huge wave swamped them and cut the line. However, the lifeboat crew still managed to draw the raft alongside the lifeboat, and successfully transferred the men.

On the journey home the lifeboat was thrown right into the air by the huge waves and her radar ceased to operate. At one point the lifeboatmen found themselves heading for Looe, not Plymouth, but the coxswain quickly corrected their course and they arrived home at 1.35 on Saturday morning. They had saved five lives.

MINUTES CAN COUNT

Not all rescues are marathons. On Easter Sunday 1985 the **Exmouth** lifeboat took just over an hour to save three people who had spent three-quarters of an hour in a sea of 47 degrees F after their speedboat sank. An observant member of the public had reported their exact position to the Brixham coastguard, so it did not take the lifeboatmen long to find them.

When the lifeboat arrived, the crew could see the three survivors in the water; none of them was wearing lifejackets.

A man was supporting two teenage girls, one of whom seemed unconscious. It was impossible to bring the lifeboat any closer without crushing the people in the water, so crew member Geoffrey Ingram jumped in to help them. His lifejacket was fully inflated, and he was able to support the two girls while the man swam to the lifeboat and was helped aboard. Geoffrey then managed to bring them to the side of the boat, where four crew members, two of them in the water, managed to hoist them on to the deck. The unconscious girl was swiftly airlifted to hospital by an RAF helicopter.

Every minute counts when it comes to saving lives at sea. On a bleak November day in 1988 the **Fowey** Deputy Launching Authority, Capt Mike Mitchell, was concerned to see a small yacht with no mainsail accompanied by a little motor cruiser, both making heavy weather of

The present-day Teignmouth lifeboat lands a man injured in a cliff fall.

their trip. He immediately told the coxswain and mechanic to stand by.

A few minutes later the cabin cruiser appeared to have broken down, and the lifeboat was launched. As it cleared the harbour the crew spotted a red flare fired from the cruiser. The pre-emptive launch meant that the lifeboat was able to take off the man on the motor cruiser only eight minutes after he had launched his flare; ten minutes later the cruiser sank.

One of the most unusual rescues in Devon's history took place in 1908, when the honorary secretary of the **Teignmouth** lifeboat, a Mr W. J. Burden, was awarded a Silver Medal for the part he played in rescuing the entire crew of a Russian schooner. At a critical moment during the rescue, Mr Burden actually took over the steering so that the coxswain could help with the rowing; the seas were so heavy that, when the lifeboat first tried to cross the Teignmouth bar to reach the wrecked schooner, a huge wave flattened the crew and washed all the oars overboard.

DENTIST AT THE HELM

On the Dorset coast, the **Swanage** lifeboat has a dentist, Chris Haw, as coxswain, which proved useful when the lifeboat mechanic chipped a tooth during a service. Once they were safely back in Swanage, Chris was able to whip him off to the surgery to carry out repairs. The boat's radio operator is renowned for his courteous messages to casualties. The other crew members claim his politeness has an ulterior motive; as an estate agent, he must always be on the look-out for potential customers!

Chris Haw was recently commended for his 'first-class boat handling and sound seamanship' in appalling sea conditions when he rescued four people from a sinking yacht. The 40-foot boat, the *Aeolian*, was lying diagonally across the waves, taking on water, when the lifeboat found her off St Catherine's Point, the most southerly point of the Isle of Wight. Her rudder had failed and one man had already been lost overboard. Coxswain Haw decided to take off the rest of the crew at once. In force 9 winds and waves 25 feet high, he several times brought the lifeboat alongside the yacht, while crew members hauled the survivors aboard the lifeboat. Shortly afterwards the yacht sank.

Further west, **Lyme Regis** is chiefly famous for the Cobb, the old harbour with grey stone walls on which the black-cloaked Meryl Streep stands to great effect in the film of *The French Lieutenant's Woman*. Much of this romantic and dramatic coastline is owned by the National Trust, and it was just off Golden Cap, a wild headland belonging to the Trust a few miles west of Lyme, that two divers went missing in May 1992. Three of their diving colleagues reported their disappearance to the Lyme harbourmaster and the town's inshore lifeboat was launched immediately.

After searching for an hour the crew decided that the divers must be further east. One of the lifeboatmen, Paul Wason, suggested that his father, John Wason, might join the search in his fishing boat, which was the only vessel that could safely leave the harbour in the force 6 winds. Shortly afterwards John Wason left the harbour in his boat, *Sea Seeker*, with two friends and his other son, Chris, acting as crew.

Using his local knowledge, John found the divers within half an hour. By this time the weather was so bad that it was impossible to get the divers on board, so a line was let down to them and they clung to this until an RAF rescue helicopter arrived and took them to Lyme.

FAMILY AFFAIRS

Many rescues from **Marazion**, on St Michael's Mount, Cornwall, have also been family affairs. For some years Bob Hunt, his wife Melanie and their daughter Emma were all members of the inshore lifeboat crew. The Hunts all live on the Mount, home to 36 islanders and a romantic old monastery that later became a fort.

'When I saw my children playing in the sea, I knew I would want someone to help them if they got into trouble,' explains Melanie Hunt. 'Then I thought, "Why should I expect someone else to do it?"'

At one stage another married couple, Robert and Juliette George, were also on the duty rota of lifeboat crews.

As there is a large, all-weather lifeboat stationed at Penlee, only a few miles away, the Marazion crew are only needed during the summer, when

Family affair – husband and wife Robert and Melanie Hunt, Marazion lifeboat crew members.

they are mainly called out to help windsurfers and swimmers in difficulties.

Two other inshore lifeboat stations have been opened in Cornwall in recent years. At **Looe**, the station that had been closed in 1929 when the rowing lifeboat was withdrawn, a new inshore lifeboat was provided in 1992. And in the Camel Estuary at **Rock**, opposite Padstow, a new station was opened with an inflatable lifeboat in 1994, clocking up 26 service launches in its first six months.

THE CHANNEL ISLANDS

The jagged coast round the Channel Islands provides some of the most challenging conditions for lifeboats anywhere in the UK. The coxswains have to make regular rounds of the islands to keep themselves familiar with the rocks; even modern radar is no substitute for personal knowledge, as Michael Berry, former coxswain of Jersey's **St Helier** lifeboat, can testify.

On a pitch black September night in 1983 during a force 9 gale, Coxswain Berry had to find a yacht caught three miles in among the rocks and take off the three crew.

'For us, because of the sea conditions and the number of rocks, the radar was virtually useless,' he recalls. 'There was no thought of careful timing. It was a case of snatching them off and getting out of it. Unfortunately just after we did get them off, they'd got so far in that we grounded.'

St Peter Port's Arun Class lifeboat Sir William Arnold.

Despite the coxswain's skill, the Waveney Class lifeboat hit the rocks twice before she found a way out into open sea again.

'We just managed it . . . we picked up two bearing lights which I knew, and which meant there was clear water. That was all we had to go on.'

Coxswain Michael Scales of the **St Peter Port** lifeboat on Guernsey had to dodge round the rocks to rescue seven people from a 60-foot transatlantic yacht that had become wedged in a rocky gully on 11 October 1983. The skipper was an experienced sailor who had sailed round the world; but disaster struck when the automatic pilot failed as he was making a cup of coffee below. The rudder locked and the next thing the skipper knew was his boat going full speed up into a gully.

Coxswain Scales was faced with an agonising decision; should he leave the people on the boat and attempt a difficult tow away from the rocks, or should he get them off and abandon the yacht?

'The main thing was to get the people, but we couldn't get them to leave the boat,' Michael Scales remembers. 'They were probably better off on the boat at that particular time as they were high and dry, but the tide was going to rise, and we didn't know if she was holed. If she was, then the boat would have sunk and then we might have had people in the water.'

In the end Michael Scales decided that the crew should stay on board;

he discovered that one of them was blind and transferring him to the lifeboat would have been far too risky. So in almost total darkness and a force 8 gale, the Guernsey crew attached a tow rope and pulled the yacht clear.

Many Channel Islands coxswains, past and present, have extremely distinguished service records, most of them gaining at least one bravery medal. Michael Scales's successor, Peter Bisson, has continued the heroic tradition. He won a Silver Medal for snatching six survivors from a dismasted yacht in a force 9 gale on 29 August 1992.

When the Guernsey crew first arrived at the scene, they discovered that the yacht's mizzen had split and was flapping wildly in the howling wind and the foresail had been ripped to shreds. Coxswain Bisson managed to bring the lifeboat close enough for the crew to grab three survivors. They had just pulled on three more when Peter Bisson saw the mast toppling towards the lifeboat. He pulled away at top speed, but the mast crashed heavily on to the lifeboat's foredeck, completely enveloping the lifeboatmen in rigging, which was still attached to the yacht. As the lifeboat was backing off, the crew were being dragged forward by the rigging and pinioned against the lifeboat's stanchions and rails.

Two of the crew were in great pain and, despite the appalling conditions, had to be airlifted to hospital. As crewmember Gary Cook was about to be winched up on a stretcher, the lifeboat plunged 15 feet into a trough, lifting the stretcher into the air before slamming it back down on to the deck. Fortunately, both lifeboatmen later made a quick recovery in hospital, and the six survivors from the yacht were taken safely back to Guernsey.

Steven Shaw of the **Alderney** lifeboat is an outstanding lifeboatman. Deputy harbourmaster of Braye Harbour, where the lifeboat is stationed, Steven has been coxswain for 11 years and has received numerous awards for his bravery.

On August Bank Holiday Monday 1986 Coxswain Shaw heard a Mayday call from a yacht with six people on board. Five minutes later the lifeboat was on its way in the force 8 gale. As the yacht's crew only spoke German, it took some time to locate the boat, and when the lifeboat reached the scene Coxswain Shaw decided to transfer Second Coxswain Martin Harwood to the *Seylla II* to avoid language problems. To achieve this two crewmen had to clip themselves to the lifeboat's guardrails and hold Martin Harwood between them while Coxswain Shaw made an approach.

The first attempt nearly ended in disaster. As the lifeboat drew near the *Seylla II*, a huge wave picked her up and brought her crashing down on to the yacht's deck. Steven Shaw immediately flung the lifeboat into reverse, driving it back up the wave and through the breaking sea; only his cool decisiveness saved both boats from damage.

As the lifeboat approached a second time, Martin Harwood leapt on to the yacht. If he had fallen he risked being crushed between the two boats or being drowned in the huge waves. However, safely on board he prepared to receive the towline. He found that the German crew were perfectly calm; in fact, below deck two children were sleeping peacefully through everything.

The towline was attached and the lifeboat set off for home again. Her decks were often awash with three feet of water as the *Seylla II*'s rudder was jammed to port and she kept pulling the lifeboat's stern round so that she was beam to sea. Both boats eventually reached the harbour in the dark, about two hours after the lifeboat crew had set out. Steven Shaw and Martin Harwood both received Bronze Medals, Shaw for his skilful boat-handling and Harwood for his heroism in leaping across to the yacht.

The **St Helier** lifeboat on Jersey has had a very unusual history, particularly during the German occupation of the Channel Islands during the war. The lifeboat, the *Howard D*, then came under the control of the Harbour Kommandant, and always put out with its English crew, plus an armed German guard.

The crew several times went to the aid of shipwrecked sailors from

The St Helier lifeboat Howard D, *subject of a cryptic wartime message.*

German naval vessels, but they were once commanded to take a party of German officers round the island's approaches. The Germans were planning the building of coastal batteries, but when the lifeboatmen pointed out that the lifeboat was not intended to be used as a survey vessel, they were sharply ordered to do as they were told.

In London the RNLI was naturally very concerned for the safety of its two boats and crews on the Channel Islands. In fact the St Peter Port lifeboat had been machine-gunned by the German invasion forces as she was trying to reach Jersey, and the coxswain's son had been killed.

The RNLI knew nothing about the fate of the *Howard D* until, in June 1943, a German Red Cross form arrived from the honorary secretary of the St Helier station. It read: 'Greetings to all. Often go out with Howard, Dee, and the boys. Howard sends regards to Groves and Guttridge, and hopes to see them soon.' (Groves & Guttridge was the boatyard on the Isle of Wight where the *Howard D* usually went for an overhaul.) Through this ingenious message, worthy of the Special Operations Executive, the RNLI were reassured to learn that the St Helier lifeboat was still functioning.

The **St Catherine's** station on Jersey has an inflatable lifeboat, invaluable for manoeuvring round the rocky coastline, which is very popular with intrepid surfers. On New Year's Day 1994 the St Catherine's crew were called out to help a surfer in distress off Plemont. He had been spotted from the shore, but when the crew arrived they could see nothing. After a search he was eventually found at about 11 pm, and was scooped quickly into the boat, despite the 10-foot waves. Only then did the crew discover that his friend was also missing.

After taking the surfer ashore to the waiting ambulance, the lifeboat continued the hunt, hugging the treacherous coastline for several hours before the search was called off. The second surfer was later found clinging to his board at St Aubins Bay, on the other side of the island and many miles from the search area.

THE WOMEN WHO WAIT

Much has been written about the heroism of lifeboat crews, but the courage and forbearance of the families who support them is less well-documented.

'It puts a lot of pressure on your relationship,' admits Debbie Vince, who is married to Steve, the **Poole** coxswain. 'The lifeboat literally comes first all the time. Sometimes it's as though he's married to the lifeboat.'

Poole is a very busy station, and unless Steve is on holiday the Vinces can never afford to leave town, in case he misses a call. On their wedding day fellow crew members were called out during the ceremony; fortunately, Steve had arranged to take the day off.

Then there are the constant phone calls from all and sundry. A modelling enthusiast once rang Steve up at 10 pm to ask advice on constructing

Lifeboatman Bob Doak kisses bride Debbie Vince as husband Steve, the Poole lifeboat coxswain, looks on. The lifeboat was called out during the wedding!

a model lifeboat. News reporters are adept at phoning at 7 am after Steve has been out on a night service. Steve always asks potential recruits to the crew how their families feel about it.

'If you had lots of problems every time you got home after a call, it would make your life unbearable,' he explains. 'It could split up a relationship. Some crewmembers might even choose the boat over their partner. It's like a drug.'

With great fortitude Debbie says that the only times she worries are when Steve is out all night in bad weather. She has her own short-wave radio so that she can follow what the crew are up to.

Another courageous woman is Jo Allam, who lives in Weston-super-Mare. Her husband was a merchant seaman who went down with the *Santampa* in 1947; all on board were lost, as was the crew of the Mumbles lifeboat that went out to help the stricken vessel. Afterwards Jo decided to dedicate her life to raising funds for the RNLI, which she has continued to do ever since.

CHAPTER EIGHT

Wales – boats and bards

'Though they go mad they shall be sane,
Though they sink through sea they shall rise again;
Though lovers be lost love shall not;
And death shall have no dominion.'

And death shall have no dominion, *Dylan Thomas*

WALES IS KNOWN for many things, not least its bards, the official and unofficial poets, storytellers and songsters of the Principality. Many Welsh lifeboatmen, past and present, fit the unofficial category and can spin a yarn that will fascinate and captivate any audience. One of them, Richard Evans, is in the official category. Coxswain of the **Moelfre** lifeboat from 1954 to 1970, he was made an honorary bard at the National Eisteddfod in 1978. A former merchant seaman who came ashore and became a butcher, Dick Evans found himself catapulted to fame as a result of two spectacular rescues, both of which earned him a Gold Medal.

The first rescue, in 1959, was from the coaster *Hindlea*, hard aground on the rocks in a full gale. It was impossible to muster a full crew as telephone lines were down and maroons useless in such a storm, so Dick put to sea with three regular crew and one volunteer who had never been in the lifeboat before. Two men short, he launched the lifeboat and, when he reached the *Hindlea*, made repeated runs in to save the crew.

Soon there was only one man left, and as the lifeboat went in for him there was a mighty crash and the coxswain was thrown from his wheel. The lifeboat had landed on the *Hindlea*'s deck.

Dick can still recall his thoughts. Lashed to the wheel, facing almost certain death, he thought of Nansi, his dear wife, and his two young sons waiting at home. He saw his crew in front of him, all family men, and realised his awesome responsibility to them for placing their trust in him. Miraculously, instead of being pounded to pieces on the deck or swept right over on to the rocks, the lifeboat was washed clear by the next wave and the last man was grabbed by the crew. But to this day Dick worries about what might have been, not fearful for his own life but

Richard Evans, double Gold Medallist from Moelfre, with his wife Nansi and their three sons.

for the fate of the men who depended entirely on his skills at the helm.

In 1966 Dick was involved in a double rescue, for it took both the Moelfre and **Holyhead** lifeboats to save the crew of the *Nafsiporos*, a ship that had lost control in a cyclone. The Holyhead boat was badly damaged when a ship's lifeboat from the *Nafsiporos* crashed down on her deck, and the Moelfre lifeboat went in to finish the job. Once again the risks were immense, but 61 year-old Evans took them and earned himself a second Gold Medal. Lifeboat inspector Harold Harvey had taken the Holyhead boat in and he, too, won a Gold.

By the time he retired Dick had a wealth of stories: his first rescue, when he launched the lifeboat to save a cow that had fallen over the cliffs; the time when he sent his own son into the water to save two men and a girl; his saddest rescue, when his son had to dive 20 feet underwater to reach a little girl trapped by her hair in a sunken boat, and the two hours they spent in a futile attempt to revive her.

So when, in 1974, the RNLI was honoured by being given a dinner in the Guildhall in London to mark its 150th anniversary, Dick Evans was chosen as the main speaker. In his beautiful lilting tones, he told the rich and influential audience: 'I don't claim to be a public speaker. I am a Welsh-speaking Welshman and I am very proud of that. Whatever I say to you tonight is thought out in Welsh, then translated into English. If you don't understand my English, I'll explain it to you – in Welsh.'

He went on to tell his tales of storms and rescues, life and death. By the end of his speech there was hardly a dry eye in the audience. Spontaneously they rose to their feet to give him a standing ovation, something that only two men, Alec Douglas-Home and Harold Macmillan, had achieved at the Guildhall before.

The same year another Welsh coxswain who could move audiences to tears, Derek Scott of the **Mumbles**, drew together into the rescue effort all the 2,500 volunteers, fundraisers and lifeboatmen at the RNLI's

Derek Scott of Mumbles, a former lifeboat coxswain and a distinguished marine artist.

Annual Presentation of Awards. Commenting on changing patterns of crewing, away from seamen and fishermen, he noted that amongst his crew at the time was a bricklayer, a draughtsman, a painter and decorator and a headmaster.

However, their individual talents were what he valued, for he wanted not heroes but hard-working volunteers who could be trained into a good lifeboat crew. In reality even lifeboating could become tedious, he said, but the boredom was usually broken by humour.

'I remember one beautiful occasion when I was asked by the coastguard repeatedly, "What is your position?" We were being thrown around really badly at the time. He said it again and before I had a chance to answer him the mechanic looked up and said, "I don't know what his position is, but ours is bloody desperate!".'

There was no false modesty when Scott went on, 'I have always believed that a coxswain is only as good as his crew. When you are setting off in the blackness of night into a gale force 9, into God only knows what, the feeling of unity between a lifeboat crew is inexplicable, and no matter how frightened you feel, you know that the crew of the ship who are waiting for you are a great deal more frightened than that.

'Then, maybe after hours of battling through heavy seas and being beaten to death, you arrive and you are wet and cold and thinking, 'What on earth am I doing here?' and then you see the casualty, which can be a terrifying situation where life is hanging by a thread, but this is the moment that we have all been prepared for.

'From the time that lady sold her flag or arranged her coffee morning to raise funds – that was when this rescue started, not when the maroons were fired.

'If you could share with me and see the look on a survivor's face at the moment of rescue, and share that marvellous feeling with the lifeboatmen when they are coming home in the boat and the job has been done, then you would all know that this last 150 years has been more than worthwhile.'

TRANSATLANTIC LEN

The anecdotes flow to this day. Listen to Ray Brown, coxswain at **Barry Dock**, called out at 4 am to a yacht in trouble off the Nash Sands, 11 miles from Barry. Approaching the yacht he commented to one of his crew, a sailor, on how short the yacht's rig seemed to be, and as they got closer, they realised the yacht had been dismasted. A bedraggled figure, in flared trousers and an anorak, hailed them from the yacht and they were now close enough to see that the side of the boat was encrusted in barnacles.

'We towed him in and got talking to him. His name was Len. I said, "When did you get dismasted, Len?"

'He said, "Five months ago."

'"Blimey," I said. "Where were you?"

'He said, "Off Halifax, Nova Scotia."

'He had come all the way across the Atlantic without a proper mast!'

Len was later interviewed by the press who were fascinated to discover that he had rationed his food so carefully that he was able to eat his last provisions the night he was rescued. Asking him if he was worried about that, he displayed a certain faith in the RNLI by saying that he was not at all concerned as he had already called for help before tucking into the last of his food, and was sure that he would be rescued and get a square meal soon.

Ray Brown took him ashore and as they climbed the steps said that Len's wife must be worried about him – would he like to ring her from the boathouse?

'He said, "I haven't seen her for two years, an extra day won't make any difference."

Although he has an admiration of Transatlantic Len, Ray is concerned about incompetent sailors – and he has seen plenty of them. He puts it gently: 'When you've plucked them and brought them in, it's nice to have a little chat and see exactly what happened.'

While he is against regulation, he does think people should do more to help themselves. 'The message that has got to be got across is, "Go somewhere and learn, don't just get in a boat and go".

An amateur fisherman lost in the fog in the Bristol Channel would have benefited from this advice. Barry Dock lifeboat found him with their direction finder and towed him back to a marina where he could not recognise the entrance buoy. Having given him a course to steer, the fisherman set off in the opposite direction, so the lifeboat chased after him in the fog and this time put a crewman on board. The fisherman had a padlock and screwdriver resting on top of his compass, the metal turning the compass's magnet so that the needle gave completely the wrong direction. Once the objects were removed, he was given a course again and was safe inside the marina within minutes.

NO REGRETS

Roy Williams, honorary secretary at **Fishguard**, in Pembrokeshire, is another seasoned volunteer with a wealth of experience. He has been involved with the RNLI for more than 40 years, 25 of them as a crew member, and has seen some dramatic changes. When he first volunteered the crew went out in an open boat, extremely vulnerable in poor weather.

'If it was a bad day, you were getting wet as soon as you rounded the breakwater. The cold and wet were killing,' he reminisces. 'Today you can go out in your shirtsleeves.'

Fishguard has recently received one of the latest Trent Class lifeboats, funded by the 1993 Blue Peter appeal. Roy Williams says the new boat handles better, and offers the crew far more comfort and speed. The week after it arrived it went on a 40-mile chase to two people lost in a high-speed inflatable.

The new technology is invaluable, Roy believes. 'In the olden days you had to have your chart out and calculate your position. Nowadays it's all done for you. You don't lose any time – you can head straight for the casualty.'

When he looks back, he has no regrets. 'I've enjoyed every minute of it. There were times when you thought, "I'm a bit of a fool. What am I doing out in this weather?" But when you came back and you'd done a good job, it was all worth it.'

CUT OFF BY THE TIDE

The jagged coastline stretching north and south of Fishguard is a paradise for walkers and climbers. The coastal path winds for many miles, offering magnificent views as it climbs the lichen-covered cliffs, then sweeps down, skirting one of the many tiny coves below. On a hot, still, summer's day, with the sun glinting on the water, it's hard to imagine the dangers that threaten unwary holidaymakers and make work for the lifeboats stationed in this beautiful area.

For the curving coastline can be a death-trap; the strong tides that batter the sandstone cliffs can submerge the inviting little bays more quickly than strangers realise, and cut off incautious walkers.

The **Borth** inshore lifeboat was called out in August 1978 to two walkers who had been cut off by the tide beneath Borth Head. As the advancing tide rapidly filled the bay, the walkers had managed to climb a rock about 50 yards from the cliff face. By the time the lifeboat arrived the rock was nearly completely submerged by the water, and green waves lashed the men as they clung there.

Speed was essential, but the force 6 wind and heavy surf made it too dangerous for the lifeboat to head straight for the rock. Instead, the helmsman, Ron Davies, decided to drop anchor 60 metres from the rock and try an approach from there. Suddenly, with six-foot waves breaking over the boat, the crew noticed that one of the drain plugs was missing. It had been ripped out on the slipway in the rough seas as the lifeboat had launched. The lifeboat rapidly became swamped with water, making it heavy and difficult to control. She would have to rescue the walkers quickly, before she became a casualty herself.

Shouting above the wind and pounding waves, Ron Davies told the walkers to jump aboard the lifeboat as it came alongside. As the boat approached them the propeller struck a rock, stalling the engine. The mechanic managed to restart it, but when the lifeboat again drew up to the rock, the nearest walker refused to jump. It was not until the third approach, each attempt risking a collision with the rocks, that one of the men managed to leap safely aboard. Encouraged by this, the second casualty jumped aboard as the lifeboat passed for the fourth time.

The two survivors were both suffering from shock and hypothermia;

Ron Davies at the helm of the Borth lifeboat.

Helmsman Davies decided that the quickest and safest way to get them ashore was to beach the lifeboat, instead of waiting for it to be winched back into the boathouse. Riding on the back of a wave, he successfully beached the boat, just 20 minutes after it had first set out!

Occasionally, people cut off by the tide will try to swim for it. As any lifeboatman will tell you, this is one of the worst things you can do. On a July evening in 1973 four people stranded on Worms Head, at the tip of the Gower Peninsula, decided to swim for the mainland. Luckily, two of their friends had alerted the coastguard, and the **Horton and Port-Eynon** inflatable lifeboat was soon heading for the area at full speed. The crew knew that the swimmers stood no chance of reaching land safely in the strong flood tide.

A crewmember soon spotted a man in the water being swept towards the boat. He was pulled aboard and, in 500 yards, the crew saw two more swimmers, a man supporting a girl in the heavy surf that was breaking over the rocks. As the lifeboat came alongside, a huge wave pushed it away and two of the crew, John McNulty and Charles Twitchett, leapt into the water and helped the casualties into the boat. The young girl appeared to be dead, so the crew administered artificial respiration. She came round, but her condition was very poor. The helmsman, Walter Grove, decided that she must be taken to hospital without delay, so the boat sped back towards the opposite shore where a coastguard Land-Rover was waiting.

This stretch of coast is studded with jagged rocks and Helmsman Grove knew that it was highly dangerous to attempt a landing here. But he was extremely anxious about the girl survivor so he took a calculated risk. He plumped for a narrow pebble gulley the other side of a rock as the best spot, realising that the rock could rip the inflatable apart if he misjudged the manoeuvre.

With the engine at three-quarter throttle, Walter Grove then used a large breaker to carry the boat in over the rock. Once they were clear of the rock he sped into the gulley, where the boat was hauled ashore by the waiting helpers. The girl and a fourth man who had been rescued by the coastguard were then taken to hospital by helicopter.

CLIFF RESCUES

Climbers and walkers all along the coast sometimes underestimate the dangers of the narrow paths winding hundreds of feet above small stony beaches far below. Welsh lifeboats have been called out many times to help people who have fallen from the cliffs.

In June 1971 the **Barmouth** inshore lifeboat was summoned to rescue a badly-injured teacher who had fallen over the cliffs at Friog. She had been with a party of students on a field study when she suddenly lost her footing and plunged 80 feet down to the beach. Two policemen, a mountain rescue expert and two of the students had reached the beach

A tricky cliff rescue for the Trearddur Bay lifeboat.

with a stretcher, but a steep overhang meant that they were unable to carry the injured woman back up the cliff. Meanwhile, the incoming tide was rapidly covering the beach.

By the time the lifeboat arrived the weather had worsened, and spray was leaping 25 feet into the air as the surf hit the large boulders on the beach. The crew managed to beach the boat without damage, although it struck several rocks on its approach and had to be manhandled the last few feet on to land.

One of the crew members, Robert Haworth, was a doctor; after examining the woman he decided that she must be evacuated as soon as possible because of her serious injuries. As it would take at least four hours to get the stretcher up the cliff, the teacher had to be put aboard the lifeboat.

It was vital for the boat to launch as smoothly as possible to avoid further injuries to the casualty, so the crew suggested that she should be taken off from a neighbouring cove where conditions were better. Even so, when the inflatable made a run into the second cove, the men on the beach had to wade shoulder-high into the surf to catch and turn the boat. Meanwhile, the woman had been carried carefully round over the rocks, strapped to a stretcher and covered with a plastic bag to reduce the risk of exposure. Once she was on board, the helpers once again had to lift the boat through the water while the waves broke over them.

The inflatable then sped away to a safe, sandy beach nearby, where an ambulance was waiting. Tragically, the teacher died a few hours after she arrived at the hospital.

Inshore lifeboats, with their speed and manoeuvrability, are particularly suitable for cliff rescues. After a climbing accident at Wylfa Headland in April 1977, two youths were rescued by the combined efforts of the **Abersoch** Atlantic 21 and a naval helicopter. As a group of three youths were climbing down a cliff, a peg pulled out, and one of the boys went hurtling 35 feet down into the sea, striking the cliff face and a submerged rock as he fell. One of the others scrambled the last few feet down to the sea and dragged his unconscious friend clear of the water, then, with the help of the third climber, he tried to drag the injured boy up the cliff to safety. Unfortunately, the boy who had fallen then became firmly wedged in a crevice only about eight feet up from the sea. While one of his friends stayed with him, the other went back down the cliff, waded and swam to a beach and ran two miles to a farmhouse to summon help.

When the Abersoch lifeboat arrived the helmsman, Barrie McGill, decided to anchor the boat and veer down on the cliff, so that one of the crew could jump on to the rocks at the foot of the cliff. After two attempts, the lifeboat narrowly missing a partly submerged ledge, crewman Michael Davies managed to climb on the rock and secure the boat to the shore with two lines.

Barrie McGill and crew member Noel Loughlin then waded and swam to the rocks below the injured boy. When Noel Loughlin climbed up to him, he found that the youth was unconscious; he and his friend were also suffering from hypothermia. In addition, the boy was so tightly wedged in the crevice that it was impossible for Noel Loughlin to move him. Barrie McGill immediately swam back to the lifeboat to radio for helicopter help.

At this stage the local coastguard officer came down the cliff on a line, followed by a stretcher. Between them, he and Noel Loughlin got the boy on the stretcher and carried him to a ledge 25 feet higher. A few minutes later both the boys were safely winched aboard the helicopter.

For William McGill, former coxswain of the **Pwllheli** lifeboat, one of his worst experiences in more than 25 years as a lifeboatman was a rescue in 1972 of a 16-year-old boy who had fallen 80 feet down the cliff face at Cilan headland. Firemen had managed to raise the boy a few feet to prevent him being swept away by the incoming tide, but they were unable to get him to the top of the cliff as he had severe head injuries.

The Pwllheli lifeboat launched with a doctor aboard in an attempt to rescue the boy from the sea. There was so much swell that it was impossible to get the doctor ashore in a dinghy, so William scrambled up to take a look at the casualty.

'It was a terrible night,' said William McGill later. 'It was dark and the

Back from another rescue, the Criccieth lifeboat is driven into a net on its trolley for safe recovery.

tide was coming in fast. The boy was in a bad way, and looked in a terrible mess. I went to go back to tell the doctor. As I moved away from where the boy lay, I took a step backwards, and felt myself falling – one of the firemen grabbed me just as I was about to go over a 60-foot drop. It was pitch black, and I couldn't see the edge of a gully.'

When William looked down afterwards, he could see the sea swirling and boiling 60 feet below him. 'I owe my life to that fireman. . . A lot of damage was done to the lifeboat, but we eventually managed to get the boy on board.'

Occasionally, lifeboatmen have to act as ambulance crews. One July morning the crew of the **Criccieth** inflatable received a call from a doctor asking them to take off a boy who had injured himself falling from the rocks at a local beach. The crew beached the boat in strong winds and heavy surf, and found that the boy was thought to have a broken leg. He was placed on a stretcher, but the crew decided that it would be too dangerous to return with him through the very rough sea. Instead, they carried him up the rocks to the ambulance waiting about three-quarters of a mile away.

THEY MUST HAVE BEEN SHORT OF HEROES

In several cases crew members have also had to demonstrate their rock-climbing skills. On 31 August 1976 Glyn Roberts, who belongs to the **Porthdinllaen** crew, had to climb 80 feet up a cliff in pitch darkness to rescue a 14-year-old boy trapped in a cleft. The cliff was about 170 feet high and almost completely vertical; it was also covered in bits of loose granite, as the place had been used as a tip for unwanted stone from a nearby quarry.

Once Glyn Roberts had been landed by a boarding boat from the Porthdinllaen lifeboat, he took off his boots and socks and began the treacherous climb up. The coxswain, Griff Jones, kept the lifeboat's searchlight trained on the boy, who was rigid with fear. The youth's friend, who had walked some distance to give the alarm, was waiting anxiously below, together with a policeman and a camper who had unsuccessfully attempted the climb.

When he reached the boy, Glyn Roberts had to use all his powers of persuasion to coax him down. Eventually the 14-year-old agreed to follow him. To the horror of those watching from the beach and the lifeboat, during the descent Glyn fell 30 feet from the cliff on to the beach. Fortunately, apart from cuts and bruises, he was unscathed, and climbed up again to bring the boy down.

As both boys were too exhausted to walk back along the shore, they were dressed in lifejackets and carried to the boarding boat. The second coxswain, John Scott, had to use the swell of the waves to bring the boarding boat into smoother waters; one mistake and the little boat would have been dashed against the rocks. However, the lifeboat was successfully reached and the crew took the boys down into the cabin and revived them with hot soup.

Glyn Roberts was awarded a Bronze Medal for his outstanding courage, yet all he will say about it is, 'I think they must have been short of heroes that year'.

Unfortunately, not all rescues involving children have such a happy outcome. On one occasion in 1966 the **New Quay** lifeboat was called out shortly after midnight to look for three boys who had been reported missing along the cliffs. After scanning the cliffs for about half an hour, the crew heard cries for help. The lifeboat's searchlight picked out a boy stranded on a ledge about 20 feet up the cliff. This stretch of coastline is riddled with submerged rocks, waiting to rip open the bottom of unsuspecting boats, and Coxswain Winston Evans decided that it would be too dangerous to bring the boat in any closer to the cliffs, so crew members Sydney Fowler and David Rees at once volunteered to swim ashore, as they could see that the boy was very distressed.

Both men were strong swimmers, but they had to struggle against the backwash to reach the cliffs. Then Sydney Fowler secured the nylon rope he had brought with him to a rock and David Rees used it to pull himself up on to the ledge. Eventually, both men reached the 16-year-old, who told them that his two friends had fallen down the cliffs. He was frozen with terror, and it took some time before the men could get him into the breeches buoy they had fashioned from the rope. Then they got him down the cliff and hauled him to the lifeboat, where the crew treated him for exposure and shock.

Soon David Rees and Sydney Fowler began a search among the boulders for the other boys, being joined by a coastguard rescue team with a stretcher. They found the boys lying on a small pebbly beach at the foot of a steep gully. One was already dead and the other was seriously injured. He was strapped into the stretcher, but he was too badly hurt to be carried up the cliff.

At considerable risk the coxswain brought the lifeboat right up to the shore so that the injured boy could be taken aboard. The boat was manhandled on to the beach by David Rees and Sydney Fowler, who were both suffering from exposure by this time. The lifeboat then set off for New Quay harbour, where a doctor and an ambulance were waiting. Tragically, the injured boy died shortly before he was taken ashore.

Deaths are always hard to cope with, particularly those of children, according to the **Penarth** crew in South Wales. The drowning of two children after a speedboat capsized on the River Taff is the most painful incident they can recall.

'We came back from that call and no one could speak,' said Andrew Rabaiotti, a crew member for more than ten years. 'To have a call out where there are children in difficulties is our worst nightmare.'

But some rescues have their comic side. 'We did have one embarrassed gentleman who ran aground on a sandbank and gave a different name and address to the police, coastguard and ourselves,' said Richard Giles, who works for the City Council. 'He thought he was going to be charged for the rescue.'

HOVERCRAFT ADRIFT

One of the most unusual rescues ever carried out in Wales was performed by the **Rhyl** lifeboat in September 1962, when the crew took three people off a hovercraft that had broken adrift from her moorings. A north-westerly gale was blowing and waves were actually rolling into the boathouse, but Coxswain Harold Campini agreed to launch, using superb seamanship to take the lifeboat alongside the hovercraft. The craft's crew managed to jump aboard the Rhyl boat just seven minutes before their vessel crashed into the promenade. Coxswain Campini was later awarded a Silver Medal for gallantry.

Another unconventional service was provided when the **Little and Broad Haven** lifeboat went to the aid of three sailors; they were not rescued from their boat, but from some rocks where they had taken refuge.

This drama began when a member of the public dialled 999 to alert the coastguard to two boats that seemed to be struggling in heavy surf near Goultrop Roads. An investigation by an RAF Sea King helicopter and a local coastguard concluded that the boats were safe. But as dusk closed in on the rough September day, the Little and Broad Haven honorary

Three women crew members at Little and Broad Haven in 1990: Vivienne Whiteright, Mandy Clarke and Philippa Lewis.

secretary began to feel concerned about the three men believed to be aboard the boats; the wind was whipping up the waves and a mysterious light had been spotted on Goultrop's rocky beach. At 8.29 pm he decided to launch the lifeboat.

Assisted by parachute flares and the searchlights of the RAF rescue helicopter, the crew soon spotted the three men, and took them back to Little Haven beach. It turned out that they were trying to move a large powerboat from its moorings at Little Haven to the shelter of Goultrop Roads, and were planning to return to Little Haven in a 12-foot dinghy. When the weather worsened they decided to take refuge on Goultrop. The dinghy owner landed two of the men on the rocks, moored his boat, then swam through the surf to rejoin them. They were just about to start a hazardous climb up the cliff in pitch darkness when the lifeboat arrived.

SHOULD WE LAUNCH?

Honorary secretaries have the key role of deciding whether the lifeboat should launch. For inshore stations this can be a very fine judgement as the boats are not meant for the worst weather and the D-Class inflatables are not night boats. However, local knowledge and a sense of extreme urgency led the **Porthcawl** secretary of 1968 to launch the inshore lifeboat in the dark and in bad weather. The crew of the sand dredger

An anxious consultation as the Mumbles lifeboat and police divers search for a local fishing boat. Twelve people were saved on this occasion, but two were lost.

Steepholm, aground on the Tusker Rock, had abandoned ship and taken to the liferafts. The **Mumbles** lifeboat was on her way, but would take another 20 minutes to arrive and the liferafts were drifting ashore. The tiny inflatable lifeboat had to battle through force 7 winds and reached the liferafts at the same time as the Mumbles lifeboat, so the Porthcawl crew held the rafts together while their occupants were lifted into the bigger lifeboat.

The captain was still on the dredger and it was too dangerous for the inshore boat to go in, so the Mumbles lifeboat struggled through the seas breaking around the ship and eventually saved the captain, Coxswain Derek Scott being awarded a medal for his outstanding seamanship.

THE FIRST OFFICIAL LIFEBOATWOMAN

Atlantic College is unique among lifeboat stations. The crew there are all students, and the college, an international school with an outward-bound emphasis, can boast the first official woman coxswain; 18-year-old Elizabeth Hostvedt from Norway became helmswoman of the Atlantic's inflatable in 1969, the first of many female students to serve in the crew.

The college actually invented the rigid inflatable lifeboat, under its inspirational, lateral-thinking headmaster, Rear Admiral Desmond Hoare. He thought that the characteristics of a surfboard could be incorporated into a boat, and set his students to work to develop the idea. After much experimentation, a wooden hull with a flat stern, mimicking

The first official lifeboatwoman, Elizabeth Hostvedt, at the helm of an early Atlantic-type lifeboat.

a surfboard, was fitted with an inflatable tube, and the rigid inflatable boat was born.

Hoare was on the RNLI's Committee of Management, and the Institution, reluctantly at first, took up the idea and developed it into the Atlantic 21, a world-leader in its field and named in honour of the college.

An Atlantic 21 now serves at **Beaumaris**, which guards the beautiful but treacherous Menai Straits, spanned by spectacular road and rail bridges. Tides rush through this gap between mainland Wales and Anglesey and have caught out many ships and yachts. The crew of the *Blue Peter II* at Beaumaris have a varied life, as illustrated by an incident in 1992. The RNLI had organised a major medical training exercise off Anglesey, involving coastguards, a helicopter and four lifeboats. The Institution's Medical and Survival Committee, which includes distinguished doctors from different branches of medicine, witnessed the exercise and gave advice.

At the end of the proceedings the Beaumaris crew took a couple of them out in the lifeboat to see at first hand the problems of treating a patient in the cramped deck space on a fast-moving small boat. Coming up the Menai Strait, the radio crackled into life with a message from the coastguard. A woman had reported a man jumping from the Menai Bridge.

Details were sparse but a search was started immediately. Soon a clattering noise announced the arrival of a helicopter whose crew seemed to relish the opportunity to fly under the bridge on their search. After about half an hour, the radio sparked into life again. The police had interviewed the woman who had reported the incident. She and her boyfriend had had a row and he had stormed off, threatening to kill himself by jumping off the bridge. But when the police checked his home they found him in front of the television with his feet up!

QUICK THINKING

The treacherous Welsh coastline, coupled with gales and storms of exceptional ferocity during the last few years, mean that the crews often have to use considerable ingenuity and initiative.

In August 1988 the **Port Talbot** crew managed to save a life without even launching the lifeboat. A small yacht had been reported in difficulties in the lee of a breakwater in New Harbour. It was anchored, but heavy waves and a force 7 wind were giving it a considerable pounding, so the station's honorary secretary and two crewmembers went down to the shore to investigate. As they were trying to work out whether there was anyone on board, the boat broke free of its moorings.

The crewmembers, who were both experienced lifesavers, at once decided to act. They waded and swam through the surf and boarded the yacht. There they found a man in his 70s, bemused and battered. He was at the start of a month-long cruise, but he had lost his dentures and had been unable to eat for three days. As the yacht went aground, the lifeboatmen were able to take the old man safely ashore to a first aid station.

The **Burry Port** crew gave a supreme example of quick thinking and rapid action when they rescued five people in 13 minutes.

At high water, one boat, *The Firm*, became stranded on the bank at the mouth of the Pembrey Channel. That evening two people waded out to try and float her off on the evening tide. Unfortunately, they could not start the engine. Another boat, the *Triple A*, went to try and tow *The Firm* off. Eventually, a towline was passed between the two boats, but in the very choppy sea the line became entangled in *Triple A*'s propeller.

The lifeboat helmsman, Hugh Owen, spotted the boats and realised that they were both in danger of being swamped. He immediately alerted the crew and the coastguard, and launched the lifeboat. As the inflatable picked its way through the surf, it was continually filling with water from the waves lashing the Burry Port breakwater. By this time all five sailors had taken refuge on *The Firm*, the larger boat, but transferring them to the lifeboat was extremely difficult. The high waves kept forcing the boats apart. Thanks to some skilful manoeuvring by the crew, the lifeboat was soon on its way back, although it was considerably weighed down with seven people and all the water it had taken on.

Speed is usually essential after a sailing accident, and the inshore lifeboats are perfectly designed to supply it. The **Trearddur** inflatable on Anglesey was once called out after a dinghy had capsized; two survivors were clinging to the dinghy as it drifted towards the waves churning round Cod Rocks. The helmsman, John Burns, realised that the inflatable had arrived only just in time to prevent the survivors from being smashed against the rocks. He quickly told them to let go of the dinghy; they were then picked up by the inflatable, which narrowly cleared the rocks at full throttle after it was caught by a freak wave. The crew returned to Porth Diana with the survivors only 15 minutes after they had set out.

INNOVATION

Around the corner, **Holyhead** has a fascinating history and a very distinguished one, for the station can boast 49 bravery medals. It has also been a place for innovation, testing new lifejackets in 1877 and receiving a steam-driven lifeboat in 1901. This lifeboat had a tragic start as a boiler room explosion killed two men on the passage to station, but she acquitted herself a few years later in the rescue, in winds of 80 miles per hour, of nine men from a Liverpool steamer.

In 1954 the Holyhead crew were awarded a case of rum by the Sugar Manufacturer's Association of Jamaica for the longest winter service, after spending 24 hours at sea in January. The whole crew won medals for their part in the *Nafsiporos* rescue, and in the 1970s Coxswain

A rescue team: Holyhead's offshore and inshore lifeboats with a helicopter from RAF Valley.

William Jones won two medals in two years for saving yachts way out in the Irish Sea.

Yachts and motorboats are the most common casualties off the Welsh coast, but the strangest vessel ever saved was a Viking longship! In July 1990 the **Moelfre** lifeboat received a call from the replica longship *Dyflin*, based in Ireland and sailing from Holyhead to Liverpool. She had suffered mechanical failure and her crew of 11 were reported to be exhausted – perhaps they had been trying to emulate the original Vikings by rowing the 76-foot boat. The lifeboat quickly found the longship and towed her the 11 miles to Amlwch on Anglesey.

OLD-FASHIONED WAYS

The **Aberystwyth** crew once used an old-fashioned lifeboat to carry out a rescue. They were out in an old restored pulling lifeboat, practising for a sponsored row, when they came across a broken-down motorboat. Using their rowing skills they towed the boat safely back to Aberystwyth.

Another unusual rescue took place when, in April 1980, two doctors from a local hospital called at the Aberystwyth boathouse looking for a boat to collect some clean seawater. A nine-year-old patient was critically ill with pneumonia, and they believed that the severe congestion in his

Old and new: a pulling and sailing lifeboat, manned by Aberystwyth lifeboatmen, meets the modern St David's Tyne Class lifeboat.

bronchial passages could be eased if he inhaled vaporised seawater. The inshore lifeboat was immediately launched, and the crew collected one gallon of water well out in Cardigan Bay, and the boy made a rapid recovery after he had received the treatment.

The Aberystwyth crew still remember a service to a man who had been swept out to sea after he had fallen asleep on an airbed. His wife had returned to the beach with some sandwiches and a flask of tea to find that the airbed, with her husband on it, was now a distant speck on the horizon.

'When the crew found him,' recalls David Jenkins, the station's honorary secretary, 'he was very red in the face, partly from embarrassment, and partly because the airbed had sprung a leak and he had to keep blowing it up again.'

FLOODS

Appalling weather conditions over the last few years have tested crews' skills to the utmost; the Welsh lifeboats have come to the rescue in hurricanes, gales and floods. The RNLI sometimes dispatches inflatable lifeboats to help flood victims in other parts of the world; Bangladesh has twice received boats from the Institution, bought by the Red Cross. But British floods are rarely severe enough to demand the services of the lifeboats.

However, the North Wales floods of February 1990 proved the exception, when unusually heavy tides and hurricane-force winds destroyed the sea wall at Towyn. For nearly five days, from 26 February until the waters abated on 1 March, the crews and lifeboat helpers in the area were all involved, some spending up to 19 hours each day in the floodwater. Altogether, lifeboatmen from **Rhyl, Llandudno** and **Flint** rescued around 580 people and numerous family pets from the rising waters.

'They said "a little flooding on caravan sites",' recalls Geraint Jones, Flint's honorary secretary. 'It wasn't until we got there that we realised the depth of it.'

'We were in uncharted waters,' says Meurig Davies, coxswain at Llandudno. 'It was very strange steering the boat with a road map on your knee instead of a chart.'

Many of those evacuated were elderly, sick or disabled; one woman was lifted into Llandudno's inflatable lifeboat in her wheelchair. Lifeboatmen also used Llandudno's Unimog launching tractor and Flint's Land-Rover to carry people to safety. Under the water, which was six feet deep in places, lurked obstructions and dangers like collapsed walls and open manhole covers.

'There was such a force in the water that the manhole covers were being lifted. You just had to tread gingerly with your feet in the best way that you could,' explains Meurig Davis. Several of his crew fell down holes and grids masked by the flood water.

'The Fire Chief was warning everybody about the street lights.

It didn't cross my mind [until then] that the street lights might have been alive under the water,' says Terry Jacklin, from Flint.

Persuading people to evacuate their homes was another problem.

The Llandudno inshore lifeboat assists during the 1990 Towyn floods with lifeboatmen and firemen on board.

Several refused to leave without their beloved pets. These included a horse, which swam to safety as soon as it was released from its stable, and a budgie, which took up temporary residence in Llandudno's boathouse.

'We came across two ladies hanging out of a window and we thought they wanted to be rescued,' says Meurig Davies. 'It turned out they wanted us to take their dogs for a walk so that they could "do their business".' The lifeboatmen duly obliged, returning the dogs on their next trip through the area.

As the floods started to recede, the water became too shallow for the engines of the inflatables to be used, so tired, wet lifeboatmen had to drag their boats along by hand. Afterwards 51 people received certificates of recognition from the RNLI for their excellent work.

SURF DARING

One of the most daring rescues during the storms of recent years took place in 30-foot waves during a force 9 gale, when the quick thinking of the **Tenby** coxswain saved a fishing skipper's life.

On a wild September afternoon in 1989, Tenby station's honorary secretary, Eric Bancroft, received a call from the coastguard; a motor fishing vessel, the *Seeker*, was in difficulties off Worms Head. Another fishing boat, the *New Venture*, was attempting a tow. Eric Bancroft immediately activated the crew's pagers and the coxswain, Alan Thomas, fired the maroons. Six minutes later the Tenby lifeboat, *RFA Sir Galahad*, was catapulted down the slipway.

The weather worsened as the lifeboat crossed Carmarthen Bay, and it soon picked up a Mayday call from the two fishing vessels. When the *RFA*

Tenby's Tyne Class lifeboat RFA Sir Galahad *returns to station after a visit to the Royal Fleet Auxiliary RFA* Sir Galahad, *whose predecessor had been lost in the Falklands War.*

Sir Galahad arrived at the scene it found that the *Seeker* had been washed on to the beach by the tumultuous seas; her crew had been helped ashore by coastguards.

But the *New Venture* and the *Silver Stream*, a fishing vessel that had come to help, were trapped in the boiling surf; they were in danger of being smashed against the shore by the huge breakers. Coxswain Thomas realised that the conditions made it impossible to tow either vessel clear of the beach. He manoeuvred the lifeboat within the surf line, close to the fishing boats, where the *RFA Sir Galahad* was constantly hit by breaking waves and her crew engulfed in water.

As daylight faded Alan Thomas decided to try and guide the fishing boats into Tenby. The *Silver Stream* was battling to get free of the breakers when an enormous wave struck her and rolled her over; a deep-freeze on the vessel's deck was hurled 30 feet into the air by the impact of the wave. Amazingly the *Silver Stream* righted herself, but she was very full of water and listing heavily. The skipper was pinned in the wheelhouse by loose gear on the deck; his boat could go down at any minute, taking him with it.

There was therefore not a second to lose; Coxswain Thomas positioned the lifeboat carefully and drove it straight towards the wheelhouse window. Using great skill he held the *RFA Sir Galahad* steady while two crew members hauled the skipper through the window and pulled him on to the lifeboat. Finally the *New Venture* managed to get clear of the beach, and the lifeboat escorted her safely back through the rough seas to moor off Tenby, landing all the survivors ashore. For his exceptional courage, determination and skill, Alan Thomas was awarded the RNLI's coveted Silver Medal.

PEMBROKESHIRE PERILS

A rescue in hurricane-force winds in February 1989 won the St David's coxswain, David Chant, the RNLI's Bronze Medal. Answering distress calls from a fishing boat, the *Stephanie Jane*, the St David's lifeboat at once headed for the South Bishop lighthouse; the fishing boat's engine had failed and she had anchored half a mile south of the lighthouse until help came.

The lifeboat's path lay through a notoriously dangerous area. Here the Pembrokeshire seascape is strewn with huge rocks and riddled with treacherous currents known only to locals like Dai Chant and his crew. Once they were a few miles clear of the coast, the sea grew so rough that the crew had to strap themselves into their seats as the boat fought its way through the 30-foot waves. At one point the sea threw the lifeboat heavily on to its beam ends, but she was soon able to resume her course.

As they approached the lighthouse the lifeboatmen saw the *Stephanie Jane*; she was rolling from side to side in the water and being dragged towards some rocks only 200 feet away. Dai Chant had to get a towline

The fishing boat Stephanie Jane *is brought to safety in Milford Dock by the St David's lifeboat.*

to the fishing boat, and he also had to succeed at the first attempt, an almost impossible task in the atrocious conditions. But before the *Stephanie Jane* could take the towline, she had to slip her anchor; and until the towline could be made fast, she would be completely at the mercy of the waves threatening to pulverise her against the rocks.

As the crew prepared the towline, the coxswain managed to bring the lifeboat to within a few feet of the *Stephanie Jane*'s bow. Both boats were rolling violently, but against all odds the towline was successfully passed between them.

After several hours' slow progress through the gale, both boats arrived safely at Milford Dock, where the four survivors were landed. By this stage the weather was so bad that the lifeboat was unable to make her way home until the following day.

Another Pembrokeshire crew braved force 10 winds to go to the aid of an oil tanker that had run aground. The **Angle** lifeboat launched in the teeth of a gale on 5 August 1973 and found the *Dona Marika* rolling heavily, with the waves breaking high over her decks.

The coastguard asked the lifeboat to take the crew off as soon as possible, as there was an imminent risk of an explosion; the tanker was carrying high octane spirit. The *Dona Marika*'s crew were told to rig a ladder on the port side and to get ready to disembark.

The lifeboat was rising and falling 20 feet in the turbulent sea, but the coxswain, Reece Holmes, managed to bring the boat alongside the ladder. At the last moment the terrified sailors refused to leave the stricken ship, although the sea was already breaking through the wheelhouse – they wanted the lifeboat to approach from the other side. This would have been impossible, as the water was too shallow there. As it was, to avoid alarming his own crew, Coxswain Holmes had switched off the lifeboat's echo sounder when it showed that there was less than a foot of water beneath them.

The lifeboatmen knew that they risked being blown to bits every time they brought their craft alongside the *Dona Marika* and her lethal cargo; the nearby village of St Ishmael had already been evacuated because of the danger. Many times the boat also came close to foundering in the heavy swell from the tanker.

For one terrible moment the coxswain of the Haven Conservancy launch, which was standing by, thought that the lifeboat had actually gone down because he could no longer see the blue flashing light on the masthead as the boat heaved up and down in the waves. Nevertheless, the lifeboat approached the tanker seven times, two from the west and five from the east, and each time the tanker's crew refused to leave.

Finally the coxswain decided to remain nearby, in case the *Dona Marika*'s crew changed their minds and attempted to abandon ship. After six hours the weather eventually improved enough for a rescue to be made from land. The tanker's crew were helped ashore by the Coastguard Cliff Rescue crew. The lifeboat returned to Angle after almost nine and a half hours in the worst conditions some of the crew had ever experienced.

CHAPTER NINE

Children of courage

'Defend, O Lord, this thy child.'

Book of Common Prayer

THE RESCUES THAT really bring a lump to the throat are those involving children, as any crew member will agree. Crews have rescued children of all ages from many perils, and have even acted as assistant midwives on several occasions! The first birth of a baby on a lifeboat is thought to have taken place on the **Barra** all-weather lifeboat in February 1960.

On the isolated west coasts of Scotland and Ireland it is not unusual for the lifeboat to be used as a floating ambulance, and the Barra boat was about to take an expectant mother to hospital. However, the birth

Coxswain Robert Harland of Whitby with a few words of advice; photographed in 1934.

Gorleston lifeboatmen pass a rescued child to safety.

occurred sooner than expected, while the boat was still under way. Fortunately, the sea was calm that night and the winds were very light.

Oban lifeboat was used to take a three-hour-old baby, Francesca Richie, and her mother to hospital. Gillian Richie needed an urgent operation so the lifeboat transferred her and the tiny baby from their home on the Isle of Mull to hospital on the mainland.

An outstandingly courageous rescue took place in **Largs**, Ayrshire, in 1983 when lifeboatman Arthur Hill dived under the hull of a capsized motor cruiser to rescue a young girl trapped in the cabin. At any moment the boat could have shifted in the water, taking Arthur and the girl down with it, but he did not hesitate.

'As I took off my lifejacket, I can remember staring down at the upturned cruiser, wondering how, on such a beautiful summer's evening, such a disaster could occur,' Arthur recalls.

After three attempts he managed to get into the hull, where he found the girl huddled in a small air-pocket. She was up to her neck in water. It was very difficult to breathe because of fumes from spilt fuel and the air was extremely stale. But Arthur recognised the girl, whose name was Tracy, as a regular at the local swimming pool where he had been a lifeguard, and started talking to her to reassure her. If he were to get her out alive, she had to stay calm.

'My first words to her were, "Hello, there! I've seen you somewhere before. . .". I asked her if she could put her face under water, but she said she didn't know. I explained to her how easy it was and briefly showed her. . . Then I explained that I had come to get her out, and that she would have to hold her breath and count very slowly to ten.'

Arthur tried to push Tracy under the coaming to get her clear of the boat, but, unfortunately, her lifejacket prevented her from diving deep enough and she resurfaced inside the hull. At that moment the boat shifted, and they both had to contort their heads to keep their mouths out of the water.

'For a few seconds it did look as though all was lost for both of us. But one thing a lifeboatman will never do is give in. It's in a lifeboatman's blood to give up everything, even if it means denying himself. There is nothing worse than having to give up hope when human souls are in peril. That's why all lifeboatmen are very stubborn, and never lose heart, no matter how grave and hopeless the situation may be.'

Suddenly Arthur heard the helmsman, John Strachan, calling that he could grab hold of the girl's legs if Arthur could push her under once more.

'I then said, "Well, Tracy, this time you're out. Take a breath." As she did so, I pushed down on her head, first with my hand and then with my foot.'

As he pushed Tracy down, John Strachan got hold of her legs and pulled her clear. By the time Arthur resurfaced he was suffering from lack of oxygen.

'Immediately after the rescue, I felt a wee bit dizzy and was not quite 100 per cent. But the feeling of relief was such as I have never experienced since.'

Arthur later received the Silver Medal for his bravery, but modestly gives a lot of the credit to his fellow crew members. 'If it were not for the speedy actions of John [Strachan] and Dave [Hewitt] on the surface, the outcome would, without doubt, have been totally different.'

With similar modesty, Steve Vince, the coxswain/mechanic of the **Poole** lifeboat, gives a dog most of the credit for the rescue of a 13-year-old boy trapped up to his armpits in mud on the edge of Poole Harbour on 1 July 1986.

'It all started with a farmer's dog,' he explains. 'When the farmer went to look at the cows, the dog kept looking at the reeds and playing up until his owner eventually rang the coastguard.'

In the inflatable lifeboat Steve and his crew headed out into the harbour. When they turned the engine off they thought they could hear shouting. The tide was quite low so Steve had to walk the considerable distance across the mud to the reeds fringing the shore, sometimes sinking up to his waist in water or mud. It was almost midnight on a moonless night and he could see nothing, but he could faintly hear a girl calling for help.

To help him find her he finally asked her to sing. Eventually he spotted the girl; she was holding up a young lad who was almost completely buried in mud.

'When I got up to them, the girl cried and just wouldn't let go of me. The lad kept saying, "Help me! Help me! It's my birthday. I don't want to die on my birthday!"'

The boy was paralysed with cold from the waist down and Steve radioed back to the boat for help. He was joined by lifeboatman Raymond Collin, and they both tried to carry the boy to the boat; it was impossible, as they both kept falling into the mud.

'It was the most painful rescue I've ever attempted,' says Steve ruefully.

Helmsman David Coles decided to use the rubber mattress from the bottom of the lifeboat as a sledge over the mud. After driving the boat up on to the shore, he heaved the mattress over to the survivors and the boy was slowly dragged to the lifeboat.

Finding a dead child is the saddest experience lifeboat crews have to deal with.

'The lifelessness of a young body stays with you for a long time. It can be very traumatic for the crew,' says Rod James, helmsman of the **Hayling Island** lifeboat. 'For some of them it may be their first experience of death.' He now tries to discuss disturbing incidents with each of the crew during the following week, so that they get a chance to talk about their feelings.

Flimsy plastic inflatables are one cause of child fatalities in the water. An offshore wind can quickly catch such a toy, and before the children know it, they are being carried far from the shore.

On a June afternoon in 1986 the crew of **Rye**'s inshore lifeboat rescued two children from an inflatable, then saw three children adrift in a rubber canoe; the youngest was only 18 months old. When they returned the frightened youngsters to their anxious families, the crew reminded the parents of the dangers of these toys.

Gaining the confidence of terrified children is a skill that all lifeboat crews have to develop. If panic sets in, the whole rescue could be put in jeopardy. On 20 July 1986 the **Weston-super-Mare** crew were called to two boys who had been trapped by the tide beneath steep cliffs. The shore was so rocky that the inflatable lifeboat could not reach the children and crew member Richard Spindler volunteered to swim the 40 yards from the boat to the boys.

When he reached them he managed to calm them down; one, an eight-year-old, was unable to swim, so Richard then swam back to the lifeboat to fetch two lifejackets and a line. Returning to the shore, Richard attached the line to himself and the younger boy. While they were being pulled back to the lifeboat, he held the boy so that his head was well above water and spoke comfortingly to him.

Once the small boy was aboard the lifeboat, Richard then swam back to the shore for a third time, and returned with the older child. In all he had swum nearly 200 yards, much of the distance against four to five-foot surf.

Three children rescued by the St Ives lifeboat in 1974.

Even quite young children are sometimes capable of astounding courage in the most daunting situations. The **Cardigan** crew were amazed by the bravery of a 12-year-old boy rescued from a motor cruiser caught on Cardigan Bar in August 1980. Twenty-foot waves were breaking over the boat and she was full of water. The owner, the boy's father, had been washed overboard, although he had managed to scramble back on to the boat. The boy had just managed to grab their dog before it, too, was swept off the boat.

After a difficult approach, crew members grabbed the boy, who was still clinging to his dog, then returned for the father. During the journey back to the shore the inflatable lifeboat several times became vertical, and the crew and survivors were thrown into the air. Yet throughout the trip, the boy clutched his dog, regardless of his own safety.

Several children have received bravery awards from the RNLI. Sixteen-year-old Simon Hall from Robin Hood's Bay in Yorkshire was awarded the Bronze Medal after rescuing a boy whose home-made raft had come to grief. The sea wall is 50 feet high here with no steps, ladders or breaks, and Stephen, the owner of the raft, was shouting desperately for help, unable to get ashore. Simon rowed his tiny dinghy out to Stephen and managed to pull the exhausted and shivering boy on board. They reached a moored fishing boat and waited there until **Whitby** inshore lifeboat came for them.

Martin Ruddy, a 14-year-old scout from **Ilfracombe**, received a Bronze Medal in 1975 for saving four people and a dog from their sinking

Martin Ruddy wearing the Bronze Medal he won for saving three adults, a child and a dog.

speedboat. He had only had his 9-foot dinghy for three weeks, and had never ventured out far in it, but he did not hesitate when he saw someone on a motor boat half a mile off the beach waving a white shirt. Using flimsy vinyl oars, Martin rowed as hard as he could through the four-foot swell. Those waiting on the motor boat were relieved to see him coming, but apprehensive as they saw the dinghy negotiating the swells, waves and rocks.

The owner of the boat swam out to Martin and clung on to the dinghy as Martin grabbed an eight-year-old boy and his dog from the water. The owner then scrambled aboard and helped Martin pull in a woman whose dress was trapped in the sinking boat. Finally they dragged on the third adult, a man whose legs were completely numb with cold. By the time a rescue helicopter arrived, the laden dinghy was already well on its way to the shore.

Fourteen-year-old Daniel Norman from **Watchet** saved the life of Leanne, ten years old and a non-swimmer, on 10 September 1981, when she was swept out to sea while playing near the water's edge. Daniel took his father's boat, a converted ship's lifeboat, out to Leanne, who by this time was floating face downwards on the water. When the water became insufficiently deep for him to reach her in the boat, he jumped into the sea and swam towards her. Returning with her, with great difficulty he clambered into the boat himself then pulled her after him, immediately starting mouth-to-mouth resuscitation. By the time Leanne was taken into the care of the coastguard, her breathing had been revived and, after three days in hospital, she had completely recovered.

Two young Welsh girls saved the life of a man trapped in mud in the Conwy Estuary. Mandy Warren and Katie Flowers were out walking when they heard shouts and shots being fired. They saw the man, who had been wild-fowling, marooned on a mud bank by the rapidly rising waters of the incoming tide. Quickly Katie ran to the nearest telephone to raise the alarm, while Mandy remained on the shore to keep him in sight.

Within five minutes the **Conwy** inflatable lifeboat had launched, not a moment too soon; when they reached the man the crew found he was now up to his armpits in the mud with the tide coming in fast. They hauled him out and soon brought him ashore.

One of the greatest child heroines of recent years was 11-year-old Jayne Edmunds, who took charge when her father was hurled from their cabin cruiser in rough seas on 10 August 1974. After he had gone overboard, Jayne had thrown her father a lifejacket and had tried to manoeuvre the boat towards him. Unfortunately, the boat then shipped so much water that it was completely unmanageable. With considerable presence of mind, Jayne then ordered her friend, Paula, 11, and Paula's younger brother, aged 9, to put on lifejackets. Before she had time to don her own, the boat sank and the three children were swept into the water.

When the **Aberdovey** lifeboat discovered them about half an hour later,

Jayne Edmunds saved two friends after her father was swept overboard and their cabin cruiser sank. With her Eric Jones, son of the Porthdinllaen coxswain, who rescued a man from an isolated rock.

Jayne was supporting Paula in the water. The lifeboat had already found the distraught Mr Edmunds, clutching the lifejacket that Paula had tossed to him. Crew member David Williams swam out from the lifeboat to reach Jayne and Paula, and helped them through the heavy surf to a sandbank where Paula's brother had taken refuge. David and fellow crew member Andrew Coghill then brought the children through the five-foot-deep channel to the beach, where the children were reunited with Paula's father. For this rescue David Williams was awarded a Bronze Medal, while Jayne received an inscribed watch and the first Churchill Award for Bravery at Sea ever to be awarded.

CHAPTER TEN

Scotland – disaster and triumph

'I have never called lifeboatmen heroes. I have always
felt that they were men who could appreciate the risks
involved better than I. The sort of men who would
train their hearts to outstrip a colleague getting to the
lifeboat because they would not let fear be their
master. Such men were these.'

Lord Saltoun at the funeral of the Longhope crew

THE MUSHROOMING GROWTH of pleasure craft, particularly in the South of
England, has given some people the idea that a lifeboatman's job is now
more of an AA patrol at sea, a get-you-home service, rather than the last
hope for shipwrecked seafarers. Even the briefest examination of the
records will disprove this. While a lot of routine rescues do involve
pleasure craft, the major successes, measured by Gold Medals, and the
terrible disasters, leaving whole communities bereft and grief-stricken, all
involve merchant ships and fishing boats.

Scotland, with its harsh winter climate and severe weather, has a
lifeboat bravery record equally matched by a tragic record of lifeboat
disasters resulting from valiant attempts to rescue fishing or merchant
craft.

Longhope, a tiny Orkney community on the north of the notorious
Pentland Firth, provides just one example. Dan Kirkpatrick had built up
a formidable reputation as a lifeboatman whose skills and seamanship
could challenge the treacherous tides and currents that run through the
Firth so quickly that nine-knot lifeboats would, at times, struggle to make
any progress at all.

In 1959 he won a Silver Medal for the rescue by breeches buoy of 14
men from the trawler *Strathcoe*, ashore in the Firth. In 1964 he received
a second Silver for another breeches buoy rescue, this time taking nine
men from the Aberdeen trawler *Ben Barvas* ashore on the Pentland
Skerries. Then in 1968 he won a third Silver for taking 15 men off the
trawler *Ross Puma* of Grimsby, wrecked on Little Rackwick Shoals.

A quiet man, Kirkpatrick gained the respect of all he met. As in so many
small communities, his sons joined him on the crew. Then on 17 March

1969 the Liberian ship *Irene* sent out a distress message. She was about five miles east of North Ronaldsay and was drifting helplessly, out of fuel. It was evening, a gale was blowing and there were rain and snow flurries. In the lifeboathouse at Longhope, Dan Kirkpatrick talked to honorary secretary Jackie Groat. Dan was under no illusions about the dangers he faced. He told Jackie that the only chance of reaching the *Irene* before she was driven ashore was to go through the North Sound.

'If we keep in close there, I think we should get through and reach her. If she comes ashore on the cliffs, they'll all be gone,' he said.

The Longhope lifeboat set out at 8 pm with eight men on board. As she fought against the flood tide and heavy swell she was seen by lighthouse keepers and coastguards making steady progress through the storm.

The *Irene* ran aground on South Ronaldsay at 9.15. At 9.28 the lifeboat called Wick Radio to acknowledge a message giving the *Irene*'s position. It was the last call ever to be heard from the lifeboat.

At 10.05 Kirkwall coastguard asked Wick Radio to tell the lifeboat that conditions alongside the *Irene* were 'almost impossible'. But there was no reply. Worried for the safety of the boat, the coastguard sent out search parties to scour the cliffs and asked the **Kirkwall** lifeboat, also at sea, to rendezvous with the Longhope boat near the *Irene*. In spite of firing flares, the Kirkwall men could see virtually nothing in the high seas,

The Longhope lifeboat crew and officials in 1963. All the crew except one died in the 1969 disaster. Back row, l to r: Robert Johnston, Dan Kirkpatrick, James Johnston, Robert R. Johnston, Ray Kirkpatrick, James Swanson, James Groat (treasurer). Front row: Jackie Groat (hon sec), Robbie Johnston, Jack Kirkpatrick.

darkness and spray. As the coastguard cliff teams worked with tremendous courage to haul the *Irene*'s crew across the gap between the ship and the towering cliffs, fears grew for the men of the Longhope lifeboat.

At daylight a huge search was mounted. **Kirkwall, Stromness, Stronsay** and **Thurso** lifeboats were joined by a Shackleton aircraft and a helicopter. All morning they searched and, as the hours passed, hope faded. It was not until 1.40 pm that the Thurso crew saw what all had dreaded. The Longhope lifeboat was floating upside down, her white hull signalling the tragedy of a capsize. The Thurso boat took her in tow and in a solemn procession, with the Stromness boat in escort, reached Scrabster harbour just before 9 pm that evening.

The young lifeboat inspector for Scotland at that time was Brian Miles, now the RNLI's Director. He had been up all night, telephoning Jackie Groat for updates. By the morning, with no news of the lifeboat, he had set out from Aberdeen to Longhope. All air services had been cancelled because of the weather, but he got on a plane chartered by Grampian Television. That got him to Kirkwall, across the Pentland Firth.

'The seas were wild, dreadful,' he recalls. 'I was determined to get to Longhope, so I got a car to Stromness, but no boats were running from there. Ginger Brown, a local boatman, offered to take me across. He warned me that he couldn't get alongside, but he anchored and veered me towards the shore in a small dinghy.

Margaret Kirkpatrick, hand to mouth, and her daughters-in-law (second and third from left) at the funeral of the Longhope crew.

'I threw my bag ashore, jumped and hit the rocks. Then I slipped down and ended up to my knees in a rock pool. My trousers and shoes were soaking and in that state I set out to see the families.'

Jackie Groat was there to meet him and the two men drove to the tiny hamlet of Brims.

'I looked down the hill and it suddenly struck me like a physical blow. We had taken someone out of virtually every house.'

Margaret Kirkpatrick had lost her husband Dan and sons Jack and Ray. Maggie Johnston had lost husband Bob and sons Robbie and Jimmy. Eric McFadyen had been home on leave from the Merchant Navy and had turned up at the boathouse to make up the numbers. James Swanson had been on duty all day as engineer on the Longhope to Stromness ferry. He had just got home when the call came for the lifeboat and, wearing his carpet slippers, went straight to the boathouse. He was swept away from the lifeboat; his body was never found.

The families first asked about their menfolk. Then, in spite of their intense personal grief, each one also asked exactly what had happened to the crew of the *Irene*. On being told that they had been saved from the shore, they all expressed relief.

'My husband would have been very pleased to know that,' said one woman.

An official enquiry examined the evidence. Everything pointed to a huge sea overwhelming the lifeboat with tremendous force. A non-self-righter, once over she would stay upside down. Dan Kirkpatrick was probably killed by the impact of the sea as he stood at the wheel. His crew, trapped inside the boat, would have drowned.

By coincidence, the day the news broke was lifeboat flag day in London, and BBC television presenter Raymond Baxter had broadcast a charity appeal on behalf of the RNLI the night before. The public response was overwhelming. The elements of heroism and sacrifice in the sombre news reports immediately struck a chord of sympathy with all who heard them and contributions flooded in from all over the world.

By contrast, another Scottish disaster, only months later, put the RNLI under intense scrutiny and criticism that led to a threat to its independence.

A GOVERNMENT TAKE-OVER?

When the **Fraserburgh** lifeboat capsized in January 1970, public debate, fuelled by the media, was so intense that Prime Minister Edward Heath called RNLI Chairman Admiral Wilfred Woods to 10 Downing Street. Politically, the RNLI had suddenly become an embarrassment. To lose two lifeboat crews in such a short time was not acceptable, never mind that the weather on each occasion had been appalling, the boats in prime condition, and the coxswains skilled men leading experienced crews. The public would take so much, then no more.

Heath's message to Woods, however illogical, was simple. Lose any more lifeboatmen and the Government will have to step in. As a sailor, Heath must have known just how nonsensical this was. But as a politician he felt he had to respond to the public mood. He had only recently been voted in, and the outgoing minister at the Board of Trade, Roy Mason, had announced in the House of Commons that he had been working on plans to incorporate the RNLI into a national air-sea rescue service, funded by the taxpayer. If the RNLI could not look after its crews, somebody else would have to take over. Although some would interpret the nationalisation threat as a party political move, it was more a naive response that supposed that Government money would prevent disasters at sea.

Labour leader Harold Wilson, whom Heath had ousted, demonstrated his personal support for the RNLI four years later on the very day the Queen sent for him to form a new Government. The RNLI's 150th anniversary was marked on 4 March 1974 by a national service of thanksgiving in St Paul's Cathedral. Harold Wilson was due to see the Queen in the afternoon and spent the morning at the RNLI service, not in the front row but unobtrusively sitting towards the back, as an ordinary member of the congregation, to pay tribute to 150 years of lifesaving.

The controversy at Fraserburgh was based on a series of criticisms, all of which were rejected by the court of enquiry. But if the Longhope disaster had been clear-cut, dramatic and heroic, the Fraserburgh disaster was portrayed as something quite different.

It all started on the evening of 20 January 1970. The Danish fishing boat *Opel* set sail from Buckie bound for the Fladden fishing grounds. At 10.30 that night the crew found seawater in the engine room, tried the pumps and found them to be useless. Gradually the water rose, and by 5 am the next morning the skipper radioed Denmark to report his plight.

While there was no immediate danger, the Danish radio operator passed on the message to Wick Radio and the information got through to Fraserburgh coastguard. The Fraserburgh lifeboat secretary was ill and Coxswain John Buchan was doubling up for him. He decided to launch the lifeboat, which set out at 6.38 am.

The situation on the *Opel* was worsening as the water in the engine room rose steadily. Fraserburgh lifeboat had a long passage with an estimated arrival time at the *Opel* of 11 am. As she ploughed on, the Russian ship *Victor Kingisepp* sighted the *Opel* and made for her. Two other Russian trawlers were already there, trying to get a towline across, and by 10.30 they had succeeded.

The lifeboat was not told of the Russians' success and kept going; by 11 am she was 36 miles off Fraserburgh. As she neared the *Opel* she reported that the Danish ship was being towed by the Russian. It was her last message.

The coxswain reduced speed to come parallel with the *Opel*. The seas

The arrow indicates the Fraserburgh lifeboat at the moment of capsize.

were rough with waves of 15 feet, sometimes twice that height. Buchan decided to go ahead to identify the name of the trawler towing the *Opel*. As he increased speed, a huge breaking wave hit the lifeboat on the port bow.

The crew clung on, as much by instinct as anything else. But this was no ordinary wave and its power was so great that it lifted the bow of the lifeboat so high that it rose up over the stern, then fell down in an arc, upside down. Men on the Russian trawler *Sarma* captured the moment of capsize on film, providing dramatic evidence of the lifeboat crew's last moments.

Four men, John Buchan, William Hadden, James R. S. Buchan and James Buchan, were trapped inside and drowned. Mechanic Frederick Kirkness was never found. Amazingly one man, Jackson Buchan, was thrown into the water and managed to clamber on to the capsized lifeboat. For 20 minutes he clung on, his feet braced against the bilge keel, vainly banging on the hull to try and get a response from inside. Eventually, one of the Russian trawlers managed to reach him. The *Victor Kingisepp* got alongside the lifeboat, but in spite of strenuous efforts by her crew, could not turn her upright. She took the lifeboat alongside and a curious stalemate developed.

Ashore, lifeboat inspector Brian Miles could hardly believe that he had another lifeboat disaster in his division. He made straight for Fraserburgh and spent the evening visiting the bereaved families. The next morning the navy provided a helicopter to fly him and the Receiver of Wrecks out to the Russian ship. Many of the crew, which included several women, had never seen a Western European before, and looked on in amazement as the two men were taken to the wardroom.

They spent all afternoon there, talking through an interpreter, who may have been the KGB officer routinely carried on Soviet ships in those days. The Russians would not release the lifeboat, which they had now righted, and to this day Brian Miles does not know whether the deadlock was broken by his negotiating skills or by shuttle diplomacy over the radio, with messages flashing between the ship, the embassy in London and Moscow. The Russians were talking about salvage, the RNLI about the need to get the bodies ashore.

Suddenly, at about 5 pm, a message handed to the captain changed everything. The atmosphere lightened and permission was given to take the lifeboat away. Miles watched sombrely as the bodies of the lifeboatmen were carefully taken down the gangplank to be laid, side by side, on the deck of the **Buckie** lifeboat, then he descended with the only survivor, Jackson Buchan. With the Fraserburgh lifeboat in tow, they began the sad passage back to land. As they pulled away, they glanced up to see the Russian factory ship's decks lined with people, all silently waving.

Memories are long at lifeboat stations, and at Fraserburgh there is good reason to remember the past, which is marked by misfortune. In 1876 the lifeboat was driven on to rocks but nobody was lost. In 1884 it capsized, but the crew were thrown out and were able to get to safety. In 1919 it capsized again a mile offshore and two men were drowned. In 1953, while escorting fishing boats into harbour, it was hit by a heavy swell breaking over her and capsized once more, killing six men who were trapped underneath.

However, Fraserburgh lifeboatmen had also built up a tremendous record of bravery. But the 1970 disaster was too much for the tight-knit fishing community. They demanded a 70-foot lifeboat, a design based on deep-sea trawlers. The RNLI refused, offering instead a smaller Solent Class, a type accepted by Longhope and already proved by service at exposed Scottish stations such as Thurso and Wick. The stalemate lasted for eight years, with **Macduff** taking a Solent to provide the necessary cover.

Then, in 1978, fishermen in Fraserburgh crowded into a public meeting with the RNLI Director, Captain Nigel Dixon, to give him an answer on whether they would re-open the lifeboat station. Discussions had been going on for weeks before the meeting, but Dixon had no idea what would happen. Even Jack Provan, who had kept the RNLI's presence in Fraserburgh alive, could only guess.

One of the fishermen's leaders got up to speak. Quite simply, he said that the time had come for Fraserburgh to have a lifeboat again. The fishermen were behind him and a new crew was soon formed under Coxswain John Sutherland. John had started his sea career as a galley boy on local fishing boats, and he later joined the Merchant Navy, got his master's ticket, bought his own fishing boat and worked the west coast of Africa and the Caribbean. Stomach cancer brought him home for treatment and, while recuperating, he took a degree, using this qualification to become head of nautical studies at the local college. Only a man of such standing could do the job, and he led the station back to action.

When he stepped down as coxswain, he was succeeded by his cousin Albert, whose identical twin brother Victor and another brother, James, are also on the crew. Since then many people have owed their lives to the Fraserburgh lifeboatmen. Thirteen-year-old Edward McDonald is one.

In October 1993 he was swept off a breakwater by a huge wave. The lifeboat crew were in the boathouse and saw one of Edward's friends throw a lifebelt into the water. They launched the lifeboat immediately and reached the boy in minutes, but he was floating face down in the water, unconscious in the heavy swell. Lifeboatman Graham Campbell jumped in to the sea, grabbed the boy's jacket and the rest of the crew pulled him on board. He and Tommy Summers then immediately started resuscitation and chest compressions on the boy, but he was not breathing and had no pulse. The lifeboatmen worked on, hoping against hope that the youngster would respond, but as the minutes ticked away it all seemed in vain.

It only took ten minutes to get Edward from the sea to an ambulance, the lifeboatmen praying that they could coax life back into the boy. But he stayed inert until, just as he was handed over to the paramedics on the ambulance, there was a faint flutter of a pulse. He was whisked straight to hospital where he was put on a life support machine. For a week he fought to live, with the doctors unsure of his chances of survival. He eventually pulled through and, as soon as he left hospital, went with his parents to the lifeboathouse to thank the crew.

One of their proudest possessions, hanging framed on the boathouse wall, is a letter from Edward: 'To Albert and the crew of the Fraserburgh lifeboat *City of Edinburgh*. I, Edward McDonald, age 13 years, would like to thank you all very much for saving my life on Saturday 2nd October 1993. What you have all done will be remembered in my heart always. E. McDonald.'

LESSONS LEARNED

The main effect of the Longhope and Fraserburgh tragedies was a reappraisal of the policy on self-righting lifeboats. Both disaster boats were Watsons, solid, trusted and seaworthy, but not self-righting. Although the last of the Watsons had been built in 1963, they were still the largest class of boats in the RNLI fleet, and out of 139 boats at lifeboat stations in 1970, only 39 were self-righters.

For over 100 years controversy had raged about the relative merits of self-righting and non-self-righting lifeboats. In Victorian times a self-righter was more vulnerable to capsize as it relied on high end boxes at the bow and the stern and a narrower hull to come back upright. These boats were more lively at sea and their excessive motion made them unpopular with the crews. Wider, more stable lifeboats were favoured, even though they would stay upside down if capsized.

Richard Lewis, the Secretary of the RNLI, analysed the number of capsizes between 1852, when self-righters were introduced, and 1874. Thirty-five self-righters were upset and, out of the 401 men on board, only 25 were killed. Eight non-self-righters capsized in this period, and out of the 140 men on board, 87 were drowned. At this time there were far more self-righters on the coast, but although the statistics were convincing on paper, few lifeboatmen were persuaded.

It was not until 1958 that RNLI naval architect Richard Oakley came up with the answer in his design of water transfer to make a good stable boat that would right herself. Then came designs that were inherently self-righting; as long as the cabin doors were shut, the boats would automatically come upright.

So by 1970 the RNLI was building only self-righting boats, but had a huge legacy of boats like those at Longhope and Fraserburgh left in the fleet. There was neither the money nor boatyard capacity to replace them all immediately and an interim solution had to be found. Once again, design ingenuity based on a very simple principle provided the answer.

If you try to hold an inflated balloon under water, the buoyancy of the trapped air forces the balloon to the surface. The idea was to attach a large balloon to the top of a boat, offset to one side, and see if it would force the boat to turn upright when it was capsized. Obviously a boat with a balloon would be ridiculous, but if an air bag could be fitted, folded flat but automatically inflated on capsize, perhaps here was a solution.

Working closely with the British Hovercraft Corporation staff, who had enormous expertise on air bag systems for helicopters and materials for hovercraft skirts, RNLI designers worked out a way of converting older lifeboats to make them self-righting. The air bag system, like the Oakley's water transfer, needed rigorous maintenance as it had to work as soon as the boat rolled more than 120 degrees. In spite of extensive testing, doubts must have lingered about its effectiveness in a real emergency. Its trial came, in Scotland, just ten years after the Longhope disaster.

RIGHT WAY UP

The weather on the night of 18 November 1979 could best be described as diabolical. Winds were gusting to force 12, waves were 30 feet high and there was a one in ten chance of meeting a mighty 60-footer. Caught at sea in these conditions, the Danish coaster *Lone Dania* took on a heavy

Islay's Thames Class lifeboat lying peacefully at her moorings.

list as her cargo of marble chips shifted. She was six miles north of the Skerryvore lighthouse, near the Hebrides, when she sent out a distress call.

Two Hebridean lifeboats responded to the call, the **Barra Island** boat, a traditionally shaped Barnett Class, fitted with an air bag, and the **Islay** boat, a more modern, steel-hulled Thames Class, designed with a watertight superstructure to right her automatically.

Islay's was the faster boat and started out at full speed of 17 knots, reducing speed in the shallower water between Islay and Oronsay as the pounding on the lifeboat became more severe. At one point the boat drove through a particularly large wave and fell about 25 feet into the trough behind it. Crew member Iain Spears fell heavily on to his right foot and broke his ankle.

A few minutes later Coxswain Alastair Campbell caught a fleeting glimpse of a very steep breaking sea, about 30 feet high. What was odd about this sea was that it was coming in at right angles to the other waves, breaking the pattern that seamen look out for; it had probably rebounded off a reef. As it surged forwards it rolled the lifeboat over by 45 degrees. The boat hung there momentarily, then slid down the face of the next wave into a deep trough. As the wave broke over the lifeboat, she rolled right over, staying upside down for five seconds before coming upright. Afterwards the crew commented on the gentleness of the boat's movement as she rolled round in the midst of the maelstrom.

The coxswain checked the crew, then made a damage assessment of the boat. One engine was out of action, and the radar and the windscreen wipers were broken. Knowing the Barra lifeboat was on her way, he decided to head back to Islay to repair his boat before carrying on with the service.

The Barra boat had 37 miles to cover to reach the *Lone Dania*. After almost three hours at sea, Coxswain John Macneil was checking to see if he was in range of the beam from Skerryvore lighthouse when the lifeboat suddenly dug her bow down into the sea and started rolling over. Glancing backwards, he saw a breaking wave of 30 feet towering over the lifeboat, a solid wall of water bearing down on him. Before he even had a chance to shout a warning, the sea hit the lifeboat, turning her upside down. The Barnett, built as a non-self-righter, had only one hope for survival – the emergency air bag.

As the boat rolled, the mercury capsize switch activated, releasing compressed gas from a bottle and inflating the bag. So smooth was the motion that the lifeboat turned in a full circle, 360 degrees, to come upright again.

Coxswain and crew were safe, but loose ropes had wrapped around the propellers and shafts, disabling the lifeboat completely. The crew tried to cut the ropes free but the boat was rolling too much and the ropes were too tightly bound. For five hours they worked on a rota, never giving up. Then the coaster *Sapphire* reached them and started to tow the lifeboat home. They eventually reached Barra at 3.40 pm, 15 hours after the lifeboat set out.

Lone Dania, meanwhile, limped towards Barra, escorted by another Danish ship, arriving before the lifeboat. The ship owners sent a large donation to the RNLI.

A Royal Navy helicopter winches an injured crew member from the Barra Island lifeboat after she capsized in 1979. The air bag can be seen inflated on top of the lifeboat.

Ten years earlier both lifeboat crews would probably have died, trapped beneath the upturned boats. They escaped – shocked and cold, but with only minor cuts and bruises. RNLI teams were sent to investigate the capsizes, Brian Miles going to Barra.

'As we flew in I saw the lifeboat lying alongside the pier, looking very battered. I remember thinking, "The last time I was in this situation there was no crew left – now they are all alive." It really brought home to me what self-righting meant.'

When the news reached Buckingham Palace, The Queen, one of the RNLI's patrons, commanded her Private Secretary to send a message to RNLI Director Wilfred Graham: 'The Queen was very impressed recently to hear that both the Islay and Barra lifeboats had turned turtle and self-righted themselves in a gale off the west of Scotland. Lord Margadale, who is president of the Islay lifeboat, wrote to Her Majesty about this and reported that it was a remarkable performance.

'I should be grateful therefore if you would convey The Queen's congratulations to the crews of both lifeboats on their remarkable efforts. Once again the Royal National Lifeboat Institution has given that outstanding service which has been so typical of all its history.'

THE FAR NORTH

The Queen Mother is the RNLI's other patron and the lifeboat at **Thurso**, which sits in Scrabster Harbour overlooked by her Scottish home, the Castle of Mey, bears her name. The distance from the town to the harbour is only two and a half miles, but in 1921 it must have caused some problems, for the crew were allowed one penny travelling money for each service or exercise. This was only stopped in 1956, when car hire was introduced.

Travelling by sea was almost quicker on some occasions, as a rescue in 1922 demonstrates. The sailing lifeboat at Thurso was launched to a steamship that had broken away from her tugs some 35 miles west of the station; under full sail the lifeboat covered the distance in under three and a half hours. The steamship's crew had been taken off by one of the tugs, so the lifeboatmen turned back for home. They were at sea for 14 hours, covering a distance of 70 miles. Even today, Thurso's Arun Class lifeboat would take two hours on a 35-mile passage.

Long distances are part of Thurso's work as there is no other station westwards to Cape Wrath, but Coxswain William Farquhar managed to win a commendation in 1982 for a rescue just outside Scrabster Harbour. The trawler *Arctic Crusader* had broken adrift in a storm, was blown outside the harbour and was drifting towards the beach; although another trawler had got a line across, her anchor was dragging and she could not hold the *Crusader*. Another line was attached and the second trawler tried to tow the *Crusader* clear, but both lines snapped.

The coxswain had to act quickly. The water was so shallow and the trawler was in the surf with high-breaking seas all around, so he would only have one chance at a rescue attempt before the *Arctic Crusader* was beyond his reach. He went in and held the lifeboat alongside, but there was no sign of the crew. Then suddenly the trawler's engines started up and she headed back for harbour! The engineers had been in the engine room and the skipper had gone down to tell them to abandon ship just as they managed to coax the engines back to life. The lifeboat escorted the trawler into the harbour, but as she approached the pier her damaged engines seized and she hit the jetty. However, she was tied up safely and the lifeboat was able to rehouse, ready for her next call.

Wick is the other station on the northern coast of the mainland, and Coxswain Walter McPhee's awards reflect the diversity of this lifeboat's work. He won praise for his high standards of seamanship and leadership when the P&O ferry *St Rognvald* was damaged by a severe storm in 1991. A wave had crashed into her wheelhouse, smashing the windows, seriously injuring the captain and knocking out the steering, radios and compass. The ferry was left circling at 12 knots off Duncansby Head in the storm.

Winds were over force 10, seas some 35 feet high. The ferry's only working radio was a hand-held set, so communication was very limited. For nine hours Walter McPhee passed instructions, based on his enormous local knowledge, to the acting master of the ferry, keeping him in safe waters until temporary repairs had been made and she was escorted to safety. The injured captain made a special point of personally presenting Walter McPhee with his RNLI bravery commendation.

The following year a small fishing boat, *Wavedancer*, ran aground on

Wick lifeboatmen launch their inflatable boat to reach the two survivors stranded on the rocks by their boat Wavedancer.

rocks two miles north of Wick, and the two men of her crew were standing on the rocks, without lifejackets. The lifeboat launched her inflatable and Second Coxswain Ian Cormack reached the men and persuaded them to don lifejackets. A line was passed and one man was washed into the sea; fortunately he was now wearing the lifejacket, so he got back on board safely.

However, as the boat cleared the rocks she suddenly sank and the men were quickly swept away by the tide. The coxswain shouted at them to swim clear of the rocks then, dodging the wreckage, ropes and treacherous rocks, he took the lifeboat round and got Ian Cormack back into the inflatable. One fisherman managed to grab the inflatable's oar and was pulled to safety. The other man had been thrown back on to the rocks and Ian Cormack managed to reach him and take him back to the lifeboat. Both survivors were suffering from cold and shock and were wrapped in blankets. Back on shore an ambulance was waiting for them and whisked them to hospital; by the evening they were fully recovered.

Services in 1993 were just as varied. In April the lifeboat towed a 450-ton cargo vessel to safety after her engines failed and the tide swept her northwards. Then in May there was a tragedy to deal with.

A helicopter had spotted a boat going round in circles, and the lifeboat was called out to investigate just before midnight. She found the yacht *Stardust* motoring round at full speed with a body being dragged behind on a safety line. In the storm and high seas it was impossible to get a man on to the careering yacht, so the coxswain came up with an ingenious solution – he told the crew to throw a rope into the sea and drift it down so that it snagged *Stardust*'s propeller. This was no easy task in the rough seas, but after several tries they succeeded and the yacht's engine finally stopped. It was still not safe to board, so the rope was used to tow the yacht back to Wick where the body of the owner was taken ashore. His family gave the large collection taken at his funeral to the RNLI.

THE ORKNEYS

Across the Pentland Firth from Thurso and Wick are the Orkney Islands. Three lifeboats guard the islands, at **Kirkwall, Longhope** and **Stromness**.

Kirkwall is the youngest station, once the base of a cruising 70-foot lifeboat that had to cover a huge area of the north-east coast of Scotland. The idea of a cruising lifeboat was copied from the Norwegians who for many years had one of their own lifeboats based at Lerwick, available to sail out to their fishing fleets and stay at sea for several days at a time. The idea never really worked for the RNLI, although the lifeboat was much liked by her crew and was eventually sold to Iceland, where she serves as the Reykjavik lifeboat.

For many years Kirkwall's coxswain was sea captain William Sinclair. He had served in the Merchant Navy, as a pilot on the River Ribble, and took over from his father as the Kirkwall harbourmaster. He reached

The Kirkwall lifeboat stands by as a coaster sinks .

lifeboat retirement age of 55 in 1988, and was just able to see in the new
Arun Class lifeboat before he handed over to a younger man.

After just six weeks on station the new lifeboat was called out for the
first time in anger. It was William Sinclair's last mission and he was to
save another sea captain, the chief engineer – and his ship.

The engines of the 500-ton bulk cement carrier *Mercurious* had failed
and the ship was drifting slowly towards the shore. A coastguard
helicopter had lifted off four of the crew, but the captain and chief
engineer stayed on board, hoping to save their ship. The winds were
increasing and the waves were up to 20 feet high, but the lifeboat kept up
full speed, arriving at the scene to find the 160-foot coaster in desperate
danger. She was rolling heavily, waves were breaking over her and she
was now only 800 yards from the shore, where a party of auxiliary
coastguards were ready if she struck. To take the men off in these
conditions would be very difficult, and anyway the captain still thought
that his ship could be saved.

William Sinclair was taking no chances. He went in close to the
Mercurious to see how she was drifting, ready to snatch the two men if
necessary. A tug was on her way, so he decided to wait. But within half an
hour things were getting too close for comfort. The ship was now only
400 yards off the rocks, the rescue helicopter was refuelling at Kirkwall,
and the tug was still miles away. The lifeboat had to move in.

In a carefully judged manoeuvre, he took the lifeboat alongside the
coaster. A line was passed, then a strong rope hauled across and the tow
began. Another hundred yards had been lost and the 30-ton lifeboat now
strained to pull the coaster, three times its length and almost 20 times its
weight. The two vessels were bucking and ranging in the rough seas and
after 15 minutes the rope snapped, leaving the coaster to drift shorewards
once more.

A second rope was attached and slowly the lifeboat edged the coaster
out to sea. After ten minutes the tension became too much, and once
again the rope snapped. For a third time the lifeboat closed in, passed a

rope and this time managed to get the coaster into deep enough water to anchor 800 yards offshore. For the first agonising minutes it all seemed in vain as the anchor slipped across the sea bed, but then it held and the ship was safe. It was another two and a half hours before the tug arrived and the lifeboat stood by throughout, the sea captain in Sinclair proud to return to the harbour and add to the record of the Kirkwall lifeboat, 'saved ship and two persons'.

Long distances distinguish many of the lifeboat rescues of the Far North. A **Stromness** rescue in 1922 was hailed as an example of the capabilities of motor lifeboats.

It was still relatively early days for engines in lifeboats, so the rescue of nine trawlermen, stranded just off Sanday, was noted not only for the 114 miles travelled in 14 hours, but also for the fact that '. . . it is a notable feature of the service that the engine ran for the whole time without stopping and gave no trouble at all – splendid proof of the care taken of it'. Splendid indeed, though nowadays it is taken for granted that lifeboats will be well maintained.

One of the most bizarre rescues at Stromness was another long-distance job, but the ship in trouble was a replica 12th-century Hebridean longboat. *Aileach* was sturdily built and was making good progress on her passage from Stornoway to Faroe, symbolising a link that goes back to Viking days. The weather was not too bad – a force 7 wind and long deep swell in the open waters. However, some 40 miles north of Cape Wrath *Aileach*'s steering gear broke. Her crew rigged up a temporary repair but this too soon broke, and they put out a call for help.

Out went the Stromness lifeboat, 70 miles, to find *Aileach* helpless but

The Stornoway lifeboat comes to the aid of the replica Viking longship Aileach.

safe. In the middle of the wide open ocean, the lifeboat's 12-foot inflatable was launched to take a rope to the *Aileach*. The three vessels together – 12th and 20th-centuries combined – made a strange sight, but there was only a helicopter crew to witness the scene so far from the land. By the late evening, 11 hours after setting out, the lifeboat had got the longboat to the safety of Stromness.

SHETLAND

Northernmost of all RNLI stations is **Aith,** on the same latitude as Oslo, and 800 miles from the most southerly station in Jersey. The work could hardly be more different. Lifeboats in the English Channel are busy, averaging 30 to 50 launches a year, and deal mainly with pleasure craft, switching to fishing boats and ships when the weather deteriorates. In Shetland the lifeboats are much less busy, with maybe only a dozen calls a year. However, when they do go out it is usually in fierce storms when even the huge Russian factory ships, the 'klondikers', run into trouble.

Hylton Henry took over as coxswain from his father, Kenny, who had held the post for 19 years. Hylton's first lifeboat rescue was when he was 16; now aged 31, he has 15 years of lifeboat experience under his belt. Brother Kevin is the lifeboat mechanic, and their younger brother was also on the crew until he moved from the area, for work is hard to find in the tiny community.

If the family worries about so many of their men being on the crew, they keep it quiet. For, as Hylton says, most people in Shetland have a great respect for the sea and for the lifeboat. In Aith there are only about 200 inhabitants.

'I've never tried counting them but it's a very small area. We have 20 on the crew list. They say there are more sheep than people, 6,000 of them.'

The remoteness is emphasised by the vast area covered by Aith lifeboat. 'We cover 10,000 square miles of sea. We rarely see another lifeboat. Lerwick is 25 miles by road but 75 miles by sea.'

Yet on the day that over 1,000 small ships and boats gathered in the Solent for the D Day commemorations in 1994, with no mishaps, four Orkney and Shetland lifeboats were out searching for a lone canoeist.

'We get some strange jobs,' agrees Hylton. 'We had one chap who we used to get called out to a lot. He lived on a small island and used to come across to get drunk. He'd stay for three or four days, then head back and fall asleep half way across. Once he slipped to the floor of his boat and it started going round in circles. The lifeboat and helicopter were called out and the winchman dropped in to wake him up, which is really an expensive early morning call!'

Aith's southern neighbour on Shetland, **Lerwick,** has its work summed up by headlines: '31 passengers rescued from ferry aground on rocks.' 'Crew snatched to safety as fishing boat sinks during salvage attempt.'

'Lifeboat rescues 33 from grounded ship in gales and darkness.' '11 men and fishing vessel saved in winds gusting to 90 knots.'

Hewitt Clark is the man who has led all these rescues, a superb seaman, soft-spoken like all Shetlanders, and a man held in great respect in the RNLI. Hewitt joined the lifeboat crew in 1965 aged 20, and became coxswain in 1979. Married with three children, he also works part time as the skipper of the Lerwick harbour pilot boat.

His son, Neil, is also a lifeboatman, and his brother William is the second coxswain. If it all seems to be a family affair, then it is conducted with good humour, for when Hewitt was away in New Zealand with his wife Margaret to celebrate their silver wedding anniversary, it was William who took command of the lifeboat in a rescue that won him a Bronze Medal. For the inquisitive it seemed an obvious question to ask whether Hewitt had not been just slightly annoyed to have missed such a rescue, but for the brothers there was no jealousy, just a job to be done.

Hewitt's record, a Silver and three Bronze bravery medals to date, is based on hard rescues in storms, from large ships and fishing boats. This is traditional lifeboat work, where skill and courage combine to beat the sea. But every lifeboat coxswain knows that each victory will be matched by a loss, the sea taking its revenge to show it can never be conquered. The accolades come for the successes. Yet the same effort is spent, the same long cold hours at the wheel, searching for missing people who are

In force 11 gales, the Lerwick lifeboat crew check the empty liferaft from the fishing vessel Premier. *No survivors were found.*

never found. The same crew is drenched with salt spray until their eyes sting and their hands become raw as they turn for home with only bodies or, worse, with nothing at all.

Lerwick men have had their share of disappointments, like searching for hours in gale-force winds for the crew of the fishing boat *Premier*, or looking for survivors from a ditched helicopter, in both cases coming home empty-handed. Still they remain ever alert, awaiting the next call.

THE HEBRIDES

The Orkneys, Shetlands and Hebrides are so exposed that in the worst of weathers their boats and their men have to face almost unimaginable hardships. Hurricane-force winds blow at over 70 mph, the effect of facing them being like standing on top of a car going full speed down a motorway. Throw in driving salt spray and pouring rain for good measure. Now put the car on a roller coaster and you are just beginning to get close to being on the foredeck of a lifeboat.

These were the conditions faced by the men of **Stornoway** one February evening in 1989, so harsh that just to breathe they had to turn their faces downwind. A crabber was being overwhelmed in the storm and the lifeboat went to her help. Getting to her was difficult enough as the lifeboat was continually knocked off course. In the steep 15-foot seas and swell, 30 tons of lifeboat could have smashed the crabber to pieces. Yet so precise was Coxswain Malcolm MacDonald's control that the lifeboat edged alongside the small boat close enough for the crew to grab a man, but without the two vessels even touching. The lifeboatmen on the foredeck, their lifelines secured, were flung into the rails and badly bruised as they tried to persuade a second man, in a state of shock, to leave the tiny wheelhouse of the crabber.

As Malcolm MacDonald fought to keep the lifeboat close in, both vessels were covered by the driving spray and were awash with solid green water. Eventually the man ventured out on to the deck and, losing no time, the lifeboatmen hauled him aboard. In a piece of understatement typical of these parts, it was said that the return passage to Stornoway was made at reduced speed 'to avoid severe motion for the sake of the survivors'. Just to be alive might be thought enough!

Across the water on mainland Sutherland are wild beautiful mountains with golden eagles and red deer. There are few towns or villages and for those who know its secret, this untamed wilderness provides a magnificent solitude. The coastline is also rugged, and had no lifeboat cover except from Stornoway until a station was opened at **Lochinver** in 1967.

Until then the Stornoway lifeboat was having to cross the Minch, 30 miles of water, and, battling against a gale, she often arrived too late. Various places were suggested for the new boat, Kinlochbervie, Ullapool, even down as far as the **Kyle of Lochalsh** (which got an inshore lifeboat

Left: Lochinver's Arun Class lifeboat Murray Lornie.

in 1995), but Lochinver was chosen for its combination of a good harbour with ready access to the sea and a big enough population to provide a lifeboat crew.

Fishing is an important part of the local economy and Coxswain Neil Gudgeon is an agent for the local fish industry. One of the big businesses is from French boats that fish further out than the locals and catch species that are unpopular on the UK market but delicacies in France. Every day huge freezer lorries set out from Lochinver for the RNLI's headquarters town of Poole in Dorset where they take the ferry to Cherbourg, then drive on to L'Orient, where the fish are on the market within 48 hours of being landed. Neil Gudgeon has fishermen on his crew, together with a garage owner, hotelier and pottery proprietor.

Lifeboat cover around the Inner Hebrides and on the beautiful West Coast of the mainland has ebbed and flowed like the tides. Until 1938 lifeboat stations were thinly scattered, then one was opened at **Tobermory** on Mull, which was judged 'the only practicable location on this part of the coast'. It was not a very good judgement as the station had to be closed nine years later due to lack of crew members, and a new station was opened at the busy fishing port of **Mallaig** on the mainland.

A rescue of a fishing boat brought a Bronze Medal for Mallaig Coxswain Tommy Ralston in 1988. In force 11 winds and total darkness, he had to take his lifeboat in amongst submerged rocks, bow first to keep his propellers in the deepest water. By the time he reached the disabled fishing boat she was only 20 feet from the shore, virtually invisible in the driving spray. The crew were already tied on with lifelines, which was just as well, as lifeboatman George Laurie had been swept overboard as the lifeboat left Mallaig harbour and had only been saved by his lifeline.

Now, as Tommy Ralston edged towards the fishing boat, the crew stood poised on the foredeck and one man monitored the radar to try and seek out the shadowy rocks. A towline was passed by hand and the boat dragged clear, but it was not until he was 600 feet from the shore and finally clear of the rocks that Tommy Ralston transferred the tow from the bow to the stern and took the boat to safety. Even then it was too

Opposite: The Tobermory lifeboat, Ralph and Joy Swann, *in 1990.*

dangerous to enter Mallaig harbour with the tow, so he headed north for Inverie.

INVENTORS

Nothing stands still in the lifeboat service, and further cover was provided by an inshore lifeboat at **Oban**, later changed to a Brede Class. Not being content with lifesaving, the crew at Oban decided to try their hands as inventors. When their lifeboat is in the thick of a rescue, all the crew tend to be fully occupied and the key task of writing down the radio messages is often impossible. Yet an accurate radio log, with exact messages and times, is not only a legal requirement but also can form evidence in an enquiry. So how could the log be kept on a small fast-moving lifeboat with a crew of four or five?

Pat Maclean, the Oban coxswain, had chewed over the problem with his crew until he and Gordon Murchison, the local doctor and a crew member, came up with a solution that was low-tech and, as Pat later said, 'blindingly simple'. A stereo tape recorder could be used to record all incoming and outgoing messages on one track and the time on the other. Another of the crew, Malcolm Robertson, is the local marine electronics engineer, so Pat asked him whether the theory could be put into practice. A Sunday in his workshop with a tape recorder, a speaking clock (cost £14.50) and some bits and pieces produced the answer. Like any new delivery, it needed a name. Dr Eleanor Wilson, wife of another doctor on the crew, came up with VITAL (voice initiated timed automated log). VITAL is now on trial with the RNLI and has already taken a runners-up prize in the prestigious Silk Cut nautical awards.

Meanwhile, Pat and the doctors are kept busy, often evacuating sick people from remote places. Heart attack victim Bob Fraser, who lives a good 50 miles by road from Oban on Morvern peninsula, was taken some 12 miles across the loch to hospital the night he was taken ill. His remote cottage is half a mile off the road and the lifeboatmen approached from the sea, tied him into a stretcher and took him off the rocky shore in an inflatable to reach the lifeboat.

The RNLI came full circle when it re-opened the **Tobermory** station in 1990. Fish farming, inshore fishing and increasing pleasure cruising in these magnificent waters had led to more casualties in the area, and a new crew was found without any difficulty. A year later another gap in cover was plugged when Skye got a lifeboat at **Portree**.

THE MULL OF KINTYRE

Paul McCartney made the Mull of Kintyre famous with his song, which romantically describes the mist rolling in from the sea. It is not so romantic when the mist turns to thick fog and you are lost in it. Even with modern navigation equipment, fog is something lifeboatmen dread. It is disorienting and dangerous when searches have to be made in rocky areas, and the eerie silence it produces can muffle sounds so that only a wake will reveal the presence of another boat, perhaps unnervingly close.

Radar is a blessing at such a time, but the **Campbeltown** lifeboat was having hers repaired when a call came one foggy night in July 1991 from a yacht, unsure of its position and running low on fuel. The crew could not see from one end of the boat to the other and could see precious little from the foredeck. The acting coxswain, John Stewart, steered from the outside position above the cabin, guided by Robert Galbraith monitoring the echo-sounder and Decca navigator. A general radio broadcast had to be made to say that the lifeboat was proceeding at speed and without radar. Then the Decca navigator started to play up, leaving only the echo-sounder to tell the coxswain if he was safe.

When the lifeboat approached the yacht's reported position, she was able to make radio contact. The yachtsmen said they would continue sailing towards Troon but the coastguard wisely intervened and asked the lifeboat to take them in tow. When lifeboatman David Cox boarded the yacht, he found the men exhausted and confused, though still insisting that they would carry on. Using either diplomacy or a lifeboatman's bluff charm, he persuaded them that a tow from the lifeboat would be better; they accepted. The Campbeltown lifeboat started the tow and handed over to the inshore lifeboat from **Arran**, which got the yacht safely to Lamlash at 3.40 in the morning.

A much more treacherous tow had taken place ten years earlier. A Spanish trawler, the *Erlo Hills*, was reported aground on the west side of the Mull of Kintyre. In fact, she was on Rathlin Island off the North Irish coast, and the Campbeltown lifeboat found her there with the coaster *Ceol Mor* standing by. A long game of cat and mouse then started.

The lifeboat passed a tow rope between the two ships and, after a struggle, the *Ceol Mor* managed to tow the trawler clear. *Ceol Mor* was low on fuel and set out for port, but soon *Erlo Hills* was in trouble again.

Alex Gilchrist was the lifeboat coxswain. He recalls, 'She started to steam round in circles, getting closer all the time. Her engine had stopped, her rudder had swung right round and her propeller had gone into it. I said, "Maybe you had better come off now", but they replied, "No, we want a tow".' The *Erlo Hills* was a 350-ton ship, the Arun Class lifeboat less than a tenth of that weight. Further, the trawler was only 200 yards from the shore. A first hurried attempt failed as the tow rope pulled through. The second tow held but Alex Gilchrist no longer had full control of his lifeboat.

'I could not get her up into the wind at all. When I crossed the sea she was rolling pretty badly, but she felt OK. The trawler would drop down the back of a wave and the tow start to snatch and pull the lifeboat away by the stern. It was none too good.'

In fact, it was so bad that the lifeboat almost capsized. As soon as he felt they were far enough from the land, Alex slipped the tow and asked the *Ceol Mor* to come back. She did, but now the Spanish fishermen would neither come off nor take a tow; they said there was a Spanish ship on the way that would help them. Having wasted three hours, *Ceol Mor* was now desperately short of fuel and had to leave again.

The trawlermen called up Spain, the Channel Islands, any number of people, trying to organise help. Eventually they decided they would take a tow. Gilchrist asked the *Ceol Mor* to come back yet again. Amazingly, the skipper agreed, though on the condition that he would tow the trawler only to the shelter of a nearby bay.

The lifeboat and trawler were now in a force 10 gale and being pushed along at six knots in a tidal race. The lifeboat had to try to get a rope between the two ships.

'We tried four times to get the tow rope alongside *Ceol Mor*. It meant getting close alongside the trawler, coming down to *Ceol Mor* and manoeuvring my stern up into the stern of the coaster. Her stern would come up and her propeller come out of the water. After a while I began to worry that the slack rope would get washed round her prop and we would drift under her stern. It was no use.'

The situation was now desperate. The lifeboatmen could see the coaster's propeller above their heads as they approached her and risked their boat being smashed to pieces. Then the captain of *Ceol Mor* said that he could stay no longer; he was imperiling his own ship as he ran out of fuel. He had to leave.

Coxswain Gilchrist did not ask the fishermen this time – he told them, 'You're coming off'. His own account makes it sound so easy, yet this was in gale-force winds and huge seas.

'All our fenders were out. We approached. They were all in the wheelhouse. One of them came out and started to go for the stern. I swung the lifeboat's bow round to try to get in, but as the lifeboat came up he got frightened and moved clear. So I swung back round and came up at the waist of the trawler. One or two of the crew began to come out and as we rose up beside the trawler the boys would pull them off. After 20 minutes we got the whole lot of them off.'

The *Erlo Hills* was later driven ashore by the storm and wrecked. Alex Gilchrist was awarded the RNLI's Silver Medal for his outstanding bravery and superb seamanship. And the long-suffering master of the *Ceol Mor*, Captain Hamilton Nixon, was awarded a special certificate by the RNLI for the tremendous efforts and considerable seamanship he showed in the rescue.

FIRTH OF CLYDE

Not all lifeboat rescues take place in storms, but most involve boats. Up at the top end of the Firth of Clyde the lifeboat station at **Helensburgh** has made over 800 rescues, the most unusual of all being to a mechanical digger stuck in the mud off Port Glasgow, bogged down by the rising tide.

Helensburgh's Atlantic 21 lifeboat covered the seven miles to the scene in just over a quarter of an hour, but by the time she arrived only the cab and the tips of the shovel were showing above the water. The digger was surrounded by the timber piles on which it had been working, and by manoeuvring her way carefully between them, the lifeboat was able to rescue the driver and land him at Port Glasgow.

In addition to Helensburgh, three other stations in the Clyde provide inshore cover, at **Tighnabruaich, Arran** and **Largs**. The lifeboat at **Arran** has a special road trailer so that she can be launched on either side of the Isle of Arran. At **Tighnabruaich** the lifeboat provides cover for the Kyles of Bute and Loch Fyne, popular cruising areas. And **Largs**, Scotland's first inshore lifeboat station, has clocked up almost a thousand rescues and saved over 300 lives.

Troon is the all-weather lifeboat station guarding the approaches to the Clyde. The station suffered a shock in 1953 when a tradition was almost literally shattered. A bottle of rum had been carried, its seal intact, for 16 years in two successive Troon lifeboats. The bottle was beginning to take on the characteristics of a talisman when, on an exercise, an American airman who was to be winched up into a helicopter was accidentally knocked out. Common sense prevailed and the bottle was opened for medicinal purposes, though the record does not say whether the airman or the lifeboatmen benefited from the contents.

Today's coxswain at Troon is Ian Johnson who has been at the helm for 16 years. He has an impressive collection of awards, one for his 'cool professional control of a rescue in difficult conditions', another praising him and the crew for their 'fine display of teamwork'. All these qualities were tested in September 1979 when a dredger was in danger of being driven ashore in a storm and the lifeboat had to go close in, while avoiding five anchor cables. The dredger was tossing and bucking in the force 10 gale with only one of the cables actually holding her. Johnson's recollection plays down the dangers.

'If that wire had parted we would definitely have been in a little bit of a sticky situation. The dredger would have carried across and we would have got the bow wire right up in our propellers.'

As he approached the dredger he could see her crew in the cabin as the rest of the ship was awash with water.

'I had to stand off a wee minute and think just exactly what was going to be done. We had to go in at an angle to keep the propeller clear of the anchor wire, and we got one man off. By this time the dredger was rising and falling 12 to 15 feet and we came down pretty heavily on one of her stanchions and bounced back off again. After that we managed to take three more off, but when the fifth man was asked to jump, he froze, so he was literally just grabbed by the scruff of the neck and hauled aboard. In that wild sea I wasn't going to take the chance of going back across the same shallows I had come over on the way out, so I set my course to seaward to clear the heavy surf. Coming back to harbour full power was required to get through the breakers. And that was about it.'

SOUTH WEST SCOTLAND

Girvan's history contains this wonderful entry: '1898. Institution's thanks were awarded to Mr McKenna, postmaster of Girvan, and Mr Lawson for riding a tandem from Girvan to Ballantrae, a distance of 13 miles, giving information of a vessel in distress as the telegraph system had broken down. The cyclists arrived at 3 o'clock in the morning covered in mud and soaked by rain.'

The **Ballantrae** lifeboat put out with the honorary secretary, a bank manager, in command as the coxswain was away. On the same day the Girvan lifeboat went out with one of the committee, a solicitor, making up the numbers due to a shortage of crew.

The station's history also shows how the RNLI gathers its support from very diverse sources. The first lifeboat was the gift of a wealthy individual. Then came *James Stevens No 18*, one of 20 lifeboats provided by the will of a Birmingham man. More recently Girvan has had *St Andrew (Civil Service No 10)*, a gift of the Civil Service Lifeboat Fund, the RNLI's single biggest supporter over the years. A legacy from Elizabeth Vaux provided the lifeboat *Philip Vaux*, named in memory of her late husband who had been the chief inspector of lifeboats from 1939 to 1951. This was followed by the *Amateur Swimming Associations*, a slightly cumbersome name but a tribute to hundreds of swimmers who raised the money to buy her. Finally, today's Girvan lifeboat is the Mersey Class *Silvia Burrell*, from the legacy of one of the Glasgow shipping family that funded the internationally famous Burrell art collection.

The Portpatrick lifeboat tackles a yacht on fire.

For a short period Girvan had a Northern Irishman, Robert Erskine, on the crew. He had been a lifeboatman at Donaghadee, served on the Girvan lifeboat for two years, then became coxswain at **Portpatrick,** where he is today. The links between South West Scotland and Northern Ireland, with the Stranraer to Larne ferry, are obvious, and it was the loss of one of those ferries in 1953 that sent the **Portpatrick** and **Donaghadee** lifeboats out on a combined search, which is described later in the book.

Not surprisingly with Robbie at the helm, Portpatrick and Donaghadee have close ties, although it was a slight surprise to a bleary eyed Salcombe lifeboatman, recovering from the previous night's hospitality, when on the day of the naming of the new Portpatrick lifeboat, he looked up and imagined he could see a lifeboat appearing over the horizon. It was, of course, the Donaghadee boat, coming to celebrate the naming at Portpatrick.

Stranraer has an inshore lifeboat, busy enough with pleasure craft but clocking up a first in 1984 when the crew rescued a Volkswagen 'Beetle'. The car had been converted for a televised attempt to cross the Irish Sea to Larne. However, a stiff breeze was blowing as the car put out into Loch Ryan and its engine failed. It was drifting helplessly and the Stranraer lifeboat, out on a regular Sunday exercise, was soon on the scene to attach a towrope. Safely back at Wig Bay slipway, the car drivers dried out their floating Beetle and tried again in the afternoon, with the same result and another tow back to the shore.

Around the Mull of Galloway on the north of the Solway Firth are two further inshore lifeboats. The **Kirkcudbright** station has a story from the First World War when men from the town were lined up in front of a recruiting sergeant. When asked his religion, one man answered without hesitation, 'RNLI, Sir'.

The Stranraer inshore lifeboat tows in a Volkswagen `Beetle'!

Unfortunately, the boathouse is over two miles from the town and, although attempts have been made to find a better site, the crew still have to start their rescues with a Land-Rover journey through woods.

At neighbouring **Kippford** the crew were amazed at the fickleness of a windsurfer they went out to rescue. As the inshore lifeboat left the shelter of the shore, she encountered force 7 winds, enough to make the waves swamp it. The windsurfer was in the water and would not have lasted long. A helicopter arrived at the same time as the lifeboat so it took the man to safety, then escorted the lifeboat back to her station. As soon as he reached dry land, the windsurfer made a miraculous recovery and decided that he had not been in any real danger. He even had the gall to write a letter of complaint to the local paper because his surfboard had not been saved!

SOUTH EAST SCOTLAND

A harbour is defined in the Oxford Dictionary as 'a place of shelter for ships'. Once in a harbour, while safety is not guaranteed, at least the chances of survival are greatly improved. But it is the mission of the lifeboat to leave the harbour when all others are seeking shelter, encapsulated in the old lifeboatman's saying, 'Drown you may; go you must'. And the going can, as they say, be rough.

At **Eyemouth** the harbour is indeed a safe haven. But the entrance is difficult and narrow and in bad weather the port is closed to shipping. In October 1992 it had been closed for two days when the coastguard received a call from the Tyne pilot launch *Norman Foster*; she had broken down in a force 9 gale and urgently needed help.

At Eyemouth conditions could hardly have been worse for launching. Spring tides meant very little depth at low water, which was only an hour away. There was just over four feet depth in the entrance channel for a lifeboat with a 4 ft 2 in draft. To make matters worse the River Eye was in full spate and a 40 mph wind was churning up the shallow water in the entrance. Not for nothing do the locals call it 'the canyon'.

The Eyemouth lifeboat enters 'the canyon'.

John Johnston, the lifeboat coxswain, had no time to lose if he was to get to sea, so he headed out, aiming for the deepest water by the training bank, at times with only two feet between it and his boat. On reaching the pier head the lifeboat started to bounce on the sandy seabed, then was hit by the breaking seas. Finally she reached deeper water.

With the greatest danger now over, more skill was needed to tow the pilot boat to safety. After talking to the coastguard, Coxswain Johnston agreed that Torness was too dangerous to enter, so he had to tow the boat for three hours to reach Port Seaton inside the Firth of Forth. After a brief rest, the crew set out again for Eyemouth. Even with deeper water the harbour entrance was still impassable, and the lifeboatmen faced the galling prospect, having already been 30 miles north, of now going past home to the south to find safety at Burnmouth. The lifeboat tied up there overnight and was taken back to Eyemouth the following day.

Two years before, the Eyemouth lifeboat had been involved in a similar coastal chase. A sudden change in the weather caught four skin-divers at sea, and the Eyemouth and Dunbar lifeboats launched. Leaving Eyemouth was again very difficult, for this time high tides made the waves crash over the sea walls, and at times the lifeboat was barely controllable. Visibility was down to about 60 yards and a remarkable piece of co-operation, backed by blind faith, between coastguard and coxswain took place off St Abbs.

The coastguard had spotted two divers, then lost them in the spray. He could not see the lifeboat, but picked out the beam of the searchlight and, with that as his only reference, guided the boat to the divers. Sixty yards from the lifeboat on either side were rocks, invisible to eye and radar in the heavy spray.

After three attempts the lifeboat got alongside the divers who were clinging to a creel buoy. The search went on for the other two, but the survivors were suffering from hypothermia and sickness. A helicopter tried to lift them off and had to abandon the attempt because of the extreme conditions.

Now the harbour-hop began. St Abbs was very close, but unsafe. Eyemouth was also too dangerous. Once again Burnmouth was tried. There the harbour lights had been extinguished by a power cut, so car headlights were used to guide the lifeboat in and land the survivors.

The other lifeboat out that day was from Dunbar. For them, too, setting out was extremely dangerous. When the lifeboat launched from the harbour the wind there was hurricane force, gusting to 100 mph and blowing straight across the harbour entrance from the north. Huge seas were breaking on to the harbour walls and the lifeboat inspector, Tony Course, later wrote, 'The crew's response was in the highest tradition of the lifeboat service. All knew they would have to pass through a maelstrom and that they would have to rely on the seamanship of their coxswain to reach the relative safety of open water; there would be no second chance in conditions which were described as the worst in living memory.'

The lifeboat was hit by a huge sea as she left the harbour and Coxswain Robert Wight had to struggle to control his boat as she rolled through the narrow channel between the rocks. Only when he had headed into the storm for three miles did he dare to make the dangerous turn to head south-east towards the divers.

Joining in the search, the lifeboat was still in considerable danger, going close inshore in the gale and the dark to try to find the divers. When the coastguard called off the search, the Dunbar lifeboat joined the Eyemouth boat in Burnmouth, the only 'place of shelter for ships' that the Forth could provide that night.

The other lifeboat stations on the south of the Forth approaches have inshore lifeboats. At **Queensferry** the lifeboat station sits virtually under the Forth Bridge and has as one of its less pleasant duties the task of searching for people who have committed suicide by jumping from the bridge.

North Berwick is best known as a Blue Peter lifeboat station, being one of the first selected by the BBC children's television programme to benefit from their appeal for the RNLI in 1966. Ever since then the inflatable lifeboats at North Berwick and all the other Blue Peter stations have been provided by Blue Peter viewers and the programme has followed their exploits.

At **St Abbs**, between Dunbar and Eyemouth, there is now an Atlantic 21 inshore lifeboat that replaced the Oakley lifeboat *Jane Hay*. This boat was named after the woman who had led an appeal by local people for a lifeboat in the town after all 17 hands from a steamship had perished off St Abbs in 1907. The passage of the *Jane Hay* to her station was full of incident.

It started innocently enough, but as the lifeboat steamed up the East Coast, thick fog set in. There was no radar on lifeboats in the early 1960s, so the lifeboat turned for the shore near Lowestoft and the engines were stopped to see if the crew could hear any fog signals. Nothing was heard, so they went in another 200 yards and stopped the engines again. Again,

Blue Peter III at North Berwick during *filming in 1994.*

there was no sound. The third time a dog barked, then there was the noise of lapping waves and people's voices. The crew shouted out and found that they were off a holiday camp to the south of the harbour entrance.

After an overnight stop they headed north and, on reaching Whitby in the dark, found that the propellers had become entangled with a salmon poacher's net. Bob Walton was the lifeboat inspector in charge of the passage; he recorded that 'A number of people appeared and helped to cut the net clear, disappearing very quickly once it was clear with nearly all the fish. The chairman and crew lunched well the next day.'

On the north of the Firth, inshore cover is provided at **Kinghorn**, a station that had the doubtful privilege of being built on top of a sewage plant. The inshore lifeboat finds itself busy with a few fishing boats, but mainly with pleasure craft and missing or stranded people, and when the crew were told of plans to replace the boat with a bigger one, needing a bigger boathouse, they readily agreed with the RNLI plan to relocate the station to the other side of the bay, away from the smells.

NORTH OF THE FORTH

Fife is a kingdom in its own right, and its ancient independence runs through the history of the **Anstruther** lifeboat station, remaining to this day. For the lifeboat is named *Kingdom of Fife* and was bought largely as a result of a local appeal. The station was set up at the request of local fishermen in 1865 and they subscribed £60 towards the cost, although a lady from Cheltenham bought the £600 lifeboat. A curious local arrangement was made whereby there were seven coxswains, each with his own crew, and all took their turn for rescues and practice launches.

There were problems summoning the crews, however, the original rocket signal being considered too dangerous to ships in the harbour. It was replaced by a mortar, but only three years later this was removed and a handbell substituted. It must have been a very big bell! The number of coxswains had been reduced to four by 1899, and the station finally came into line in 1903 with one coxswain only, rather grandly described as coxswain superintendent.

The current honorary secretary, Peter Murray, is a joiner and also the town's undertaker. He took over when he retired as coxswain and, in spite of much joking, mostly from Peter himself, nobody has accused him of a conflict of interests in saving some people and burying others!

Anstruther exported their mechanic to become the coxswain at **Broughty Ferry**, the lifeboat station near Dundee at the mouth of the Tay. The inshore lifeboat often gets called to 'jumpers', people who are about to try, or have already tried, to take their lives from the Tay Bridge. The Arun lifeboat has a varied life, as shown by a service giving very practical if low-key help to a grounded tug on the Gaa Sands, five miles from the station.

The Broughty Ferry lifeboat and a helicopter assist the tug Defiant.

The tug *Defiant* had run aground and one of the crew was in a state of severe distress. Because of the shallow water the lifeboat could not get close enough to take the men off, so a helicopter was called. The ill man was duly taken off and the master and mechanic of the tug were also winched off and landed on the lifeboat. While the helicopter took the first man to hospital, the lifeboat waited for over two hours until the tug refloated on the tide, then put the two crew back on board. All was well and the lifeboat was able to return home, notching up another record of help to fellow seafarers.

NORTH-EAST HARBOURS

Scotland's oldest lifeboat stations form a group on the north-east coast, with **Montrose** having been established in 1800, **Aberdeen** in 1802 and **Arbroath** in 1803. All were set up by harbour boards before the RNLI had been formed, and all had boats built by Henry Greathead, builder of the world's first lifeboat

The links between harbour authorities and lifeboats remain strong in Scotland. In many ports the job of lifeboat secretary is an unpaid extra that the harbourmaster is, by tradition, expected to assume. Most harbour authorities still regard the lifeboat as a public service, provided by the community for all seafarers, and charge peppercorn rents for lifeboat buildings and moorings. There is a workmanlike, rather than benevolent, relationship between harbour and lifeboat, a relationship that has been soured by commercialism in many other parts of the United Kingdom, where port and marina owners (and, in one case, even a golf club, whose course the crew have to cross to reach the lifeboat station) are happy to see what profit they can make out of the RNLI.

THE LONELIEST JOB

One of the loneliest jobs in the lifeboat team is that of the honorary secretary. The importance and yet isolation of this role was epitomised by a situation facing David Chappell, hon sec at **Arbroath** in 1953. In October of that year the lifeboat had been called out after a report of red flares. It was later established that the flares were from a dredger that sank with all hands, in spite of extensive searches by the Arbroath and Anstruther lifeboats. David Chappell received a message from his lifeboat to say that she was returning to harbour, and suggested that she should instead make for Anstruther, as the conditions at the Arbroath harbour entrance were appalling. The coxswain replied that he would assess the situation when he reached the harbour mouth, and took the decision to come in, using his drogue.

Coastguards were on the pier with a line-firing pistol. The harbour entrance was a boiling cauldron as the gale blew against the tide and the backwash off the piers threw the seas into a wild confusion. As the lifeboat approached, suddenly her lights reversed, the red going over the green, then both disappeared. She had been hit by a huge cross sea and was capsized.

Instinctively the coastguard grabbed his pistol and, in desperation, fired into the darkness. By a miracle the line fell across Second Coxswain Archibald Smith who grabbed it and was hauled ashore. The rest of the crew, six men, were lost.

Within days a new crew had been formed and the station tried to get back to normal. Then, at 3 am one morning, another terrible storm hit the town; slates were rattling on roofs, trees were blown down. David Chappell was told that there was a coaster in trouble and the lifeboat was needed.

Down in the boathouse the crew were already gathering and a lot of the old fishermen and townsfolk were there, in two distinct factions. Some were saying 'If you go out tonight, you'll be dead', others 'You'll

The Arbroath lifeboat disaster of 1953, when six lifeboatmen died.

have to go, you owe it to the boys'. The new coxswain, Henry Smith, was in an impossible position. Straight away David Chappell knew where his duty lay. He called the coxswain over and made very sure that there were plenty of people within earshot. Then, in a loud voice, he told the coxswain, 'As honorary secretary, I am forbidding this boat to launch'. The coxswain protested, but Chappell repeated his order.

He was a man who had commanded troops in the war and had been decorated for his bravery, but he later recalled, 'I have never seen, even in the war years, such a look of relief come over a man's face. He was absolutely on a hiding to nothing. If he had gone and lost the boat, then he would have been damned. If he hadn't gone, he'd have been branded forever in a community that had just lost a crew, told he wasn't the man for the job. I took the weight off him.'

In **Montrose** the lifeboat secretary is another sea captain, Niall McNab, who has 32 years at sea under his belt. Having worked in commercial shipping, it came as a surprise to him to discover the care and attention given to the maintenance of RNLI boats.

'Our ships were time-chartered. If they weren't at sea, they weren't earning money, so we allowed ten days a year for maintenance. But the standards for lifeboats have to be exceptionally high if we want and expect volunteers to go out in them in any weather.'

Captain McNab does not worry about sending his crew to sea. 'I am not a natural worrier. We have a superb crew and I have every confidence in the coxswain, who has a mate's ticket, and in the lifeboat. Being a professional seaman means being sensible enough to know when to get frightened. I am sure there are times when multi-denominational prayer meetings are going on all over the boat.'

He always makes sure that he is there in the boathouse all the time that the lifeboat is out so that he can see the crew when they return. 'They appreciate that.'

Apart from anything else, it means that there is somebody to thank the crew. 'A lot of survivors are too embarrassed to say thank you, particularly if they are locals. We rely on help and support from the community and don't want to embarrass people. The fishermen mostly have well-found boats. If there's some chancer putting to sea in a

The Montrose lifeboat
Moonbeam.

motorised wash-basin, we'll pick up the pieces. I always tell the coxswain – we're here to help people. Nothing's too small. You don't hang around. You launch the lifeboat and sort out the paperwork afterwards.'

FISHING AND OIL

Fishing and oil exploration dominate the coastal economy of Scotland from Aberdeen right up to Orkney and Shetland. Inevitably, both industries make work for local lifeboats and over a third of Scottish lifeboat calls are to fishing vessels.

While fishing is in severe decline, harbours such as **Peterhead** still boast a healthy home fleet. Scotland's only Gold Medal this century was won at Peterhead.

Coxswain John Maclean and his crew had, in three days at sea in 1942, met heavy seas, blinding snow and winds up to 105 mph while they rescued 106 people from three separate ships. His namesake in 1987 won an award for his seamanship and devotion to duty when the lifeboat stood close by the fishing boat *Constant Star*, which had run aground.

There seemed to be nobody on the boat so the lifeboat started to search and found lifebelts and a liferaft, but no survivors. Instinct told the coxswain that he had to check the boat again. As the lifeboat approached, the crew could see signs of movement in the wheelhouse. The lifeboat called up a helicopter that had been on the search, and the fishermen were airlifted to safety. But for John Maclean's vigilance, the men would have been swept to their deaths by the huge seas battering their boat.

Up the coast at **Buckie**, the lifeboat coxswain, John Murray, used to be a fisherman. He joined the crew one night to make up the numbers and about six months later the coxswain invited him to become his deputy. Some of his crew also have fishing experience, while others now work on the oil rig standby boats. The lifeboat has some work from pleasure craft, some from fishing boats.

But according to John, 'The fishermen tend to look after themselves.

The Peterhead lifeboat puts out in January 1984 – storm force 10, 40-foot waves.

They don't want to bother us. There's an element of pride. They'll wait a couple of hours until someone else has taken up their gear, then ask them for help.'

The calls do come, though, and in August 1991 John Murray had one similar to John Maclean's Gold Medal rescue at Peterhead. The fishing vessel *Fidelity* had run aground at night on a dangerous reef near Buckie and was near to capsize. As the lifeboat set out it was reported that the fishermen were taking to their liferaft, so when a red flare was spotted and no survivors could be seen on the *Fidelity*, the coxswain assumed that they were in the liferaft. However, as the lifeboat trained its searchlight on the fishing vessel, the lifeboatmen spotted a flashing torch. The fishermen had only thought of getting into the liferaft, but had decided to stay with their boat when they heard the maroons calling out the lifeboat.

As the lifeboat approached, John Murray could see the fishing boat being lifted by the swell, in danger of turning over completely at any moment. Speed was of the essence. Normally he would have sent the lifeboat's inflatable across, but if the fishing boat capsized on top of her, the two lifeboatmen could be lost as well as the fishermen.

Murray knew these waters well. The *Fidelity* would have only about five feet of water under her. Taking the lifeboat in could damage his propellers, so he put the starboard engine in neutral and crept towards the *Fidelity* as slowly as he could, using his port engine to stop the swell pushing his lifeboat on to the rocks. He got within feet of the boat and his crew reached out and grabbed the fishermen as they lunged for the lifeboat's bow. The port engine was then coaxed into neutral and the lifeboat taken gingerly astern. Three times she struck the bottom as she edged out, but soon she was in deeper water and turned for harbour.

The whole rescue took only 27 minutes, from first alert to landing the three survivors, for John Murray had shown the age-old qualities of a lifeboat coxswain – superb seamanship and all-important local knowledge, combined with just a touch of daring.

Calls connected with oil exploration have involved supply ships, standby vessels, helicopters and rigs themselves. The **Invergordon** lifeboat was summoned to an unusual and gruesome accident in January 1992 when two men fell 120 feet trying to lower a small launch from an exploration drilling rig. The rig was anchored in the Cromarty Firth and the weather was calm as the men set about lowering the launch, but it slipped and plummeted down to the sea, hitting the surface with a massive force. The lifeboat took out the local doctor, not knowing what they would find.

They discovered the launch in the water, her keel split, taking in water, so they had to put a pump on board. It was dark and they used their searchlight and hand-held lights to illuminate the injured men as the doctor set about administering pain-killers. One man was trapped between the engine and the side of the launch. He had broken arms, legs and pelvis. In the confined space it was impossible to slide a stretcher under him, so the metal tubing trapping him was cut away and ropes were passed under him to lift him on to a stretcher.

Coxswain David Lipp recalls that the doctor had only given a limited amount of pain-killer lest the man lose consciousness. 'We just had to ignore his screams and get on with the job.'

The other man had already been taken off by a local work boat and, because of his broken limbs, he was not put on the lifeboat but taken straight ashore.

Invergordon sits on a huge firth and in 1993 a new inshore lifeboat was established at **North Kessock**, some 20 miles away and opposite Inverness, to cover the upper reaches of the firth.

SAVED − ONE HELICOPTER!

Aberdeen has seen almost all types of rescues, and while many medals have been won at the station for rescues from fishing boats in very rough seas, the station took a certain pride in towing in a ditched helicopter used to take men out to the oil rigs.

The helicopter had been returning from a rig in the Clyde field with 15 people on board and had to ditch in the sea 17 miles off Aberdeen. By the

The Aberdeen lifeboat tows in the ditched helicopter.

time the lifeboat arrived eight people had been lifted off by another helicopter and the remaining seven, who had taken to a liferaft, were safely aboard a nearby ship.

Lifeboatmen sometimes get annoyed at being 'beaten' to the rescue by helicopters, but now they could do something that no aircraft could – tow the stricken helicopter to land. A line was attached and flotation bags were supplied to ensure that she stayed afloat, then the slow, careful tow began. It took over five hours to get the helicopter back into Aberdeen Harbour, and there were broad grins on the faces of the crew when they arrived.

It was not, however, Aberdeen's strangest rescue. During floods in 1993 the inshore lifeboat was taken eight miles inland by road to a flooded caravan site where the River Dee had burst its banks and water was up to ten feet deep. The lifeboat took people off the top of their caravans, found a man and his dog lying on a partially submerged bed inside an isolated caravan and had to break a window to get him, found two cats floating on a settee, and a wild rabbit marooned on top of a fence post.

But nothing in the lifeboat service is new. During gales in 1937 the Dee flooded, causing widespread damage and isolating scores of buildings. The lifeboat was called out to rescue a woman and two men from a farmhouse; the coxswain took the lifeboat in stern first through the front door. The farmhouse is now included among the local landmarks pointed out on coach tours.

CHAPTER ELEVEN

Ireland – Hibernian future

'And the sea flint-flake, black-backed in the
regular blow,
Sitting Eastnortheast in cursed quarter, the wind;
Wiry and white-fiery and whirlwind-swivelled snow,
Spins to the widow-making unchilding
unfathering deeps.'

The Wreck of the Deutschland, *Gerard Manley Hopkins*

IRELAND POINTS THE way to the RNLI's future; in the last ten years more new lifeboat stations have been opened in Ireland than anywhere else, plugging gaps to help meet the comprehensive cover the RNLI is committed to provide. Modern all-weather and inshore lifeboats are strategically positioned at the new stations, some of which are in towns and villages that had their lifeboats withdrawn many years ago. And Ireland can also boast more female crew members than anywhere else in the RNLI.

Some people find it strange that a Royal Institution should work in the Republic just as it does throughout the United Kingdom, but the traditions of lifesaving go back just as far, the history of the stations is just as distinguished, the spirit of the crews and fundraisers is just the same as anywhere else in the British Isles. Political divides play no part in the straightforward humanitarian task of the lifeboat service. Lifeboats from Ireland frequently join boats from Scotland, the Isle of Man or Wales on searches in the Irish Sea, all using the same procedures, training and equipment.

Far more unusual is the lead that Ireland has taken in appointing women to lifeboat crews. Elizabeth Hostvedt at Atlantic College has already been mentioned as the first female crew member of modern times, but the barrier to recruiting a woman to an all-weather lifeboat crew only fell in 1981, when Frances Glody joined the **Dunmore East** boat.

Frances was no stranger to the sea. She held a trawler skipper's licence and became the port's radio operator, taking over from her father; her brothers, Patrick and Brendan, were already on the lifeboat crew. It was

Frances Glody of Dunmore East, the first woman crew member of an all-weather lifeboat.

Coxswain Stephen Whittle, a much respected lifeboatman with three bravery medals, who invited Frances to join the crew. Some of the men had reservations. For one thing, was a woman strong enough to pull a person from the water?

'One strange thing is the strength you find in an emergency,' says Frances. 'I've never been what you call petite, but ordinarily I probably couldn't pull a dead weight from the water. But on the boat, from somewhere you get the strength. Once you've got hold of a guy, there's no way you're going to let go.'

One mission in particular helped to cement her place in the crew. On a calm summer day two children drowned not far from the lifeboat station. Divers found one body and the lifeboat picked up the second, a little boy. Lifeboatman Dermot Murphy recalls, 'You see some terrible things at sea – smashed limbs, people already dying when you haul them aboard – but a dead child is by far the hardest to take. So after we'd got the little lad aboard and covered him up, the fellas stood there with our faces turned away, feeling awful for ourselves. But not Frances. She made the sign of the cross over him and said a prayer. That changed my attitude completely. I've never seen anything so cool and yet so soft-hearted.'

Frances also has the wry humour typical of a crew member. 'In the summer you get called out for a lot of amateur yachtsmen who don't know much about what they're up to. You throw them a line and they ask "Where shall I tie the rope?". Comes a voice from the lifeboat, "Round your neck will be fine".'

Media attention has caused problems for other lifeboat women. Ruth Lennon at **Donaghadee** joined the crew while her father was the coxswain. After a while it began to jar with the men on the crew when Ruth became the centre of unsought newspaper and magazine articles. The publicity was good for the RNLI, but not so welcome for Ruth. After all, if the men accepted her as an equal, why should the press treat her as someone special?

Like most women on lifeboat crews, Ruth found that she needed to do something a little extra to prove her worth. A trained nurse, she came into her own when the lifeboat was called to take a woman suffering from a miscarriage off a ferry. Ruth calmly went about her task, offering as much reassurance as possible in a way that the men simply could not have done.

On another occasion, Ruth, with crew members Shane McNamara and George Thompson, went to the help of an injured climber who had fallen down a cliff. It was night with torrential rain and a stiff wind, and the lifeboat could not reach the base of the cliffs because of rocks, so the three crew set off in the inflatable. They had to scramble up the cliffs, slipping on the sodden grass that covered deep holes and gullies. Eventually they found the badly injured man and, again, Ruth's training came to the fore.

She decided that he was too badly hurt to be taken down the cliff to the boat, and insisted on a helicopter lift. It was later discovered that he had broken ribs, a cracked pelvis and a collapsed lung. Ruth's assessment had been right; manhandling the climber down the slippery cliff could have killed him. As the media pressure has died away, so Ruth has been able to settle into the crew just like any other new recruit, though unlike others, she married a fellow crew member, Shane McNamara.

A rescue off the north-west coast has emphasised Ireland's lead in recruiting female crew members. The **Lough Swilly** lifeboat made history in August 1992 with the first award-winning rescue carried out by a crew that included a lifeboatwoman.

Every crew member and helper turned out to join in a difficult search for a missing speedboat. The search was on a night with poor visibility caused by light rain, but the inflatable lifeboat coped easily with the choppy sea. A six-mile journey up the coast in both directions revealed nothing, even though the lifeboat was firing parachute flares to light up the scene.

Baby Hannah McNamara, daughter of crew members Shane and Ruth (nee Lennon) of the Donaghadee lifeboat.

As the lifeboat was working in the dark, beyond her normal limits, one of the crew launched his own boat to act as a back-up. By now there were seven lifeboat crews at sea in two boats and more searching the shore. Just before midnight they found one of the missing men, who told them his companion was near Dunree Head. The speedboat could be seen crashing against the rocks and the second man was stranded at the bottom of a 35-foot cliff, in considerable distress and in danger of being swept away.

As the boats headed for the spot, lifeboatman Mark Porter climbed down the slippery cliff face to reach the man, who was weak, suffering from hypothermia and in no state to climb to safety. When the boats arrived crew member Bernard Devlin swam ashore with a rope. The man was hauled from the rocks to the lifeboat, then Devlin and Porter swam to the boat, which reached the lifeboat station an hour later.

Devlin and Porter were singled out for special recognition, but the lifeboat inspector wrote, 'The station as a whole are commended for their joint efforts. Every crew member and helper turned to on the night.' George and Frank O'Hagan received framed letters, and certificates went to Sean Smith, Aidan McLaughlin, Mark Bennett – and lifeboatwoman Bridgita Kelly.

Irish women can even boast of preceding Grace Darling by some 70 years with a rescue by two sisters named Pigeon. Their father, John, had built a house on the south bank of the River Liffey and used to supplement his income as a watchman by rowing sightseers out to the Poolbeg anchorage. However, John died, and when his son Ned was killed by burglars, Mrs Pigeon died of shock on hearing the news.

The two daughters, Rachel and Mary, were left as orphans and took over the boating business. One wild October night in the 1760s Dublin Bay was hit by a severe storm and two sailing ships were wrecked up the river at Ringsend. The girls set out in their boat and, with tremendous bravery, rowed across to one of the stranded ships where they found and rescued a man and his child. The man turned out to be a wealthy widower from Philadelphia and promptly married Mary, who took Rachel to America to live with her new family.

In traditional fishing communities, some of the old seafaring superstitions still linger on; green should not be seen on a boat, whistling and talking of salmon are out, and carrying clergy – or women – on boats is said to be unlucky. So it may be some years yet before it is commonplace to see lifeboatwomen, but Ireland has shown the way forward.

IRISH ORIGINS

The history of the lifeboat service in Ireland boasts several remarkable rescues. The service itself predates the RNLI; it has its roots in the independent Irish parliament, which ran from 1782 to 1800 and established the Dublin Port Authority in 1786.

Wrecks in Dublin Bay were common as ships at anchor waited outside the sandbar across the mouth of the River Liffey. Improvements were made to the harbour and its approaches, and the Port Authority ordered three lifeboats in 1800. The first went to Clontarf in 1801, the second to Sandycove two years later and the third to Sutton in 1805. By 1818 there were also boats at **Howth** and **Dunleary** (now **Dun Laoghaire**). These are the two surviving Dublin Bay stations, which the RNLI took over in 1861.

The outstanding figure associated with the Dun Laoghaire station in those days was William Hutchinson, a Dublin pilot and coxswain of the Dalkey lifeboat. Records still exist of the early rescues – in one report, a crew member is described as 'William Grimes, a poor man' – and they show very generous rewards. Hutchinson, for example, received 15 guineas for a rescue in 1820, and 50 guineas worth of silver plate for another, in which he was nearly drowned. His own account only hints at the immense dangers faced in vulnerable open rowing lifeboats.

'It blew a most violent gale from the south-east. With a volunteer crew of 14 men, I embarked and with much difficulty reached the stern of the vessel, where we received a hawser to hold by. At this time the vessel was lying nearly head to the sea which broke completely over her, and while the crew were getting into the lifeboat she filled. While we were bailing out water with our hats, a sea, of which I shall never forget the aspect, overwhelmed the boat and washed six of us out of her.

'Two fortunately caught hold of the rope they had been holding and three unfortunately perished. I, with difficulty, regained the lifeboat and with the remainder of her crew were drove among the breakers without oars'.

Hutchinson was obviously made of strong stuff both physically and mentally. His modesty evaporated when the RNLI committee in London awarded him a Silver Medal in 1829 for another very dangerous rescue. He declined the medal and persuaded the Inspector General of the coastguard in Dublin to write to the RNLI, whose records report: 'Read a letter from J. Dombrain saying Lieutenant Hutchinson RN . . . declines accepting the silver medal, conceiving the committee may, on perusing the several papers therein enclosed, consider him deserving of the highest distinction they are in the habit of bestowing.'

The committee duly read the papers, including accounts of his earlier lifesaving escapades, and concluded that they '. . . felt much gratified in voting the gold medallion of the Institution be presented to him'.

The establishment of the Irish Free State in 1922 made little difference to the lifeboat service. Certainly at lifeboat stations the crews continued their work uninterrupted, in spite of incidents such as the arrest of the lifeboat mechanic at Dun Laoghaire for having a revolver at the boathouse. Readers of *The Lifeboat* magazine might hardly have suspected that anything was changing in Ireland. There was no mention at all of any discussions about whether the RNLI, with its London headquarters and British origins, would continue to operate in the new republic; perhaps it was taken for granted.

However, in 1921 it was reported that the ladies collecting for the flag day in Dublin had to face 'trying' conditions, as there was fighting going on in the streets. There were two ambushes, leaving several people wounded, and all were witnessed by some of the collectors, who administered first aid before resuming their collecting. Again in 1922 fighting got in the way of fundraising, with many collecting boxes destroyed or raided. One station reported, 'During some recent trouble here, a down spout on the lifeboat house was damaged by gun fire and requires repairs'.

The magazine devoted more space to an account of a voyage from Cowes to Wexford to deliver a new motor lifeboat. On arrival a rat was found in the boat and the lifeboat inspector reported that, due to the prompt action of the crew, armed with a lead cane, axes and hammers, the rat was killed. It had, however, eaten '. . . the best part of one oilskin jacket', which obviously amused the editor of the magazine, who added the footnote, 'This statement caused much interest among the experts of the Institution, who had been of the opinion that every part of an oilskin, except the buttons, would taste exactly the same, and have the same food value. The matter still remains in doubt, the rat being dead (without having expressed any opinion) and the experts, so far, refusing to verify their opinion by personal experiment, in spite of the Secretary's warm appeal to their public spirit.'

LOST ON CHRISTMAS EVE

As one rescue from Wexford shows, Irish stations share in the triumphs and tragedies of RNLI crews everywhere. It was 1.15 am on Christmas Eve 1977. Four red flares were reported off Bannow Bay, Co Wexford, and the **Kilmore Quay** lifeboat *Lady Murphy* launched ten minutes later. On board were six regular crew and one extra, Finton Sinnott, a local fisherman who volunteered to join the lifeboat when numbers were short. South-westerly winds had been blowing for days, piling up a heavy swell across the whole of the Irish Sea's western approaches from Cornwall to Ireland. As the *Lady Murphy* set out on her search, a nightmare was about to unfold.

Seamen know that there is a pattern to waves. Every seventh is likely to be higher, then one in 35 higher still, and 'freak' waves of enormous proportions are agreed by oceanographers to come at one in every 350. However, the luxury of counting waves is not available to a lifeboat crew at night in the thick of a storm. They keep their eyes peeled, but the freak waves can rise up, seemingly from nowhere.

Tom Walsh was coxswain at Kilmore that Christmas Eve. He recalls, 'There were pretty big seas running all right but there was no heavy breaking water whatsoever. We had come for miles and we had seen nothing like that. Then we seemed to come on a wave that was just coming to the point of breaking and we just rolled with it and went right over. There was no sound at all. Then the noise started coming like breaking water in and around and under the boat.'

The lifeboat had come back upright after the capsize and Tom Walsh shouted out for a roll call. To the crew's dismay, one man, Joe Maddock, was missing.

'We couldn't believe we had lost one of our crew overboard,' says Tom. 'Every second seemed like hours going back to look for him. I thought we would never find him again.'

For Maddock, in the chilling sea, the greatest fear was that he would not be found.

'First of all I thought that there was nobody else left in the world but myself; everybody else had gone. I thought, "Christmas Eve – terrible night for something to happen. What will they think at home? Will the boat come back for me? Will I kick off my boots? Will the lifejacket keep me up?".

Maddock was picked up in the beam of the searchlight within three minutes and was hauled back on board the lifeboat. The mast was broken, the windscreen shattered and the radio would not work. Joe was taken forward in the boat and Dermot Culleton and Finton Sinnott stayed with him. Sinnott had a badly cut head and loosened his lifejacket to get more comfortable.

As Walsh turned for the harbour the sea struck again, capsizing the lifeboat for a second time. Four men were pitched into the water, leaving only three on board. David Culleton was in the sea, close to the stern; Walsh and Devereux got him first, then grabbed brother Dermot Culleton who was hanging on to a lifeline at the bow. Joe Maddock was in the water for a second time, but quite close to the lifeboat, and, as Walsh took the wheel, the other three men, weakened and in shock, struggled to keep a grip on him. Walsh had to drive the lifeboat forwards to regain control

Lady Murphy, *the Kilmore Quay lifeboat that capsized twice on Christmas Eve in 1977.*

and avoid another capsize, and as Maddock dragged through the water, it seemed as though he must slip out of their grasp. Somehow they managed to hang on, then bundle him back on board, suffering from shock and exposure.

Maddock knew he was in poor shape. 'I called out to Dermot Culleton. I said, "Keep talking to me, whatever happens, keep shouting and I'll shout back. If I don't shout, make sure you get an answer from me." Because, you see, I have this thing that if you fall asleep you are a gonner. I knew I was badly shocked because I was shaking all over.'

Meanwhile, Finton Sinnott, his lifejacket loosened, drifted away from the other men. After an unsuccessful search for him, Walsh knew that he would have to get the rest of the crew to land for medical treatment.

Waiting ashore were men who had missed the call. Second coxswain John Connick had not heard the maroons in the storm and mechanic Liam Culleton had been on leave, so he helped launch the lifeboat but did not go out, as his relief, John Devereux, was already there.

Connick and Culleton set out at first light with a fresh crew of volunteers. Fate was to play another cruel trick as a rope wrapped around one of the propellers, leaving the lifeboat with only one engine working, but the men pressed on, hoping against hope that Sinnott was still alive. The search went on for two and a half hours. By now a helicopter had joined in and, half way through the morning, a winchman was dropped to the lifeboat to break the news that Sinnott's body had been found on the shore by a local farmer. At 11.30 am on Christmas Eve the lifeboat returned to a shocked village.

There were no news reports of Sinnott's death, as newsrooms were closing for Christmas. But news travels fast in the RNLI and lifeboat crews all around the coast made collections for Sinnott's young widow and children. The St Ives lifeboat, the same type as Kilmore's, had been out in the same storm. She had suffered a knockdown that had put the whole crew under water, but had just avoided capsize. The lifeboat was damaged and the crew worked until 10 pm on repairs. Then, two hours before Christmas, they emptied their pockets of all they were carrying and collected £60 in Finton Sinnott's memory.

CHASING HALF A TANKER

In shipping circles nowadays a furious debate rages over safety standards, crew competence and the fierce competition that demands cost-cutting in all areas. The world's tanker fleet is growing steadily older as the low price of oil makes it impossible to recover the huge capital costs of building new ships. Shipping registers of tiny countries such as Liberia and Panama – the so-called 'flags of convenience' – have been criticised for accommodating sub-standard ships, although statistically their safety record matches that of many of their critics. And finally, the issue of crews of mixed nationalities, taken on to save money but with no common language, has been raised time and again at disaster investigations.

But none of these problems is new. Forty years ago, many of the elements were present when a bizarre double lifeboat rescue took place in November 1954. The 20,000-ton Liberian tanker *World Concord*, sailing from Liverpool to Syria, broke in two when she was hit by exceptionally violent storms in the Irish Sea. Both parts of the tanker stayed afloat, with seven men in the bow section and 35 in the stern.

The lifeboat from **St Davids** in Pembrokeshire was launched into the storm and found the stern section of *World Concord* three hours later. The tanker was rolling heavily, her huge propellers still churning the water, threatening the tiny lifeboat. The coxswain, William Watts Williams, made a dummy run in to assess the chances of a rescue, then gave his orders.

A rope ladder was hung from the tanker, well clear of the propellers and at the lowest point of the deck, and five of the seven lifeboatmen were sent forward to grab the survivors as they came down. Tossed around by the 20-foot waves, Coxswain Watts Williams made his first careful approach, plucked off one man and immediately broke away from the tanker. With enormous skill he spent the next hour repeating this tricky manoeuvre 34 times, taking one man off every time, never missing, never taking the risk of staying alongside the tanker to take more. Thirty-four Greeks and one Egyptian, none of whom could speak English, were taken on board the lifeboat without even a scratch.

Meanwhile, the bow section of *World Concord* continued to drift, and as the St Davids lifeboat was heading for home, the **Rosslare** lifeboat was asked to launch, reaching the tanker in the early evening. Coxswain

The St David's lifeboat takes 35 men off the stern section of the tanker World Concord.

Richard Walsh now had a difficult decision. Should he try a rescue in the darkness, risking the lives of the survivors, or should he and his crew take the risk themselves of waiting by the tanker for the next 12 hours, their boat being pummelled by the storm, and give the tanker men a better chance in a daylight rescue? The bow of the tanker seemed to be in no immediate danger so the coxswain decided to stand by.

All night he and the second coxswain took turns at the wheel, trying to keep their crew safe while tracking the tanker as it drifted northwards, without lights, at four knots. Conditions were already so bad that the lifeboatmen could hardly have noticed that the wind was actually increasing, reaching full gale force around midnight. By morning the tanker was listing five degrees to port, surrounded by a heavy swell with waves up to 25 feet high.

The Irish coxswain, like his Welsh colleague the day before, made a dummy run to see how to get alongside the tanker without smashing his boat on the jagged metal of the broken ship. Once again a rope ladder was lowered and once again a coxswain's skill was put to a severe test. As the lifeboat ranged up and down the side of the tanker, Coxswain Walsh used his engines to keep alongside until, in 15 minutes, he had taken off the seven survivors – again, without a scratch.

During the night both the lifeboat and the bow section of the *World Concord* had been drifting north up the Irish Sea. Having started from the south-east corner of Ireland, the Rosslare crew now found themselves nearer to the north-west corner of Wales and headed for Holyhead, whose lifeboat came out to escort them in to harbour. After 26 hours at sea they finally reached dry land. For Coxswain Walsh, though, the land was too dry. The story is told that his only complaint about the whole escapade was that, having landed in Wales on a Sunday, all the pubs were shut and he could not get a well-earned drink! The next day the crew sailed back to Rosslare to a heroes' welcome – more than 1,000 people lined the harbour walls and brass bands were playing.

Unfortunately, perhaps, such homecomings are no longer the vogue. In weather conditions very similar to those that split the *World Concord* apart, an arduous rescue by today's Rosslare lifeboat, the Arun Class *St Brendan*, took the crew 53 miles south of the station. The casualty was less dramatic – a yacht with a fouled propeller – but lives were at risk as the lifeboat punched straight into the gale-force winds. It took four hours to reach the yacht, then eight hours to bring her to the safety of Rosslare harbour. The coxswain and crew received special thanks from the RNLI headquarters for their skill and determination, but this time there were no brass bands on the quay.

FAMILIES

The Rosslare crew on the *World Concord* rescue had two Walshes, brothers, and three Duggans, two brothers and a son. Close family links

Arklow mechanic John Hayes talks to a young John Tyrell in 1956.

are less common at lifeboat stations nowadays, but at **Arklow** they continue with the Tyrell family. Arklow is a port with a long history of shipbuilding, and Tyrells of Arklow has a reputation as a shipyard that extends far beyond Ireland, renowned for its workmanship in the building of the beautiful Irish sail training ship, *Asgard*. Tyrell's was also one of the RNLI's main repair and maintenance yards, but the decline in the fishing industry that provided much of the other work of the yard put it into financial difficulties in the recession of the 1990s. However, the Tyrell family link with the Arklow lifeboat was too deep-rooted to be affected. At one time the three brothers were the second coxswain (John), honorary secretary (Jimmy) and deputy launching authority (Michael). In 1991 all were involved in an unusual family rescue.

On a pleasant July evening Jimmy set sail in his 18-foot dinghy with a friend. However, as the evening wore on the wind unexpectedly increased, making the sea too rough to return to harbour. The sails were lowered and Jimmy decided not to run the dinghy ashore in case they capsized in the breaking seas on the beach. The two men tried instead to attract the attention of a man ashore at Porters Rocks.

Meanwhile, Michael and John were trying to find out why Jimmy had not returned when a call from the Shannon rescue co-ordination centre told them of a 999 call they had received about a boat in difficulties. The maroons were fired to call the crew and were spotted by the two men in the dinghy, 'a most heartening sight' as Jimmy said later. They knew the lifeboat was on her way.

The dinghy was now drifting rapidly, and although they dropped the anchor it would not hold. Water was breaking over the side and the rope parted, leaving the dinghy drifting helplessly towards the rocks, when the men saw the welcome lights of the lifeboat. A rope was passed but soon snapped as the conditions deteriorated to very rough seas and a force 8 gale. The dinghy was just 20 feet from the rocks when the tow was reconnected and it was towed clear of the rocks and the tidal race.

READY FOR SERVICE

Every official lifeboat report ends with the words 'The lifeboat was refuelled and ready for service at. . .'. For the crew this means that, no matter how long they have been at sea they must check the equipment, replenish any used stores, fill the boat's fuel tanks and wash her down. For the next call could come at any time, and although it's an extra chore, particularly at the end of a long night at sea, rescues come in all shapes and sizes and the lifeboat must be at constant readiness.

Howth lifeboatmen might have expected a routine night when they were called out to search for an overdue sailing dinghy on a July evening in 1988. Only minutes after leaving harbour they were recalled, as the dinghy had been found, safe and sound, but as they turned back a radio message was picked up from a yacht saying that she had seen a second yacht in trouble near Baily lighthouse, just two miles south of the station. Changing course, the lifeboat soon found the yacht, the *Birgitz*, anchored near the lighthouse having lost her rudder.

The official report, noting southerly force 6 to 8 winds and 10-foot seas, described conditions as 'poor'. The four yachtsmen may well have had stronger words. They were taken in tow and were safe in Howth harbour just before 9 o'clock.

After less than an hour at sea, the lifeboat crew were just tying up the yacht when a third call came. Sixteen miles north-east of the station the trawler *Riki Pia* was taking in water, and although another trawler, *Christmas Tide*, was towing her through the storm (the gale-force winds and heavy seas out in the open water could still not move the author of the RNLI account to report anything more dramatic than 'the same poor conditions'), there was a strong chance that the *Riki Pia* would sink before reaching port.

Howth lifeboat set out once again, making full speed to reach the trawler within an hour. A pump was put aboard the *Riki Pia* and she was kept afloat while the lifeboat escorted the trawlers to Skerries, where she took over the tow and put the *Riki Pia* safely alongside the pier. There was then the short passage back to Howth, the job of refuelling and mooring the lifeboat and, by 3.40 am, when the rest of the town was safely in bed, the lifeboat was once more 'ready for service'.

THE FASTNET RACE

The Fastnet Race is known worldwide in yachting circles, but it sprang to international public prominence in 1979 when 13 yachtsmen died as the fleet of 303 yachts was hit by south-westerly hurricane-force winds sweeping across the Atlantic and funnelling into the 150-mile gap between Land's End and the Fastnet Rock.

The result was the biggest ever co-ordinated search in the history of the RNLI. Thirteen lifeboats from Ireland, England and Wales, together with helicopters, naval and merchant ships and fishing boats, went out to help the yachts, and the lifeboats alone clocked up 187 hours at sea.

Baltimore was the first lifeboat to launch, and was out for 24 hours. Next to launch was the **Courtmacsherry** boat, where a veteran relief lifeboat, *Sir Samuel Kelly*, was on station. This 29-year-old lifeboat had served at Donaghadee at the time of the 1953 *Princess Victoria* disaster (of which more later), and was in her last months of service with the RNLI.

Setting out at 2.40 in the morning, the eight-knot lifeboat faced a 27-mile passage to the yacht *Wild Goose*, and jokes about a certain type of chase were probably cracked as the lifeboat was diverted to another yacht, the *Pepsi*, some 30 miles out. Coxswain Stephen Mearns kept his throttles pressed hard down, but with seas smashing on to his bow and the tide and winds pushing against his boat it was only possible to make six and a half knots. After six hours the lifeboat reached the reported position of the *Pepsi*, but there was no sign of the yacht and a square search was started.

Two other yachts were sighted and found to be in full control. At 10 am the yacht *Casse Tete V* reported the loss of her rudder. Modern carbon fibres, with tremendous uni-directional strength, had succumbed to the battering and the rudder stock had snapped. On board was a very

The Courtmacsherry lifeboat towing the yacht Casse Tete V *during the 1979 Fastnet Race.*

experienced crew, including Lord Greenway, a well-known marine photographer as well as an accomplished navigator. He managed to take pictures of the lifeboat during the 12-hour tow at an agonisingly slow two to three knots, the violent yawing and surfing of the rudderless yacht making any greater speed impossible.

He recalls, 'We gave our position but the weather was so bad that the lifeboat could not see us when they were only 50 yards away. The crew fired flares but the wind blew them sideways into the sea. When they got us in tow, the yacht was overtaking the lifeboat all the time so we streamed sails over each quarter to act as drogues.'

The wind was moderating all the time and the crew on the yacht were reasonably comfortable. 'We were in a stripped-out ocean racer, but could easily have cooked a four-course meal. The lifeboatmen, on the other hand, were absolutely soaked through and couldn't even make a hot drink. When we got into Courtmacsherry there were over 200 people on the quay at three in the morning. We were taken to a local hotel, given showers and a meal, followed by a day or two of festivities on the quay.'

The point Lord Greenway stressed when he subsequently wrote to the *Daily Telegraph* was that although the helicopters got most of the publicity for the Fastnet rescues, it was the lifeboat crews who suffered real hardships and were able to rescue both people and boats.

JUDGE AT THE WHEEL

Wicklow lifeboat is crewed by the usual mixture of men. There is a butcher, a factory worker, a motor mechanic, a garage director, a printer, a factory manager, an electronic engineer, a docker, a tug boatman, a ship's engineer and a sea captain.

The sea captain, a Swede, is not the coxswain, nor is the man who describes himself, jokingly, as an environmental technician (dustman!). Wicklow surely has the most unusual coxswain in the whole RNLI, for Gerard Houghton is a judge. When he joined the crew in 1985 he was a well-known local solicitor and an experienced yachtsman who was soon appointed second coxswain in recognition of his seamanship and navigation skills. Then in 1991 he became coxswain and was also appointed a judge of the district court, working on the circuit travelling from court to court, leading to the nickname 'the floating judge'. Unfortunately, there is little chance of a trial being abandoned as the judge rushes out, robes and wig flying, to answer an emergency call. For Judge Houghton's professional work takes him out of Wicklow and, when he is away, Second Coxswain Sean Byrne or Emergency Coxswain Nick Keogh take the helm.

Wicklow's crew also spans a tremendous age-range. The RNLI introduced a retirement age of 55 when fast lifeboats became the norm, for fitness and speed of reaction tend to deteriorate with age and a long rough service can be physically punishing, even on a young person. Many of the older hands were upset by the decision; some were grateful, as they realised the strain imposed by the new boats. But one point used by the detractors, that years of experience would be lost, can be dismissed by looking at ages on a crew list. At Wicklow the range is from 19 to 46, with an even spread through the 20s, 30s and 40s.

A young man joining the crew in his teens can expect to work his way through, gaining experience and local knowledge all the time, spending over 30 years in the boat before he has to retire. The experience at Wicklow suggests that when that man retires, there will be plenty of other young people following on. While there are fewer family connections than previously, there is no shortage of volunteers to crew the boat.

THREE DAYS AT SEA

One of the greatest feats of endurance in the RNLI's history was carried out by the crew of the **Ballycotton** lifeboat when, in 1936, the lightship at Daunt Rock broke away from her moorings. Any storm that could snap the gargantuan chains designed to hold a lightship in place would have to be severe, and the storm that night combined all the worst elements; a whole gale blowing, a very heavy sea, rain and snow. The waves were so high when the lifeboat set out that spray was flying over the lantern of a lighthouse 196 feet high. The lifeboat was away from Ballycotton for three days, spending 49 hours at sea, during which time the crew got only three hours sleep. For 25 hours they had no food.

Robert Mahony, the lifeboat secretary, wrote a vivid account of the storm and the rescue: 'The gale increased until it was blowing a hurricane force never before experienced by the oldest inhabitant in Ballycotton. The harbour was a seething cauldron. Stones, a ton in weight, were being torn from the quay and flung about like sugar lumps.'

During the night the coxswain's own boat broke from her moorings and he had been up all night trying to save her. Then came the call for the lifeboat. It was 8 am on Tuesday 11 February.

'I gave the coxswain the message and he made no reply. I had seen the weather. Seas were breaking over the lifeboathouse, where the boarding boat was kept. I did not believe it possible for the coxswain even to get aboard the lifeboat at her moorings. I was afraid to order him out.

'He left and went down to the harbour. I followed a little later. To my amazement the lifeboat was already at the harbour mouth, dashing out between the piers. The coxswain had not waited for his orders. His crew were already at the harbour.

He had not fired the maroons, for he did not want to alarm the village. Without a word they had slipped away. As I watched the lifeboat I thought every minute that she must turn back.

But she went on. People watching her left the quay to go to the church to pray.'

The lifeboat headed for the lightship and, failing to find her, put into

Queenstown for the latest information. Out in the storm again the lightship was located at midday and during the afternoon a destroyer made attempts to get a rope across. The storm was too severe and snapped the towing wire as soon as it was connected, and as darkness fell the destroyer agreed to stand by all night while the lifeboat went back to Queenstown for more ropes and food.

Some of the crew snatched a little sleep, but three were on the lifeboat all the time, ready if the call came. Early in the morning of the 12th the lifeboat set out again and stood by the lightship all day and all night, 25 hours with the seas breaking continually over the lifeboat and her crew.

By now petrol was getting low, so the coxswain again headed for Queenstown, refuelled the boat and set out again. It was now 4 pm on the 13th.

When the lifeboat reached the lightship again, at dusk, the storm that had been calming down began to whip up again. The lightship's crew had wanted to stay with their vessel to be able to warn others of the dangerous Daunt Rock, but they were now perilously close themselves – only 60 yards away – and the wind was shifting, threatening to drive the lightship to destruction. The crew had to be taken off the violently plunging ship.

Mahony takes up the story again: 'The coxswain knew the dangers. The lightship was only 98 feet long. If he ran too far, the lifeboat would

The Ballycotton lifeboat rescuing the crew of the Daunt Rock lightship in 1936.

go over the anchor cable and be capsized. As he came alongside the lightship might crash over right on top of the lifeboat.'

The coxswain went ahead of the lightship, pumped out oil to calm the seas a little, went astern of her, then drove full speed alongside. One man jumped and the lifeboat went astern. A second time she raced in, but no one jumped; a third time and five men jumped; a fourth time – the lightship sheered violently and crashed on top of the lifeboat, smashing the rails and damaging the fender and deck. No one was hurt, but the man working the searchlight sprang clear just in time. The lifeboat went in a fifth time. Again no one jumped.

There were still two men on board the lightvessel, clinging to the rails. They seemed unable to jump. The coxswain sent some of his crew forward, at the risk of being swept overboard, with orders to seize the two men as the lifeboat came alongside. Then he raced in for the sixth time. The men were seized and dragged in. As the coxswain said, 'It was no time for "By your leave"'.

The long strain on the crew of the lightship had been tremendous and shortly after the rescue one of them became hysterical. Two lifeboatmen had to hold him down to prevent anyone from being hurt or being knocked overboard. The lifeboat made for Queenstown, arriving at 11 pm on the night of the 13th. The crew stayed overnight, then set out for home the next morning. By the time they got back to Ballycotton, triumphant and with all eight of the lightship's crew safely ashore, the lifeboatmen were able to assess their own condition.

All had severe chills and stinging saltwater burns. The coxswain had a poisoned arm. Yet the same men, drawn on this rescue from just two families, the Slineys and the Walshes, went on under Patsy Sliney to win more honours in the war, facing tremendous dangers and enduring prolonged searches. Patsy Sliney did not retire until 1950, by which time he had been in the lifeboat 39 years, 28 as coxswain, and had saved 114 lives.

THE GOOD SHEPHERD

'I thank God for the RNLI, for the discipline and spirit of those who man its lifeboats,' said Dr Robert Runcie, then the Archbishop of Canterbury, as he christened a new lifeboat, the *Good Shepherd*, in 1988. But he can hardly have foreseen just how far that discipline and spirit would be tested in the very boat he had named.

The endurance of the *Good Shepherd* and her crew was to be stretched to the limit on an October day in 1991, when a southerly storm force 10 gale blew up over South West Ireland. In the open sea, winds of over 50 knots were kicking up seas 20 feet high. And in the late afternoon the engines of the *Japonica*, a 120-foot fishing boat, failed, leaving her without power only 13 miles west of the notorious Fastnet Rock, and drifting steadily towards the jagged shore.

It took **Baltimore** lifeboat coxswain Kieran Cotter and his crew two and a half hours to reach the *Japonica* and a further hour, in the tumult of the waves, to get a rope across to her. Then the lifeboat gingerly began to tow the fishing boat, which was almost three times her size, nursing her through the high winds towards the shelter of Bantry Bay.

All went well for a couple of hours until a large wave wrenched the boats apart and the towrope broke. After several attempts it was reconnected, and after a tow that lasted all night, the *Japonica* anchored safely in Bantry Bay as dawn broke.

The lifeboat crew had now been 12 hours at sea and were exhausted after their hard night's work. But two minor mishaps delayed their return trip to Baltimore still further. One crew member gashed his head while repacking the gear used on the tow. He needed stitches, so the lifeboat diverted to Castletownbere to land him, and also replace a blocked fuel filter. After two hours ashore, they were ready to head for home with a new filter and two fresh crew members. Then came the call they could happily have done without – a 60-foot yacht was in trouble south of the Fastnet Rock.

The *Good Shepherd* set out again, straight into the teeth of the gale. It was over two hours before the lifeboat reached the yacht. Once again the lifeboat crew connected a tow and at last set off for Baltimore, arriving just before 7 pm, 25½ hours after they had first set out. But their marathon trip wasn't yet over. First the crew had to see the lifeboat safely in the boathouse once more, wash her down and refuel her, ready for the next 'shout'.

For his outstanding leadership and skilful seamanship, Kieran Cotter was summoned to London the following May to receive a Bronze Medal. When he arrived at his hotel he was handed a letter from the new Archbishop of Canterbury, George Carey. It read, 'At Lambeth Palace we receive regular reports about the relief lifeboat *Good Shepherd*, which was substantially funded by the churches. I was delighted to see that you are being awarded the RNLI's Bronze Medal for gallantry for your remarkable service in October. I am sure you and your crew will receive many expressions of appreciation. I simply wanted to add my own admiration for your skill, dedication and tenacity.'

THE WILD WEST

The next stop westwards from Ireland is America. Over 3,000 miles of rolling Atlantic Ocean heaves up and spills its fury on cliffs and beaches that rival the best in the world. Communications, geography and economics mean that the West Coast of Ireland is composed of small isolated communities. Inland, farming is all important. Even now hay is gathered in pitchforked haycocks, and turf dug from peat bogs is an essential and very economical source of fuel. There are active fishing fleets in harbours such as Killybegs and Rossaveel, freighters plying up and down the West Coast and now an expansion of marina berths and cruising.

For many years the RNLI had only three lifeboat stations to cover the huge stretch of coastline from Donegal to Kerry. **Arranmore, Valentia** and **Galway** all had traditional Barnett Class lifeboats, rugged in the extreme, but slow; rescues lasting 10, 11 or 12 hours were common as the boats drove on for mile after mile to reach the casualty. Because of the distances between the lifeboat stations, they were completely self-reliant; if one of the lifeboats hit trouble, there was nobody else to help them.

The last few years have changed things quite radically. Recognising the increasing sea traffic, the RNLI opened new stations at **Ballyglass** and **Fenit** with inshore boats at **Bundoran, Clifden, Galway City** and **Kilrush**. Modern lifeboats now serve all the stations. But the weather remains unchanged.

Valentia used to be the radio station for transatlantic traffic, and although the lifeboatmen look out on huge Atlantic swells, none will describe them graphically. Former Valentia coxswain Dermot Walsh merely said, 'We don't bother with weather forecasts. We can feel it'. His mechanic, Joe Houlihan, added, 'You know your own waters. If you cannot see the swell, you can feel the motion.'

Houlihan won a medal in 1963 for a single-handed rescue in which he launched the lifeboat's boarding boat to rescue two men after their dinghy capsized. He hauled one man into the boat, but the second, a clergyman, was too heavy for him to heave out of the choppy seas. He therefore told the clergyman to hang on to the stern of the boat, causing a tremendous drag as Houlihan exerted all his efforts to row back to the shore. By the time he beached the boat he was completely exhausted, but two more lives had been saved.

The incident did not end there. Eagle-eyed officials at RNLI headquarters in London spotted a gap in a report from Valentia. The machinery log showed that the mechanic had been absent for four days and no explanation had been given. A polite letter was sent to the honorary secretary, who must have taken great delight in sending the following reply: 'I acknowledge receipt of your letter re Mechanic J. Houlihan being absent from 4th to 9th April. Houlihan was attending the Annual General Meeting in London where he received the award of the Institution's Bronze Medal.'

Even with new faster lifeboats, rescues can last many hours. Joe's son John took over from his father as the lifeboat mechanic and was repairing the valve gear on the starboard engine one wild January morning in 1989 when a call for help came in. A Brixham trawler, the *Big Cat*, had been driven ashore in a force 9 gale. She was taking water rapidly as the high seas broke right over her.

Officially the lifeboat had been placed 'off service' while the repair was carried out. If there had been another lifeboat station close by, they would have gone, but at remote Valentia this is not an option. After an anxious

An anxious group of rescuers check the fishing boat Big Cat, *wrecked on Beginnis Island.*

consultation between mechanic, coxswain and secretary, the decision was made to go out on only one engine.

When Coxswain Seannie Murphy reached the *Big Cat*, he realised that the trawler, which was hard on the rocks of Beginnis Island and being battered by the waves, could not be reached from the sea. He would have to put men ashore to attempt a rescue from the cliffs. The lifeboat went back to pick up the local cliff lifesaving team, took on some more volunteers from a Spanish trawler nearby and, with the help of a local fishing boat and the lifeboat's boarding boat, landed them all on the island.

The 15-man party trekked overland until they were above the *Big Cat*, then set about lifting 11 survivors up the 30-foot cliffs. They were hampered by diesel fuel leaking from the trawler, which made the cliffs treacherously slippery. Three men were still missing, so the lifeboat now had the dispiriting task of searching for men who had almost certainly drowned.

Waves 30 to 40 feet high made the search difficult enough and, with only one engine operating, the coxswain had to keep an anchor at instant readiness as he searched the rock-strewn waters for any sign of life. After an hour and a half a body was sighted and picked up; it was the *Big Cat*'s engineer. The search went on until darkness fell, and after nine hours at sea the crew finally got home. John Houlihan once again set about his engine repair.

Most remote in the whole of the RNLI's domain is the **Galway Bay** lifeboat station on Inishmore, one of the three Aran Islands. Inishmore has two Bronze Age forts perched on cliff tops and the windswept landscape is broken into tiny fields by a maze of drystone walls. The island's romantic past, the Gaelic language spoken by islanders and the old canvas and tar coracles, or curraghs, draw thousands of summer visitors eager to taste the island's magic.

But in the winter it is a harsh life for the islanders, and the lifeboat becomes the last link with the mainland, acting as an ambulance when the light aircraft from Galway City cannot reach the island's grass landing strip. The crew have never yet had to deliver a baby on board, but there have been some close shaves, with island mothers giving birth in the mainland ambulance minutes after being taken ashore.

Once again, it is the wild winter storms that take their toll. Former coxswain Bartley Mullin describes the hazards: 'In the wintertime it can be a bad coast . . . all the Atlantic swell is coming on top of us, a long swell when you get around the back of the islands . . . you get it very bad with a west or north-west wind.' But he plays down the perils. 'You get used to it,' is all he will say.

Mullin was assistant mechanic under Coxswain Coley Hernon for a rescue that earned them both a Bronze Medal in 1962. A Dutch coaster had been driven aground and the crew took shelter on Mutton Island. The lifeboat could not reach them, so Mullin and crew members Thomas Joyce and Patrick Quinn took turns to try to row a small boat across to them. The wind was gusting to force 10, putting the tiny boat in great danger, but at the first attempt six men were taken off. Five more times they tried to row in to the island, each time being driven back by the sea. On the seventh attempt they got in to bring off the last two men – and their dog.

Bartley Mullin's account is typically modest: 'It was a bad night and there were plenty of seas running. We had to launch a little dinghy and row to the island. We were getting swamped. We took off the crew and landed them in Galway.' Yet Bartley is all too aware of the dangers. Cruelly, the sea has taken two of his sons. One drowned when he was fishing, and the other was lost in the harbour at Rossaveel where he worked on the ferry serving the islands.

Bartley Mullin (left) and Coley Hernon of the Galway Bay lifeboat.

Modern lifeboats are finding a new range of problems, and divers occupy more of the RNLI's time, even in remote places. In the summer of 1989 two divers got caught in bad weather at Doolin, County Clare, and could not get ashore; they were being battered by big seas and the strong tide was keeping them away from the land. A helicopter had been sent from Shannon, but was forced to land by the heavy squalls.

For Padraic Dillane, coxswain of the Galway Bay lifeboat, the problem was acute. The divers were close inshore in dangerous shoal waters; the lifeboat echo sounder readings fell quickly from 120 feet of water to a mere 17 feet, and a sea swell of 30 feet meant that the lifeboat could crash down on the rocks at any minute.

Dillane could not risk going in any closer and took a brave but risky decision. He would launch the lifeboat's small inflatable boat to cover the last 50 vital yards to the divers. Without hesitation Seamus Flaherty and Mairtin Fitzpatrick jumped into the inflatable and drove it through the waves, snatched up the divers and drove back to the lifeboat. The divers had been in the water for four hours and were in poor shape. Eventually the helicopter was able to take off again and airlifted them to safety.

COUNTY DONEGAL

Arranmore, County Donegal, completes the trio of long-established West Coast lifeboat stations, and its history shows that there is no pattern to sea rescue, no easy logic to explain why some lives are saved, others lost.

Early one October morning in 1981, while it was still dark, a fishing vessel struck a reef off Aran Island and her sister vessel fired red flares. Within 15 minutes of being alerted the Arranmore lifeboat launched into the gale-force winds; ten minutes later she was on the scene. Four men had been washed ashore and survived; three more were washed up but either drowned or died from hypothermia. The remainder perished nearer the wreck. The lifeboat spent over nine hours on a harrowing search, to no avail.

Another tragic search started when a man from a party of six students who had been out on a small dinghy swam ashore to say that his five companions were missing. He rushed to the first house he saw, which by good fortune was the home of Mary Conlon, sister of the lifeboat mechanic. She raised the alarm and rang all the crew, who were afloat in the boarding boat within 15 minutes. On their way to the lifeboat the crew heard shouts from the water and found a young woman from the missing dinghy. They picked her up and took her straight to Mrs Conlon's house, where both survivors were looked after.

The lifeboat crew then returned to the lifeboat and started a long search, firing parachute flares to illuminate the whole area. Local boats joined in right through the next day, and the lifeboatmen used their boarding boat to search the shallow areas. Divers came from the Garda, the naval service and volunteers from diving clubs. For seven days the search went on until the last body had been recovered. The lifeboat crew manned the boarding boat on a voluntary basis all week to provide surface safety cover for the divers.

In the Arranmore lifeboathouse is a plaque that reads: 'In memory of Isabel Pryse Lloyd, Alexander Ricketts, Justin Arbuthnott and Matthew Hallifax who tragically lost their lives off this coast on 28 July 1989'. Alongside it on the wall is another plaque recording the Gold Medal awarded to Coxswain John Boyle for a wartime rescue in which he saved 18 men from their wrecked steamer driven ashore off Tory Island, 24 miles north of Arranmore. At sea, tragedy and triumph are never far apart.

CHANGING PATTERNS

The lifeboat service is constantly evolving, changing in response to the different uses of the sea. Fishing ports grow or decline, marinas are opened and fill with pleasure craft of all shapes and sizes, and faster lifeboats mean that some stations can be regraded.

Originally, when the only power was sails and oars, lifeboats had to be spread thickly, one to cover each port or harbour. Then scores of stations were closed as motor lifeboats were introduced, one boat covering two or three former stations. Now, as more and more people go to sea for pleasure, many former lifeboat stations are being re-opened, often with speedy inshore lifeboats.

At **Tramore** the lifeboat station was closed in 1924 when a motor lifeboat went to Dunmore East. However, the station re-opened in 1964 with the first inshore lifeboat in Ireland, and the versatility of the inflatable boat, particularly when working close inshore among rocks and below cliffs, has proved itself time and again, performing feats that a larger lifeboat would find impossible.

Bangor was the second inshore lifeboat station in Ireland, opened in 1965. When a replacement lifeboat was needed, George and Lynne

The Tramore inshore lifeboat was twice thrown clear by breaking seas before the boy stranded on the rocks could be rescued.

Ralston, stalwarts of the station as lifeboat secretary and fundraiser, set up an appeal to young people throughout the province, which bought the Atlantic 21 *Youth of Ulster*. It was appropriate that Prince Edward agreed to name the boat, although as soon as his red helicopter of the Queen's Flight came over the harbour, the heavens opened leaving the reception line of VIPs bedraggled and sending the assembled guides and scouts rushing for cover.

North of Dublin the small harbour at **Skerries** lost its lifeboat in 1930, when Howth got a motor lifeboat. Once again the inflatable inshore lifeboat, sent to re-open the station in 1981, has proved invaluable.

Courtown, in County Wexford, closed in 1925 shortly after Wexford received its motor lifeboat, but re-opened with an inshore lifeboat in 1990.

Youghal has a different tale to tell, having been sad to lose its big lifeboat, the *Grace Darling*, in 1984, but pleased to see its versatile replacement Atlantic 21 inshore lifeboat. And although the two craft could hardly be more different, the traditional Liverpool Class afforded no more crew protection and, arguably, only marginally more safety in heavy weather than the rigid inflatable Atlantic with four times the speed.

Fenit is different again. The station was closed in 1969 because there were few effective services, and problems with crewing. But in 1994, because of an expanding harbour and marina development, the lifeboat station was re-opened with an Arun Class all-weather lifeboat.

In communities with a lifeboat history, it might be thought an easier task to re-establish a lifeboat station than in places where there has never been a lifeboat. But plugging gaps in the cover in Ireland has shown that new stations will attract ready volunteers and after a training and weeding-out process, a new lifeboat crew will emerge.

At **Clifden**, Connemara, the breathtaking cliffs and the high-banked, narrow country lanes posed the problems when the station was opened in 1988, for the extent of the coastline to be covered meant that several launching sites had to be identified, and the inshore lifeboat has to be towed along the road to the most appropriate place. But a Land-Rover and a trailer take up a lot of road, and negotiating the narrow bends can be more hazardous than the subsequent sea passage.

At **Kilkeel** the Atlantic 21 is launched into the narrow harbour entrance with a derrick, which swings the lifeboat over the harbour wall. With over 100 fishing boats active in the port, this can be a hazardous operation, as the entrance is too narrow for two boats to pass safely, so there is a blue flashing light on top of the lifeboathouse to warn of a launch, though the crew have their own, rather more effective, verbal means of communication.

The versatility of inshore lifeboats was shown by a rescue at **Portaferry**, a station set up in response to increasing pleasure craft traffic in and around Strangford Lough. The Lough is strewn with islands and rocky reefs, many hidden just below the surface at high tide. When Belfast

Kilkeel's Atlantic 21 lifeboat leaves the busy fishing port.

coastguard telephoned one cold December evening in 1982 to report that the yacht *Frieda* was overdue, there was a difficult decision to be taken. Conditions, even within the Lough, were marginal for the inflatable lifeboat, but the honorary secretary and the helmsman decided to launch.

Des Rogers, at the helm, drove the lifeboat out to search the islands and shoals, using a searchlight and firing parachute flares. After just an hour the yacht was spotted, wedged between two rocks and stranded by the falling tide. The winds had increased and were now force 8 gusting to storm force; the lifeboat was well beyond her safe operating limits. A helicopter arrived to help light up the scene with searchlights, but was withdrawn because of the severe weather. The lifeboatmen managed to find a sheltered gully, land and get across the rocks to the yachtsman. They now had to get home.

The wind was almost continuous storm force 10 and the seas so high that the 16-foot lifeboat was both hidden and sheltered in the troughs. The spray stung the eyes of the crew and visibility was almost down to zero. Des Rogers had to navigate with extreme caution, drawing on his extensive local knowledge backed by his wits, as the lifeboat was constantly awash. Coastguards and lifeboatmen gathered ashore to light up a safe landing spot and the three-hour ordeal was over. Only a small tough boat could have made the rescue; only local knowledge and determination brought the crew back safely.

The newest stations are **Bundoran, County Mayo, Kilrush**, on the Shannon Estuary, and **Larne**, all opened in 1994. An inshore lifeboat was sent to **Galway City** in 1995 and an all-weather station was added at Larne in the same year. If these are infants in lifeboat history, then **Ballyglass**, set up in 1989, has shown how quickly a lifeboat station grows to full maturity.

Belmullet is not at the end of the line – it is 50 miles beyond it. A long drive across peat bog, passing a peat-fired power station, will take you to this village of 1,100 people, which provides the crew for the lifeboat at Ballyglass, six miles further on. When the lifeboat arrived for the first time in 1989 over 2,000 people turned out from all over County Mayo, jamming the narrow lanes with their cars and crowding the small quay to the point of nearly falling in.

It was not long before the new crew, raw recruits only weeks before, were put to the test in a typical West Coast service. In February 1990 the lifeboat was still being evaluated when a 100-foot Spanish fishing boat, the *Xisti*, put out a distress call. Forty miles out at sea in a gale and very rough seas, she was holed and taking in water. Until then the Ballyglass crew – including a policeman, a forestry worker, a farmer, a shop assistant and just one fisherman – had been training, learning, working hard certainly, but enjoying the new experience of being lifeboatmen.

Now came their first real test, and for the next nine hours they were battered and pummelled as the winds gusted up to force 12, blowing at 100 mph, and the waves towered up to 60 feet in the open Atlantic.

The *Xisti* had her pumps working and her only hope was to run downwind to Killybegs, 70 miles away. In the horrific conditions the lifeboat escorted the damaged fishing boat until, in the darkness of the wintry night, they finally reached Killybegs. The official report is a masterpiece of understatement: 'With the casualty safely secured at 2115, the coxswain decided that having been at sea for almost nine hours and in the prevailing conditions, it would be prudent to remain there overnight.' The next day the crew took the lifeboat back home; it took just five hours this time, from breakfast to lunchtime, and the winds were only force 9!

HYDROGRAPHER

Francis Beaufort was born in Navan, up the river from the port of Drogheda, in 1774. He joined the Royal Navy, eventually becoming Hydrographer, and invented the Beaufort Scale, which measures wind speed. The basis of the scale was to match visible signs (waves and spray at sea, smoke and trees on land) with a series of numbers, 0 to 12, to indicate the strength of the wind. Force 12 is a hurricane with winds over 64 knots, waves over 40 feet and described in modern almanacs as 'air filled with foam and spray; sea completely white with driving spray; visibility very seriously affected'. Beaufort had a more direct description, 'that which no canvas could withstand'.

Sadly the RNLI's tradition of the Hydrographer of the Navy serving on the Institution's Committee of Management started after Beaufort's time, for he would have undoubtedly made a significant contribution to the work. But he is proudly remembered in his native County Meath, as well as in neighbouring County Louth, where the handbook of the history of local lifeboats records his achievements.

Today there is only one lifeboat station, at **Clogher Head**, but there used to be two at the mouth of the River Boyne, one on each shore, and also one at Blackrock in Dundalk Bay. Clogher Head is a quiet fishing village, modern bungalows alongside thatched fishermen's cottages, and its small harbour is looked after by harbourmaster Patrick Hodgins, who is also the honorary secretary of the lifeboat. He took over from one of the few women ever to hold the post, Maire Hoy.

Mrs Hoy was persuaded to step in as honorary secretary 'as a temporary measure' to take over from her husband who died suddenly. She carried on for 20 years, finding no difficulty in being in charge and taking the crucial launching decisions for the lifeboat. As she was also responsible for fundraising, she used to enlist the whole crew for collections.

Coxswain Fergal Sharkey runs a pub, as does his second coxswain, Declan Levins, but there is no rivalry either in business or on the lifeboat. Perhaps the only competition the Clogher station would enter, and win, is that for hospitality, for the welcome in this small community is always warm.

The new Mersey Class lifeboat delivered in January 1993 showed within six months the diversity of work at the station.

Four weeks after arriving she was called out to tow a disabled tug to Carlingford. Six weeks later there was a 30-mile dash to a Kilkeel trawler, the *Karen Mary*, taking in water, which the lifeboat towed to safety through heavy seas. In May there were three calls, to a merchant ship, a

Clogher Head's Mersey Class lifeboat Doris Bleasedale.

fishing boat and a yacht. In June there was a huge search, with lifeboats from Newcastle and Kilkeel and a helicopter, for a small boat sailing to the Isle of Man.

COUNTY DOWN

The Mountains of Mourne sweep down to the sea at **Newcastle** in County Down, and on a clear day their legendary beauty can be seen from the coast road running into the town from Carlingford Lough. On the other side of that coast road is Dundrum Bay, a traditional anchoring point for ships waiting for the tides to enter the Lough or local harbours, and also the sight of many wrecks.

The first lifeboat in Northern Ireland was established in 1825 at Rossglass near Newcastle, County Down. The lifeboat was under coastguard control and, as was typical for that time, many of the rescues were made by coastguard officers. Soon a gallantry record started to build; by the time the SS *Great Britain* ran aground nearby in Dundrum Bay in 1846, three Gold Medals and ten Silver Medals had been awarded to local men, many of them coastguard officers. The number of wrecks in the Bay led to the placing of a lifeboat at Newcastle, the Earl of Annesley MP paying for the boathouse, and the medal count continued to rise, with a further six being won by the end of the century.

The station was very active during the war, when the hazards were increased enormously, not only from enemy action but also because all coastal lights were extinguished. The vital supply convoys, being natural targets for the enemy, also became an extra problem for the lifeboat service.

In January 1941 the Newcastle lifeboat launched twice within eight days to merchant ships from the other Newcastle, on the Tyne, and Coxswain Patrick Murphy won a Bronze Medal for each rescue. But his real test was to come exactly a year later. A south-easterly gale was blowing, pushing the seas right into Dundrum Bay, and it forced a small convoy of ships to run aground.

The Newcastle lifeboat had a 20-mile journey through the gale to reach them. A very rough sea was running, and the night was so dark with rain and sleet that sometimes the coxswain could see for less than the length of his boat. By the time the lifeboat arrived one of the ships, the *Browning* of Liverpool, needed help. The tide was rising fast and earlier rescue attempts from the shore had been abandoned. Horses on board the steamer had gone wild with fear and had broken loose; the captain had to give orders for them to be shot, and in the confusion the seaman who did it put two bullets through his own hand.

For over an hour Coxswain Murphy tried to get his lifeboat alongside the steamer, but the seas were breaking right over him, and one moment he would see the ship towering above him, the next he would be lifted by the seas to look down on its deck. The only chance of a rescue was to go between the steamer and the rocks.

The shallow channel between them was 16 feet wide at its narrowest; the lifeboat was nine feet broad. The seas were surging through, but Patrick Murphy put on full speed and drove the lifeboat through unscathed. He was now on the sheltered side of the ship and took 20 men off with ease. That was one more than the safe quota for his lifeboat in rough weather, and a further ten men were still on the *Browning*.

The coxswain knew the risk that he would run in taking them. They would add three-quarters of a ton to the lifeboat's load, and would bring the deck almost awash. And he had to go back into the storm, then travel for miles with his boat overloaded. At the same time he knew that it would be impossible to return. He accepted the risk and took all the men on board.

The survivors were packed into the lifeboat and told to lie down and keep still. The lifeboat had no space to turn round and the only way out was to go straight ahead, across the reef on which the steamer's stern lay. Yet there was only enough water on the reef when a wave broke across it, and any mistake would leave the lifeboat aground, ready to be capsized by the next wave.

Picking his moment, Patrick saw three huge breakers rolling in and put the engines full ahead – he crossed the reef without even touching it. He had not told anybody of his plan and when the mate of the *Browning* saw what he had done, he said that had he known, he would never have left the wreck.

The RNLI, awarding Patrick Murphy a Gold Medal for conspicuous gallantry, summed up the contradictory qualities he had shown when they praised his 'reckless daring, great coolness and superb seamanship'.

The Irish Sea continues to take its toll of shipping to this day. While fishing is generally in decline, Kilkeel, just south of Newcastle, still has an active fleet of over 100 boats, making it the biggest fishing port in Ireland. Much smaller fleets operate out of Newcastle and Clogher to the south, and the three lifeboat stations at these ports often work together on searches for overdue boats.

These searches are one of the most difficult jobs for lifeboat crews. The fishing boats are usually local, their crews known to the whole community. By the time they are reported overdue there is a good chance that they will already have foundered and their crews drowned. But there is always hope, and even the grim task of bringing in bodies is of value to the bereaved relatives, whose grieving is so much more difficult if their men are never found.

When huge resources are committed to a search, they must be co-ordinated from both the land, by the coastguard, and at the scene itself. RNLI coxswains are trained to become on-scene commanders, and Francis Morgan, coxswain at Newcastle, found himself with this role when a local fishing boat, the *Silver Quest*, failed to return after attending to her creels in Dundrum Bay on 7 September 1990.

Coxswain Francis Morgan (second left) and the crew of the Newcastle lifeboat.

The lifeboat was alerted in the evening and launched at 9.45 pm to start a search that was to last well into the next day. She was soon joined by the Atlantic 21 inshore lifeboat from **Portaferry**, and eventually lifeboats from **Kilkeel, Clogher Head** and **Port St Mary**, along with seven fishing boats, two helicopters, a Nimrod aircraft and an Irish warship.

Throughout the night Morgan took responsibility not only for his own boat but also for the complicated search patterns of the small fleet, painstakingly plotting courses over an ever-expanding area to try and find the *Silver Quest*. The Newcastle and Portaferry lifeboats spent over 16 hours at sea, extra fuel and meals being ferried out by a fishing boat. Portaferry's Atlantic 21, being a fast inshore boat with little crew protection, needed crew changes every two or three hours, yet still the search went on until 2 pm the following day, when there was no further chance of finding the fishermen alive.

Six days later the body of one of the men was found and local fishermen organised a renewed search for the second. The weather was rough, so the Newcastle lifeboat joined them and for nine long hours Francis Morgan and his crew searched with them, but nothing was found. At the end of these gruelling missions there are no expectant crowds on the quayside to welcome the crew home, no handshakes from bedraggled survivors as they step ashore, nobody to say thank you. Wet, cold and tired, the lifeboat crew have to rehouse and refuel their boat, wash her down, stow all the gear ready for action then go home and wait for the next call.

FERRY DISASTER

The disaster most feared by coastguards, lifeboatmen and helicopter pilots alike is the sinking of a passenger ferry. With so many people at risk, the only hope is that passengers will be able to use the ferry's own liferaft and lifeboats and that they can be found quickly. Tragically, three major post-war disasters have proved that hope to be a frail one. The rescuers' nightmare remains.

Lessons were certainly learned when the Stranraer to Larne ferry *Princess Victoria* sank in the gales of January 1953, which also claimed hundreds of lives in the floods on the East Coast of England. As the ferry left Stranraer at 8 am it was obvious to both passengers and crew that they were in for a rough crossing, but this was a well-found ship, only six years old, and she had made the trip scores of times before.

But less than an hour out of harbour the captain was having to contend with more than just the storm. The stern doors, used for loading and unloading the cars, had been buckled when a huge wave hit them, and in spite of efforts by the crew to force them back, water was pouring on to the car deck. Shortly after 10 o'clock the ship's tannoy system announced that the vessel was in difficulties – something that the passengers already knew as they could only move around the decks by clinging on to the rails as the list increased. Then came the order over the tannoy; all aboard to don lifejackets.

The 127 passengers and 49 crew remained calm and obeyed the order, but the ferry was now drifting and, as the passengers assembled on the weather deck, rescuers were being given inaccurate positions as the ship careered about. Suddenly at 1.45 pm she heeled over, and the passengers were thrown against a side wall that suddenly became a floor as she started to sink.

The last message was sent at 1.58 pm. Two minutes later the *Princess Victoria* sank. In a last desperate bid to attract the rescuers' attention, the crew fired distress rockets, but because of the list the rockets did not go high enough to be seen.

John Fitzpatrick was travelling on the *Princess Victoria* to visit relatives in Northern Ireland: 'I jumped on to a deck shelter and from there into the sea, which was only a few feet below me. I managed to grab a raft and haul myself on board. Then I was joined by a young girl, but a couple of minutes later a huge wave overturned our raft. We were both thrown into the water. I managed to grab the raft again and the girl grabbed it too. Just at that moment another big wave washed her overboard. I never saw her again.'

The **Portpatrick** lifeboat from Scotland had been searching for the *Princess Victoria* since 11 o'clock, as the ferry had given a position four miles from the Scottish coast. But the position was wrong and the communications chain, with no direct links between the lifeboat and the coastguard, and all messages being passed through coast radio stations, caused confusion about which messages had been passed and received. Direction-finding bearings were taken by the radio stations, but did not give an accurate position for the ferry. By the time she sank, she was only a few miles from the Irish coast.

The first that Hugh Nelson, coxswain of the **Donaghadee** lifeboat, heard of the trouble was when a newspaper reporter telephoned his home. Immediately he and his son went down to the lifeboat and minutes later the coastguard asked them to launch. The lifeboat went straight to the ship's last reported position, but it was wrong – by over five miles. A destroyer and several merchant ships were also searching, and all were going the wrong way; southwards, away from the wreck. By good fortune, one ship, the *Orchy*, was further north than the rest and she came across wreckage. The other ships turned immediately and headed for the spot.

The Donaghadee lifeboat, with great skill, took 29 men from one ship's lifeboat, a solitary survivor from another boat, then lifted out John Fitzpatrick, who had spent three hours on his liferaft. The Portpatrick boat found two men on liferafts, a trawler rescued one and the destroyer eight. In all, 133 people died in the Irish Sea that afternoon; not one woman or child survived. The Court of Inquiry found that the stern doors were inadequate and that the arrangements for clearing water were

The Donaghadee crew of 1953 who took part in the Princess Victoria *rescue.*

insufficient. Once the sea had entered the ship, she was doomed.

Thirty-four years later the roll-on-roll-off ferry *Herald of Free Enterprise* sank off Zeebrugge. The reasons were that the bow door was not properly shut, and that once water had entered the ship it could not be cleared. She capsized, and 194 people died, in spite of a massive rescue operation co-ordinated by Belgian sea captain Marc Claus. Later Claus was to describe how, as he mobilised everything at his disposal, he knew that he needed time to think, but that every second wasted meant another life lost. His efforts earned him an OBE, an award very rarely given to foreign nationals.

In 1994 disaster struck again. The huge Baltic ferry *Estonia* on the run from Tallin to Sweden sank at night in a storm with the loss of over 800 people, most asleep in their cabins and trapped as the ferry sank within minutes. In this instance the force of the sea had broken off the bow doors.

Roll-on-roll-off ferries have vast car decks with no subdivisions, and if tons of water pour in and swill around, capsize is inevitable. While the *Princess Victoria*, her stern doors buckled and letting in seawater, took over four hours to sink, the *Herald* and the *Estonia*, with bow doors gaping open, capsized in minutes. The rescuer's nightmare remains.

SEA DOCTORS

Bad fortune seems to dog some ships just as it follows some people. The Hull trawler *Junella* ran aground on the Isle of Skye in 1980 in a severe storm and her crew of 29 was taken off by the **Stornoway** lifeboat. A year later *Junella* was back in action, when one of the crew was taken critically ill. The **Portrush** lifeboat was called to take Dr William Hill, the station's medical advisor, to tend to him.

It took less than an hour to reach the trawler, in spite of a storm, and Dr Hill boarded the *Junella* with lifeboat first-aider Albert McQuilken to find that the man had a brain haemorrhage. A Wessex helicopter arrived overhead, but the doctor decided that the patient should be taken ashore by the lifeboat to avoid undue stress.

The helicopter was then called away as the lifeboat set off at half speed to avoid too much slamming. Suddenly a message came through about a

The Portrush lifeboat leaves harbour in a gale gusting to hurricane force 12 with waves over 45 feet high.

second medical problem. The trawler *St Jasper* also had an injured seaman, and the single-engined helicopter would have to withdraw, as dusk was falling.

The lifeboat landed the first patient at Portrush, then set out for the *St Jasper*. Using the same tactics as before Coxswain James Stewart asked the trawler skipper to make a lee and the lifeboat tied up alongside as both vessels steamed slowly north-east to maintain steerage in the heavy seas. Dr Hill and Albert McQuilken scrambled aboard to find an unconscious man who had accidentally inhaled fumes. The Wessex helicopter had been replaced by a twin-engined Sea King, with a night capability, but again the doctor decided that the patient should be taken ashore by lifeboat, and the helicopter was released. Although the weather was moderating, the sea was still rough, and with care the coxswain made full speed back to Portrush, anxious to get the man safely to hospital.

Dr Hill was awarded a special doctor's Thanks on Vellum certificate for the strenuous efforts he had made, particularly in the risky act of boarding the trawlers as the lifeboat steamed alongside them.

SAVING SHEEP

Portrush lifeboatmen were joined by the crew from **Red Bay** in another unusual task when floods swamped nearby Ballycastle and Cushendall in October 1990, putting householders at risk. Taking the Arun Class lifeboat into Ballycastle Bay was one thing – that was at sea. The next job was to launch the inflatable – on to a lorry!

Lifeboatmen Trevor McCullen and Trevor Creelman were driven to the centre of the town, where the River Tow had burst its banks, stranding a large number of people. Seamanship gave way to improvisation as the two Trevors pushed and paddled their boat from house to house, unable to use the engine because of fences and posts underwater. In places the water was eight feet deep and the men could not tell what was under the boat, waiting to rip through the inflatable hull. For two hours they searched the houses, ferrying 22 people to high ground and safety.

Meanwhile, the Red Bay crew had decided that their larger inflatable inshore lifeboat was too big and heavy to negotiate the flooded streets of Cushendall, so they borrowed two open boats and teamed up with the fire brigade to check all the flooded houses and cars. One family was stranded in a bungalow with water four feet deep coursing through their kitchen – they had to be rescued through the window!

Later in the morning one team was diverted to Glengarriff to rescue stranded sheep, another team sent out to Ballycastle to help there, and in the afternoon a second foray was made to Glengarriff where 14 sheep were rescued. By 4 o'clock the flood waters receded and the emergency was over, leaving the lifeboat crews with the more familiar work of going to sea, where underwater obstructions are marked on charts and there are few sheep to be rescued.

CHAPTER TWELVE

Survivors' stories – saved from the sea

'WHEN I SAW her [the Yarmouth lifeboat] . . . I stood up and started waving my coat. And I couldn't stop. I kept on waving until I could actually see the lifeboatmen, smiling. They gave us such a feeling of security. It was like being reborn. I had so much trust in them. If they had asked me to jump into that rough water I would have done it.'

Dorset fisherman David Gimson

'I don't know how long I was in the water, but I remember I started to panic and shout, as I was very cold and had been in the water a long time. All of a sudden what seemed like a red log appeared in front of me, and a hand came over and grabbed me. I have never been so pleased to see anyone.'

19-year-old Cornish angler Stephen Quayle

Few emotions can equal the sheer relief felt by the victims of the sea, in fear of their lives, when they at last see a lifeboat coming to rescue them. The eye-witness accounts of survivors like these spell out the unique value of the RNLI's work.

David Gimson's ordeal began on 16 January 1983, after a quiet day's fishing with a friend, Nigel Fitzgerald, off the Isle of Wight. The two men had just decided to return home to Poole when the engine of their fishing dory failed. They sent up flares and tried in vain to attract the attention of passing boats. As the January night fell, their anchor broke free and they began to drift towards the rocky coastline, buffeted by the increasingly rough seas, before they could attach another anchor.

'All night, every time I thought of my wife and children, I was

The Dover lifeboat lands a man with mild hypothermia, sustained after he swam out to rescue a parachutist who came down in the sea.

frightened for them as well as for myself,' explains David. 'I began to think I should never see them again.'

But seasoned fishermen like David know that it is vital to try and stay in control, no matter how powerless you feel.

'Every time, I tried to wipe all such thoughts from my mind because I did not want to get so worried and so frightened that I would perhaps do something silly and make my children orphans.'

Despite their desperate situation, David had faith that the RNLI would eventually find them. 'Somehow, I suppose I knew that as long as the boat stayed upright and at anchor, and we stayed in the boat, the RNLI would rescue us.'

At daybreak their wives reported them missing, and the fishermen were hugely relieved to see the maroon flares go up – they knew that help was on its way.

'We were full of hope and enthusiasm,' recalls David. 'But the sea had got up. It was very rough with waves probably 12 to 14 feet high; the crests were breaking and coming into the boat. It wasn't serious enough to cause us trouble because the water was draining out as fast as it came in, but when you are helpless it is still frightening.'

As a rescue helicopter came over to search for them, David took off his coat, which had a bright red lining, and frantically waved it. To his dismay the helicopter failed to spot them, and the two men began to give up hope.

'When I saw the helicopter disappearing I thought, "That's it, we are not going to survive", the seas were so bad by that time. I thought about my family and wished that I had never come out fishing that Sunday.'

David was just about to smoke his last cigarette, one he had decided to save until there was no hope left, when he thought he heard an engine. It was the **Yarmouth** lifeboat!

'I had never realised how beautiful a boat can be, and I had never seen seven men look so beautiful in all my life,' says David.

The lifeboat quickly came alongside and the crew tossed David a towline. When they had made it fast and cut the anchor free, David and Nigel were helped into the lifeboat.

'I can never explain how wonderful I felt, partly because the lifeboatmen themselves were so happy,' David remembers. 'The coxswain told us that when they first spotted us, everyone was just jumping up and down for joy because they had found two live men when they had been afraid it might have been two dead men.'

David had been expecting a telling-off for causing the crew so much trouble; instead, they were welcomed aboard with coffee and brandy and plied with chocolate and cigarettes. The coxswain reassured them that anyone could have found themselves in the same predicament.

David will always be deeply grateful. 'No matter what I can do, I can never repay those lifeboatmen, or the RNLI. It was the men from Yarmouth who saved my life. I owe them everything, not only that I am living today, but that my children have a father.'

Angler Stephen Quayle also owes the RNLI his life. At sunset on 30 November 1984 he set off with his father and a friend for an evening's fishing off the rocks at Newquay's Fistral Beach. He was not to know that the peaceful angling trip would soon turn into a nightmare as

Nine-year-old Jennifer Stone of Onchan, Isle of Man, says thank you to Coxswain Robbie Corran of Douglas who saved her and her uncle when they were cut off by the tide.

he struggled to survive in icy waters for over 40 minutes.

At first all went well, until, at about 6 pm, Stephen's line became jammed in rocks by the waterline. The sea was fairly flat at that moment, although there had been big waves breaking against the rocks a little earlier. Stephen decided to climb down to release the line.

'As I was leaning over I happened to look up and saw a big wave coming towards me,' recalls Stephen. 'It was like a wall of water. I crouched down into a ball, hoping that the sea would go over me. The next thing I knew, I was being thrashed around in the sea near the rocks and decided to swim away from them. I started to shout, then I heard father and Dave shouting back.'

Stephen's father quickly cast his rod so that the line fell within his son's grasp. Unfortunately the young man was so anxious to get back that he pulled too hard on the line and it broke. He tried to swim for shore but the sea forced him back.

'I could see I was drifting outwards. I decided to tread water.'

Stephen then found that he was dangerously encumbered by his protective clothing. 'My boots filled with water and I kicked them off. My jacket was also very heavy and the hood kept going over my head, but I couldn't get it off.'

At last he saw a flare go up from the rocks, but the sea was getting rougher and he was becoming increasingly exhausted.

'I kept seeing these big waves coming in. I would duck under them to pop up behind; they dragged me down. I tried several times to shout back ashore.'

Just as Stephen's strength was about to give out he was hauled aboard Newquay's inflatable lifeboat. Mike Morris, then honorary secretary of

The Whitby inshore lifeboat takes a party of 27 schoolchildren and three teachers to safety after they were cut off by the tide.

Newquay lifeboat station, had been in two minds whether to launch the inflatable; it was pitch dark, there was a strong south-easterly breeze, a force 6, and a very choppy sea. Luckily for Stephen, Mike decided that the lifeboat could and should be sent out.

Once on board, Stephen was given emergency first aid by the lifeboat crew. He was suffering from shock and hypothermia. At one stage he lost consciousness, and worried crew members were unable to find his pulse. Back inside the harbour he was given oxygen and rushed to Truro hospital by ambulance, still numb with cold. Once in hospital he made a rapid recovery and was fit enough to return home with his parents that night, full of gratitude.

'I can never thank the lifeboat crew enough for rescuing me,' he said later. 'I know that the sea was very big, but I never gave up hope and I knew that they would try to get me.'

Yachtsman Roger Cole also has cause to be grateful to the RNLI. As he described in a letter to *The Lifeboat* magazine, Roger and his crew were rescued by the **Salcombe** lifeboat during an extremely rough trip from Plymouth to Dartmouth. They left Plymouth in a 'bumpy' sea, then, as they approached the Bolt Tail, the seas suddenly became very steep.

'We came up behind a large wave and came off the other side as though we were falling off a block of flats. The vessel submarined into the next wave,' wrote Roger. The impact removed the windscreen and most of the roof, throwing Roger through the teak aft doors and breaking his forearm and collar bone.

'I was washed into the aft cabin with about 1,000 gallons of water and thought, in fact, that I had gone overboard. I might add that the sea is like ice at the end of March!'

As he felt around him it became obvious that he was in the cabin, which was filled to the roof with water.

'I thought at this point that the boat had sunk with me in it.

On surfacing in the cabin stairwell, you can imagine my relief in finding not only that the other crew members were not washed overboard, but that we were still afloat with both engines running.'

However, Roger and his crew were in desperate trouble. The force of the water had ripped away the instrument console, leaving the throttles immoveable. Roger immediately made a distress call to Brixham coastguard, and asked for the lifeboat to be launched. He believed that the yacht might go down at any minute, as huge waves were continuing to break over the boat.

Roger managed to head the yacht east towards the Salcombe River and soon spotted the Salcombe lifeboat, which escorted the crippled vessel over the treacherous bar in Salcombe harbour and saw it safely into the inner harbour.

'I think we had a narrow escape and it was only by the narrowest margin that we weren't all in a watery grave, being searched for by the lifeboat crew, who came out without a thought for themselves in the terrible weather that day,' concluded Roger.

Some survivors and their families express their gratitude to the RNLI by writing to the Poole headquarters, or to the crew that rescued them. The **Lowestoft** lifeboat coxswain received a particularly touching letter from the granddaughter of Mr George Bird, an elderly man who had been rescued:

'Dear Mr Catchpole,
Just a few lines of very dear thanks.
Mr George Bird, who you and your crew saved, was and still is my grandad thanks to the bravery and courage of you men.
My grandad is 73 and I love him very much, if he had have died, a big part of me would have died as well.
So once again I just can't thank you enough.
Love,
Debbie

Surprisingly, victims are not always grateful at first.

'We rescued a young girl who'd been in the sea for hours,' recalled Joe Adams, former honorary secretary of the **Hastings** lifeboat. 'I took her home, my wife gave her a hot bath and a nightie and our bed to sleep in for 12 hours, and she walked off without a word of thanks.'

Joe puts this apparent bare-faced ingratitude down to a mixture of shame and shock, 'shame that they've put themselves in such a position, shock that they've been staring death in the face for hours. . . Ten days later, she wrote us a marvellous letter.'

Selsey in Sussex is another station that provides a five-star service to survivors, who are often given a bed for the night by crew members' families or the station's voluntary workers. On one occasion the wife of lifeboatman Ernest Scott acted as a valet to three people picked up from a capsized yacht. The survivors had been clinging to the hull for four and a half hours by the time they were rescued; while they were recovering in hospital, Mrs Scott washed, dried and aired their clothes. When they were discharged they stayed overnight at the home of the station's honorary secretary, Clive Cockayne.

However sympathetically they are treated, experienced sailors often find it difficult to come to terms with the fact that they needed rescuing.

'Regardless of all the reassurances that I have received to the effect that I made the right decision in accepting the offer of assistance, I still cannot help feeling an element of embarrassment and keep asking myself what we would have done if no help had been at hand,' wrote Lawrence Phillips in his letter of thanks to the **Hastings** crew. 'I will, of course, never know, but I do hope that I never have need of your services again!'

Lawrence Phillips and his two fellow sailors were rescued by the Hastings lifeboat in July 1991 when their yacht got into difficulties.

'I found the whole experience humbling in the extreme,' recalled Mr

Phillips, 'especially reflecting upon the number of you employed and the enormous resources employed purely for our well-being.'

'Having sailed for 35 years, such a course of events was not one I ever thought would happen to me,' wrote Paul Williamson, who was rescued off **Galway** when his motor sailor ketch suffered fuel failure. 'This was the one situation everyone fears, and it was very reassuring to see the Arun coming to our assistance.'

But not everyone is relieved to see the lifeboat coming for them. Some even indignantly refuse to be rescued, like one elderly gentleman out in his yacht in gale-force winds. The coastguard had expressed concern for his safety, so the **Ramsgate** and **Margate** lifeboats launched to help him. When the Ramsgate crew found him, in the diplomatic terms of the RNLI's daily summary of services, he 'refused any assistance and indicated the direction the lifeboat should take, then went below refusing to communicate further'.

Undeterred, both Margate lifeboats again went to his aid two days later. This time the yacht had run aground on Margate sands, and the old man was perched on the stern. When he did not respond to calls from the crew of the all-weather lifeboat, the inflatable went alongside; they found that he was confused and seemed unaware of anything that was going on around him. As he also had a head injury, the crew immediately took him ashore to the waiting ambulance. Both lifeboats then towed the old man's yacht into Ramsgate harbour.

* * * * *

So the work of the lifeboat crews goes on. It is often unremarkable, in reasonable conditions and without much drama. A rescue takes place, on average, every two hours, day and night, every day of the year. The men and women who carry out these rescues never know what they will face. Yet still they remain ready to go to the help of complete strangers, whatever the time, whatever the conditions. They make the RNLI an organisation of which everybody in Britain and Ireland can be proud.

Christie and Caroline Brown recover from their ordeal after being rescued from the ketch Donald Searle *by the Hayling Island lifeboat.*

APPENDIX ONE

'The lifeboatman's VC': Gold Medal awards in the 20th century

1901	James Haylett, Caister	Aged 78, he waded into the surf to pull two men from the capsized lifeboat.
1907	Daniel Rees, Barry	Saved two men from the capsized yacht *Firefly* by putting out in small dinghy.
1908	William Owen, Holyhead	Saved nine men from the SS *Harold* of Liverpool.
1911	Rev John O'Shea, Ardmore	Parish priest who led the rescue attempt in an open boat for the crew of the schooner *Teaser*.
1914	Thomas Langlands, Whitby Robert Smith, Tynemouth H. E. Burton, Inspector	For rescues from the wrecked hospital ship *Rohilla*.
1917	Henry Blogg, Cromer	Rescued 11 men from the SS *Fernebo*, blown in half by an explosion.
1920	John Howells, Fishguard	Rescued seven men from the wrecked schooner *Hermina*.
1922	John Swan, Lowestoft William Fleming, Gorleston	Rescued 24 men from the wreck of the SS *Hopelyn*.
1927	Owen Jones, Moelfre William Roberts, Moelfre	Saved three men from the ketch *Excel*; one lifeboatman died from exposure on this 17-hour rescue.
1927	Henry Blogg, Cromer	Rescued 15 men from the oil tanker *Georgia*, broken in half on Happisburgh Sands.
1934	Robert Patton, Runswick	Saved a man from the SS *Dispenser*, but was crushed between the ship and the lifeboat and subsequently died.
1936	Patrick Sliney, Ballycotton	In a rescue lasting over three days, he saved eight men from the Daunt Rock lightship.
1940	Robert Cross, Humber	Rescued the crew of the trawler *Gurth* in a blizzard and onshore gale.

1940	John Boyle, Arranmore	Saved 18 men from the SS *Stolwyk*, hauling them through the water for over four hours.
1941	Henry Blogg, Cromer	Rescued 88 men from four ships in a convoy aground on Happisburgh Sands; twice he drove his lifeboat on to the submerged decks to reach the men.
1942	Patrick Murphy, Newcastle	Rescued 39 of the crew of the SS *Browning*.
1942	John Maclean, Peterhead	In three days he rescued 44 crew of the SS *Runswick*; 26 crew of the SS *Fidra*; and 36 crew of the SS *Saltwick*.
1942	William Bannison, Hartlepool	After three separate attempts he rescued five from the SS *Hawkwood*.
1943	Robert Cross, Humber	Saved 19 men from the grounded trawler *Almondine*.
1944	William Gammon, Mumbles	On a bitter winter night, with two crew in their 70s and two in their 60s, he saved 42 men from the frigate *Cheboque*, aground in the surf.
1949	Thomas King, St Helier	After nine hours searching for a plane in a gale, he went in amongst rocks to save the yacht *Maurice Georges* and crew.
1959	Richard Evans, Moelfre	Took the lifeboat into boiling surf to rescue eight crew from the MV *Hindlea*.
1963	Hubert Petit, St Peter Port	Took nine men off the MV *Johan Collett*, six while she was under tow.
1966	Richard Evans, Moelfre Harold Harvey, Inspector	In a combined rescue, he saved 15 crew from the MV *Nafsiporos*, whose own lifeboat crashed down on to the Holyhead lifeboat during the rescue.
1976	Keith Bower, Torbay	Rescued 10 from the MV *Lyrma*; at one point the lifeboat was trapped under the ship's gunwales.
1979	Brian Bevan, Humber	Rescued four from the MV *Revi* in a winter gale; the captain was taken off minutes before the ship sank.
1981	Michael Scales, St Peter Port	Rescued 29 people from the MV *Bonita* in a violent storm; over 50 runs in were needed to take off the survivors.
1981	Trevelyan Richards, Penlee	Rescued four from the MV *Union Star* before the lifeboat was destroyed in the storm and crew and survivors all perished.

APPENDIX TWO

Lifeboat disasters in the 20th century

THE LIST BELOW records lives lost in capsizes and when lifeboats were damaged on service. Lifeboatmen have also been lost or killed from other causes such as being washed overboard or injured.

Date	Station	Lifeboatmen lost	Date	Station	Lifeboatmen lost
1900	Padstow	8	1939	Cullercoats	6
1901	Caister	9	1942	Newburgh	2
1903	Mumbles	6	1947	Mumbles	8
1907	Ryde	2	1952	Bridlington	1
1908	Newquay	1	1953	Fraserburgh	6
1910	St Davids	3	1953	Arbroath	6
1914	Fethard	9	1954	Scarborough	3
1914	Peterhead	3	1959	Broughty Ferry	8
1915	Worthing	1	1962	Seaham	5
1916	Port Eynon	3	1969	Longhope	8
1916	Salcombe	13	1970	Fraserburgh	5
1920	Rhoscolyn	5	1977	Kilmore Quay	1
1928	Rye Harbour	17	1981	Penlee	8
1939	St Ives	7			

Index

Aberdeen 204, 209–10
Aberdovey 171–12
Abersoch 150
Aberystwyth 159–60
Admiralty 11, 58
Aith 189
Aldeburgh 57, 73, 80–1
Alderney 138–39
Amble 40, 46, 110
Angle 164–65
Anstruther 203
Appledore 123–24
Arbroath 204–6, 254
Ardmore 252
Arklow 221
Arran 195, 197
Arranmore 229, 232–33, 252
Atlantic College 156–57
Ballycotton 225–27, 252
Ballyglass 229, 236
Baltimore 223, 228
Bamburgh 30, 45
Bangor 233–34
Barmouth 148–50
Barra Island 166, 182–84
Barrow 21–3, 25
Barry Dock 145–46, 252
Baxter, Raymond 176
Beaufort Scale 236
Beaumaris 35, 157
Bembridge 83–4, 94
Berwick 40
Birmingham 13, 67
Blackpool 18–21
Blue Peter 104–5, 128, 146, 202
Blyth 47–8
Borth 147–48
Bridlington 51–2, 54, 110, 254
Brighton 93–4
Broughty Ferry 203–4, 254
Buckie 179, 207–8
Bude 124–5
Bundoran 229, 236
Burnham 76–7
Burry Port 158
Caister 252, 254

Calshot 96–7
Campbeltown 195–96
Canterbury, Archbishop of 227–28
Cardigan 170
Churchill, Sir Winston 56
Clacton 81
Cleethorpes 73–5
Clifden 229, 234
Clogher Head 237–38, 240
Coastguard 42, 44, 69, 82, 116–17, 133, 144, 165, 174, 201, 206
Conwy 171
Cook, Captain 50
Courtmacsherry 223–24
Courtown 234
Coventry 67
Craster 46
Criccieth 151–52
Cresswell 43–4
Cromer 53, 64–6, 77–9, 252–53
Cullercoats 41–2, 254
Darling, Grace 43, 45, 214, 234
Donaghadee 199, 212–13, 223, 242–43
Douglas 9, 10, 25, 28, 247
Dover 58, 60, 71–2, 88, 95, 97–5, 246
Dublin 214–16
Dunkirk 33, 57–61
Dun Laoghaire 215
Dunbar 96, 201–2
Dungeness 60–1, 95, 103–4
Dunmore East 211–12
Eastbourne 56, 61, 95, 98
Estonia, lifeboat service 28
Exmouth 133
Eyemouth 200–1
Falmouth 131–2
Fastnet Race 120, 222–24
Fenit 229, 234
Fethard 254
Filey 50–2
Fishguard 146, 252
Flamborough 51–2

Fleetwood 20–2, 25
Flint 161
Formby 11
Fowey 133–34
Fraserburgh 176–80, 254
Fundraising 12–15, 145, 216
Galway Bay 229–32, 251
Galway City 229, 236
Girvan 198–99
Greathead, Henry 31–2
Great Yarmouth & Gorleston 65, 70–2, 252
Grimsby 53, 63, 73
Happisburgh 67, 68
Hartlepool 37–40, 48, 252
Harwich 73
Hastings 8, 96, 100–1, 250
Hayling Island 82–5, 99, 168, 251
Heath, Edward 176–7
Helensburgh 196–7
Helicopters 7, 20, 25, 37, 39, 41–2, 72, 83–4, 86, 95–6, 100–1, 111–12, 116–17, 119–21, 124–25, 130, 133, 135, 148, 157, 178, 183, 189, 209–10, 218, 223–24, 232, 246
HM The Queen 128, 184
HM The Queen Mother 184
HRH The Princess Royal 102, 128
HRH The Duke of Kent 100
Hillary, Richard 62
Hillary, Sir William 9–11, 25, 28, 62
Holyhead 143, 158–59, 220, 252–53
Horton & Port Eynon 148, 254
Howth 215, 222, 234
Hoylake 15, 18
Humber 51–55, 57, 63–4, 66, 75, 77, 252–53
Hunstanton 69, 99
Hythe 60–1
Iceland 111–13, 186
Ilfracombe 130–1, 170

Invergordon 208–9
Islay 182–84
Kegworth, air crash 51
Kilkeel 234–35, 240
Kilmore Quay 216–18, 254
Kilrush 229, 236
Kinghorn 203
Kippford 200
Kirkcudbright 24, 199
Kirkwall 174–75, 186–88
Kyle of Lochalsh 191
Largs 167–68, 197
Larne 236
Leicester 67–8
Lerwick 189–91
Lewis, Richard 181
Little & Broad Haven
    154–55
Littlehampton 104–6
Littlestone 95
Liverpool 11, 12, 64, 109
Lizard 117, 131
Llandudno 161–62
Lochinver 191–92
Longhope 173–76, 254
Looe 136
Lough Swilly 213–14
Lowestoft 67–9, 70–2, 76,
    250, 252
Lukin, Lionel 30, 32
Lyme Regis 135
Lymington 101–3
Lytham St Annes 12, 13, 18,
    20, 25
Mablethorpe 81
Macara, Charles & Marion
    13–5
Macduff 179
Mallaig 192–93
Manchester 13, 14
Marazion 135–36
Margate 59, 60, 62, 99, 100,
    251
Matthew, Brian 35
Minehead 126
Moelfre 25, 142–43, 159,
    252–53
Montrose 204, 206–7
Morecambe 16–8
Mudeford 101–2
Mumbles 57, 110, 141,
    143–45, 156, 253–54
New Brighton 16
Newburgh 254
New Quay (Dyfed) 15, 153
Newbiggin 43–5
Newcastle (Co Down)
    238–41, 253
Newhaven 91–2, 95–6,
Newquay (Cornwall)
    125–26, 247–49, 254
North Berwick 202

North Kessock 209
North Sunderland 45–6
Norway 29
Nottingham 67
Oakley, Richard 34, 181
Oban 167, 194
Padstow 128–30, 254
Peel 28–9
Penarth 153–54
Penlee 115–19, 121, 131–32,
    135, 253–54
Peterhead 207, 253–4
Plymouth 131–33
Poole 122, 130, 140–41, 168
Port Erin 28
Port Isaac 126–27
Port St Mary 25–8, 240
Port Talbot 157–58
Portaferry 234–35, 240
Porthcawl 155–56
Porthdinllaen 152–53, 172
Portpatrick 199, 241
Portree 194
Portrush 243–44
Portsmouth 99
Pwllheli 150–52
Queensferry 33, 108, 202
Ramsey 25–6
Ramsgate 57–60, 86–7, 95,
    251
Red Bay 244
Redcar 32, 41
Red Cross 140, 160
Rhoscolyn 254
Rhyl 154, 161
Robin Hood's Bay 40, 170
Rock 136
Rose, Sir Alec 47
Rosslare 219–20
Royal Air Force 39, 41–2,
    62, 72, 124–5, 130, 133,
    135, 154–5
Royal Humane Society 69
Royal Navy 30, 57, 111,
    123, 178, 183
RSPCA 108
Runswick 41–3, 252
Ryde 254
Rye 95, 169, 254
St Abbs 201–3
St Agnes 128
St Bees 22–4
St Catherine's 140
St Davids 160, 163–64, 219,
    254
St Helier 136–37, 139–40,
    253
St Ives 127–28, 169, 218, 254
St Mary's 117, 119–22
St Peter Port 137–38, 253
Salcombe 113–15, 199,
    249–50, 254

Savile, Sir Jimmy 34–5
Scarborough 33–7, 254
Seaham 254
Self righting 34, 180–84, 217
Selsey 57, 92–3, 250
Sennen Cove 111–13, 117
Sheerness 7, 8, 87–90
Sheffield 14
Sheringham 62, 79
Shoreham 90–2
Silloth 24–5
Skegness 64, 67
Skerries 234
Southend 79, 80
Southport 12, 13
South Shields 32
Southwold 75–6
Staithes 42–3
Stornoway 191, 243
Stourbridge 15
Stranraer 199
Street collections 15, 216
Stromness 175, 186, 188–89
Stronsay 175
Sunderland 48
Swanage 85–6, 107, 134–5
Teesmouth 7, 33, 36, 38, 39,
    41, 48
Teignmouth 134
Tenby 162–63
Thurso 175, 184–85
Tighnabruaich 197
Tobermory 192–94
Torbay 130, 253
Tramore 233
Trearddur Bay 149, 158
Troon 197
Tyne, River 30, 47
Tynemouth 31, 33–4, 47–50,
    66, 252
Valentia 229–30
Walmer 60–1, 94–5, 107–8
Walton & Frinton 72–3
Wells 52, 54, 58, 63, 77
West Kirby 15, 108–110
West Mersea 69, 70
Weston super Mare 141, 169
Weymouth 122–3
Whitby 32–4, 36–7, 49, 50,
    170, 203, 252
Whitstable 100
Wick 185–6
Wicklow 224–5
Wilson, Harold 177
Withernsea 51
Wolverhampton 67
Wordsworth, William 10
Workington 23–4
Worthing 254
Wouldhave, William 31
Yarmouth 85–6, 245–47
Youghal 234

Severn
Length:	*17 m (55 ft 9 in)*
Range:	*250 miles*
Speed:	*25 knots*
Introduced:	*1993*
Last built:	*Current*

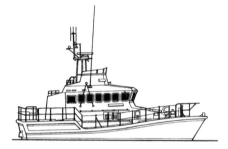

Trent
Length:	*14 m (45 ft 11 in)*
Range:	*250 miles*
Speed:	*25 knots*
Introduced:	*1993*
Last built:	*Current*

Arun
Length:	*15.9/16.5 m (52/54 ft)*
Range:	*330 miles*
Speed:	*18 knots*
Introduced:	*1971*
Last built:	*1990*

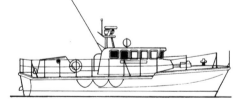

Tyne
Length:	*14.3 m (47 ft)*
Range:	*240 miles*
Speed:	*17.6 knots*
Introduced:	*1982*
Last built:	*1990*

Mersey
Length:	*11.6 m (38 ft)*
Range:	*140 miles*
Speed:	*17 knots*
Introduced:	*1988*
Last built:	*1993*